THE

ARMY OFFICER'S

POCKET COMPANION ;

PRINCIPALLY DESIGNED

FOR

STAFF OFFICERS IN THE FIELD.

PARTLY TRANSLATED FROM THE FRENCH OF M. DE ROUVRE, LIEUTEN-
ANT-COLONEL OF THE FRENCH STAFF-CORPS, WITH ADDITIONS
FROM STANDARD AMERICAN, FRENCH, AND
ENGLISH AUTHORITIES.

BY WILLIAM P. CRAIGHILL,

FIRST-LIEUTENANT U. S. CORPS OF ENGINEERS, ASSISTANT PROFESSOR
OF ENGINEERING AT THE U. S. MILITARY ACADEMY.

NEW YORK:

D. VAN NOSTRAND, 192 BROADWAY.

1862.

C. A. ALVORD, STEREOTYPER AND PRINTER.

PREFACE.

THIS book in its beginning was intended to be a translation from the Aide-mémoire of the French Corps d'Etat-Major, prepared by Colonel de Rouvre. There is no such corps in the army of the United States. The duties of the Corps d'Etat-Major, or Staff-Corps, are very extensive and important, as will be perceived from an examination into their details. An officer of this corps, to be fitted for his position, should be capable, among other things, of filling the place of almost any other officer of the army. It readily appears, therefore, that an Aide-mémoire for such officers is an Aide-memoire for the whole army, but especially for staff officers.

The matter may be divided into three classes: 1st, *those portions applicable only to the French army, which are specially stated as so belonging,* being retained here because they furnish valuable and interesting information to the officers of the army of the Union, and give indications of what might well be added to our system; (this is a small part of the work.) 2d, *those portions applicable only to the army of the United States,* being drawn from existing laws and regulations; 3d, those portions applicable to service in any well organized army. The 3d is the largest part of the book. Every thing not specially stated as *French* is applicable to our own army.

Much of de Rouvre's work has been omitted in the translation, while modifications and great additions have been made. The authorities for these changes are the following: the laws and regulations for the government of the army, Scott's Military Dictionary, Mahan's Field Fortifications, the authorized works on the tactics of the three arms of the service, Younghusband's Hand-Book for Field Service, Maxims and Instructions on the Army of War, and others.

This book, like most others of the present day, is a compilation. Nothing in it is original with the compiler except its arrangement, and that is perhaps its worst feature.

A few blank pages have been added at the end of the book for the convenience of those who may wish to add notes to the text.

U. S. MILITARY ACADEMY,
WEST POINT, N. Y., *November 4th*, 1861.

DESCRIPTION OF FIGURES.

ARMY OFFICER'S POCKET COMPANION.

PART FIRST.

ART. 1.—Composition of the Corps d'Etat-Major or Staff-Corps in the French Army.

It consists of thirty colonels, thirty lieutenant-colonels, one hundred chiefs of squadron, three hundred captains, one hundred lieutenants.

The lieutenants of the corps are appointed from the sub-lieutenants, pupils of the school of application, in the manner prescribed by regulations.

There are fifty sub-lieutenants, drawn, first, from the sub-lieutenants in all arms of the service on active duty; second, from sub-lieutenants coming from the polytechnic school; third, from sub-lieutenants coming from the special military school. (See arts. 4 and 6.)

Officers of all arms, of the grade of captain and below, if they are able to pass such an examination as they would upon leaving the school of application, may be admitted into the staff-corps by exchange with officers of their grade. However, they do not take in the corps their position according to seniority unless their date is later than that of the officer replaced.

Officers of the staff-corps, up to the grade of captain inclusive, may, at their request, be placed in certain cases in the infantry or cavalry, but they then lose their places in the staff-corps, and no longer belong to it.

ART. 2.—Employment of Officers of the Staff-Corps in the French Army.

The colonels, lieutenant-colonels, chiefs of squadron, and captains of the staff-corps, are employed as chiefs of staff, officers of staff, and as aides-de-camp.

Officers of the corps are sent to certain bureaus of the war department, where they are occupied in compiling the map of France, and all similar duties.

Officers of the corps may be placed at the disposal of the minister for foreign affairs, to be attached to embassies, or employed on diplomatic missions.

The lieutenants of the corps are attached as supernumerary officers for two years to the infantry, then two years to the cavalry. After four years' service in these two arms, they may be for another year attached to the regiments of artillery or engineers. In time of war, lieutenants thus attached to the cavalry, artillery, or engineers, may be recalled by the minister of war to perform their proper duties in the staff-corps.

The minister of war may also, in the same circumstances, call upon those officers for duty in the staff-corps, who have previously left that corps, either by exchange or otherwise, or been pupils of the school for the staff, and passed the necessary examination for admission into the staff-corps, but who never entered it because of the want of vacancies. These officers may have their places in their regiments filled, if the exigencies of the service require it. In this case only they become supernumerary officers of the staff-corps, take rank in it from the day of entrance, and are eligible for promotion in it. The officers, not thus replaced, continue to be borne on the rolls of their corps, and lose none of their rights in them. They receive, during the performance of staff duties, the pay and emoluments belonging to the same grade in the staff-corps.

When officers of the staff-corps are not to be obtained, general officers may receive authority from the minister of war, and in the field from the commander-in-chief of the army or army-corps, to employ, with the title of orderly officers and to transmit their orders, junior captains of cavalry and lieutenants of infantry and cavalry from the troops they command. Such officers are still borne on the rolls of their own corps, and lose no rights of promotion in them.

ART. 3.—Officers of the Staff-Corps attached to Troops (French Army).

The lieutenants of the staff-corps, attached to the infantry and cavalry, serve in companies and squadrons during the first year they pass in each of these arms. They are candidates, during the second year, for duty as adjutants of regiments, when they are considered suitable therefor by the inspector-generals.

Lieutenants, who are promoted to the grade of captain before the expiration of the four years they should pass with regiments of infantry and cavalry, continue their service with them for the remainder of the time as supernumerary captains, and perform the duties of adjutant.

The service of officers of the staff-corps, who are

attached to other corps, is performed in all the arms in accordance with the regulations prescribed for the government of all supernumerary officers.

Their seniority regulates their right to command, but a lieutenant performing the duties of adjutant is superior in rank to all the lieutenants of the corps.

Lieutenants detached from the staff-corps cannot be attached to the regimental schools. They accompany the active battalions or squadrons, go with the larger fraction of the corps, and in case of equal division of the regiment, they go with the colonel, unless they perform the duties of adjutant to one of the other fractions.

The inspector-general of infantry and cavalry cause the detached captains and lieutenants of the staff-corps to undergo examinations upon the theory and practice of manœuver, as well as upon the parts of their duties; they examine them, moreover, as to the special duties of the staff-corps, making them execute military reconnoissances, and giving them never more than forty-eight hours in which to make their sketches and memoirs. Report of these examinations is made to the minister of war, which is accompanied by the sketches and memoirs, and these are sent to the examining board of the staff-corps.

ART. 4.—Pupils of the School of Application of the Staff-Corps (French).

Every sub-lieutenant who desires to compete for admission into the staff-corps, makes an application before August 1st, through the proper military channel, to the inspector-general; or, in his absence, to the general commanding the division, who sends it to the minister of war before the 20th of the month, accompanied by his own recommendation and all the information he has collected respecting the applicant.

The minister designates what officers shall be entered as competitors for the staff-corps. They continue to receive full pay of their grade.

Those pupils of the special military school, who graduate from it among the first thirty of the class, compete with the sub-lieutenants of the army for admission into the school of the staff-corps. The places in their own corps, of those sub-lieutenants who are admitted to the school, are not filled.

The first thirty graduates of the special military school, destined, according to their examination number, to compete for the school of application, are assigned at the same time with the others of their class, to the cavalry schools or to regiments of infantry.

Those graduates who have been admitted into the school of application, are counted in the corps of infantry or cavalry to which they have been assigned. The three graduates of the polytechnic school are placed, according to their choice, in the cavalry or infantry.

The graduates, not admitted, go to the cavalry school or into infantry regiments.

The graduates remain two years at the school of application of the staff-corps, and are there separated into two divisions. They are next, after the final examination, divided into two classes—1st, those who satisfy the requirements of this examination, are eligible for admission into the staff-corps; 2d, those who fail at the examination are not thus eligible.

The sub-lieutenants who are found eligible, are assigned to duty as lieutenants of the staff-corps, when vacancies exist, in the order given them after their examination above referred to. When there are not vacancies, they are sent to regiments of infantry or cavalry as sub-lieutenants, and are borne of the right upon the list for promotion, in addition to the number determined for yearly presentation. The second class above referred to are also sent to regiments, but have no special advantages as to presentation for promotion. (*See Art.* 6.)

Promotion to the grade of captain takes place in the proportion of two-thirds by seniority and one-third by selection; that to the grade of chief of squadron in the proportion of half by seniority and half by selection.

ART. 5.—Examining Board of the Staff-Corps (French).

There is established, for the purpose of holding the examinations or admission into the school or into the staff-corps, and to direct the studies both of pupils and officers, an examining board, composed of generals and other high officers.

The professors of the school of application are added to the board, in order to participate in the examinations for admission and exit.

The board arranges and submits to the minister of war, regulations for the internal organization, the course of studies, and the discipline of the school of application.

Competition for entrance into the school, and examinations for leaving it, take place before this board.

They also attend to the examination of officers who present themselves for admission into the corps by exchange.

The board determine the studies to be passed through each year by the lieutenants and captains attached to other corps, as well as by the captains in the corps who have not been two years captains, and have not, during two years, performed the duties of the staff-corps. These officers are, as far as these duties are concerned, under the supervision of the chief of the staff-corps, who is their intermediary with the board.

The captains who have, during a longer period than two years, performed the duties of the staff-corps, and the higher officers employed in the divisions, either as officers of staff, or as aides-de-camp, or attached to troops, execute, in accordance with the orders of the minister or the generals commanding the divisions, certain works of reconnoissance and collecting statistics as to frontiers, and important military points, as well as certain historical and critical treatises relating to the wars of which these points have been the theatre.

The plans and memoirs, both those made by order and those conceived and executed voluntarily, are sent to the minister by the generals of division, in order to be placed before the examining board, unless otherwise decided by the minister.

The secretary of the board receives the plans and memoirs, as well as other works of the kind, and places them before the board, by whom they are classified.

There is opened, by the secretary of the commission, a register giving the name and date of commission of all the officers of the corps, which serves for the reception of the annual notes and reports of the inspector-generals and the generals commanding, for an indication of the works of reconnoissance, &c., executed by the officers, and the opinion of the board with reference to them. A duplicate of this register is deposited in the bureau of the staff-corps, to be consulted in every case, and especially when there is a question as to the most suitable duty or station to assign to an officer.

Each year a special temporary staff board, composed of five generals, and presided over by the oldest general of division, arranges a table for promotion by selection. With this view, they consult the reports of inspector-generals, the notes of generals or high officers under whose orders are the officers set down for promotion, and the classification in order of merit of the works of these officers as made by the staff examining board. They take note, in like manner, of the manner in which these officers have performed special duties, which, by their importance, or the daily application they require, may have debarred these officers from additional duties.

ART. 6.—Modifications of preceding Regulations.

Among the fifty sub-lieutenants, twenty-five are annually taken as follows:

Three from the pupils of the polytechnic school;

Twenty-two from thirty of the pupils of the special military school, arranged in order of merit, and having asked to be permitted to compete; and from not more than thirty sub-lieutenants on active duty, who, having served at least a year in that grade, present themselves for admission into the staff-corps.

The thirty pupils of the special military school, designated in conformity to the requirements of the preceding article, compete with the sub-lieutenants of the army for admission into the school.

ART. 7.—Employment and duties of the French Staff-Corps.

The officers of the corps are employed upon the general staffs of military departments, or with generals as aides-de-camp, or attached to embassies. The staffs are the centres from which the generals, in accordance with the superior orders of the head of the war department, direct all the operations of the army, with the assistance of a certain number of officers not attached to troops.

The staff of a military department is composed of a colonel or lieutenant-colonel of the staff-corps, and several additional officers, either chefs d'escadron or captains. The staff of an army is similarly composed. The assignment of the officers is made by the head of the corps, when not by the minister of war.

An army commanded by a marshal of France has for its chief of staff a general of division, and for an assistant chief of staff a general of brigade, or a colonel of the staff-corps.

When several armies are united in one command, the chief of staff of the command takes temporarily the title of *major-general*; the general officers employed under the major-general receive each the title of assistant major-general. An army commanded by a general of division has for its chief of staff a general of brigade, or a colonel of the staff-corps.

An army-corps has for its chief of staff a general

of division or brigade. For the wings, the centre and
the reserve of an army, the chief of staff is a general
of brigade or a colonel. A division has for its chief of
staff a colonel or lieutenant-colonel of the staff-
corps.

ART. 8.—Chiefs of Staff (French).

The duties of a chief of staff are—1st, to transmit
the orders of the general, and to execute those he
receives himself for detached duties, such as the
marking out of camps, reconnoissances, inspections,
&c.; 2d, to correspond with the chiefs of artillery and
engineers, and with the commissaries, quarter-masters, &c., in order to keep the general exactly
informed of the condition of all branches of the service; 3d, to keep up such correspondence with the different corps as will suffice for a thorough knowledge
of their condition in detail; 4th, to furnish to the commander-in-chief, and to the head of the war department tables of the strength and position of corps and
posts, reports of marches and other operations, and,
in a word, all necessary information.

Next to the commander, the chief of staff is the man
of the whole army who can do the most good if he is
capable, and the most harm if deficient in ability. It is
his duty to cause to be executed all the designs of the
general which are connected with the service. It is
equally his duty to communicate to the general all
information he collects, and to make such sugges-
tions as he thinks will be of interest and benefit to
the army. His duty to the army requires him to give
most anxious and watchful attention to all its necessities, even the most minute. It is his duty to make to

the war department the most exact and circumstantial reports of every thing relating to operations and the troops.

The chief of staff has under his orders an assistant, whose exclusive duty it is to assist his senior, and replace him when necessary. The assistant performs such duties as are assigned him by his chief, and in the best manner his capacity and means permit.

The sphere of action of the chief of staff of a division is more contracted than in the case of an army, but in that sphere his duties are the same, and his relations the same.

A chief of staff can fulfil all the duties required of him only by the zealous and methodical cooperation of the officers attached to his department; one of his first cares should then be the proper subdivision of duties or the organization of bureaus.

The points requiring the attention of a staff may be classified, as indicated in the following table, which contains at least the most usual and important; if circumstances increase these, it will be always easy to classify them in a manner similar to that shown below:

ART. 9.—First Bureau—General Correspondence. (French.)

PRINCIPAL OBJECTS.	DETAILS—REMARKS.
1. Organization of the army.	Relative rank of the troops. Assignment of general officers, of officers of the staff-corps and others not attached to troops. Composition of garrisons and posts of communication. Eventual commands and head-quarters. Regulations of the general officers and chiefs of staff.
2. Weekly and other reports to the war department.	1st. Organization of the army, changes introduced, special commands formed and the reasons therefor, instructions given. 2d. Movement of head-quarters. 3d. Condition of the staff; its wants 4th. Every thing relating to the service of the army, the wants of the troops, recruiting, discipline, clothing, instruction, equipment, general police, the condition of hospitals, the mortality, the destination of prisoners. 5th. Copy of the topographical works. 6th. Information as to the enemy, his condition, his projects. 7th. Projected operations, the reasons therefor and the means proposed to be employed. 8th. Movements of troops, works constructed, operations ordered, corps employed, results obtained. 9th. Detailed events of sieges. 10th. Remarkable actions, as follows: The reasons, the antecedent circumstances, the position of the troops before the fight, the movements which brought it on, the hour at which the action commenced, the points upon which the real and false attacks were made, the names of the corps coming into action together and in succession, the names of their chiefs, the precise hour of the crisis, the hour when firing ceased at different points, the ground passed over by the troops, the position

FIRST BUREAU.—GENERAL CORRESPONDENCE (CONTINUED).

PRINCIPAL OBJECTS.	DETAILS—REMARKS.
2. Weekly and other reports to the war department (continued).	taken up after the affair, its strong and weak points, the works construction and projected, the enemy's position, his plans, his forces, the faults committed, the beautiful feats performed, the results obtained, the losses sustained; a statement of the losses and captures is added to the report, which may be made out as below.

Statement of Losses and Captures in the Engagement of ——.

		By the enemy.	By our troops.
Men {	killed,		
	wounded,		
	captured or missing,		
Arms captures,			
Cannon {	captured,		
	dismounted,		
Caissons & {	taken,		
carriages {	destroyed,		
Horses {	killed,		
	captured,		
Money captured,			
Munitions "			

PRINCIPAL OBJECTS.	DETAILS—REMARKS.
3. Instructions relating to all the operations of the army.	
4. Organization of depots in rear of the army. Depots of convalescents.	The depots of convalescents are established in secure positions, convenient to the grand hospitals of the army, upon the most direct lines of communication. The chief of staff, with the approval of the commander of the army, designates the officers to command them. Each corps of infantry sends to that depot assigned to it a sub-officer to oversee and bring back at a proper time the men belonging to it. A medical officer is appointed to visit the depots.
Cavalry depots.	These are established to receive sick or weak horses. They serve also for convalescents belonging to the mounted corps.

FIRST BUREAU.—GENERAL CORRESPONDENCE (CONTINUED).

PRINCIPAL OBJECTS.	DETAILS—REMARKS.
5. Relations with the commanders of artillery and engineers.	Orders, plans, works to be executed, requisitions for munitions, inspections of same. Service in sieges. Recording and numbering. Special orders always indicate the authority whence they proceed.
6. Special orders and supplemental instructions.	These orders should be communicated to all persons who must assist in executing them, or whose position requires their being informed of them. They imply details and recommendations which make additional instructions necessary. Orders include every thing relating to their execution; instructions include what may relate to their modification. Orders should be as concise as possible, instructions detailed as possible. Orders, always more or less extensively promulgated, ought to be known to all persons who assist in their execution; but instructions, which are almost always special and secret, should be made known only to those who are actually in charge of the operations in hand and responsible for their management. For example, instructions should show what any body of troops will have to do, where to be placed: when movements are to be made, the instructions should indicate to each chief of a column the position or movements of the neighboring troops, in what direction either at night or in the day he must look for succor and support: they should define exactly the places and lengths of halts, the times of arrival and departure. Officers detached for reconnoissances daily, special or offensive. Encampments, cantonments. Tracing out camps and every thing relating thereto. Grand guards, their position, orders, duties.

PRINCIPAL OBJECTS.	DETAILS—REMARKS.
Special orders and supplemental instructions (continued).	Positions, intrenched posts.
	Detachments, partisans, convoys.
	Different military operations.
	Service of the army; service of superior officers; movements of troops. Special orders concerning movements to be effected are the most frequent.
	For movement of head-quarters, the chiefs of staff address orders to the masters of transportation, and they then contain, 1st, the order of setting out, the manner of transportation, whether by carriages or packhorses; 2d, the place of reassembling; 3d, the composition of the escort; 4th, the road to follow and the places to halt; 5th, the special dispositions to which the movement may give rise; 6th, the directions as to reports to be made upon the march to the chief of staff.
	For movements of troops, the orders are addressed to their commanders. They point out, 1st, the corps to march; 2d, the points of departure and of reassembling; 3d, the hour of departure, and, if necessary, that of arrival; 4th, the destination, the itinerary to be observed, the principal points to be passed, the points where to receive or expect new orders; 5th, recommendations as to the route to be pursued, if necessary—as to equipments, baggage, sick persons, provisions to be carried—as to inspections to be made; 6th, depots and hospitals established along the road; 7th, directions as to the return of detachments, guards, pickets; 8th, information relating to distant detachments, to detached officers; 9th, munitions to be taken, recommendations as to armament, clothing and equipment; 10th, order in which the troops should march, composition of the advanced-guard, the

FIRST BUREAU.—GENERAL CORRESPONDENCE (CONTINUED).

PRINCIPAL OBJECTS.	DETAILS—REMARKS.
Special orders and supplemental instructions (continued).	rear guard, of the main body, of escorts; 11th, the designation of the commander of the column when there are several bodies of troops; 12th, if there are several columns, the route of each; 13th, recommendations as to what employees should follow the troops; 14th, in case of the evacuation of a fortified place or a cantonment, recommendations as to magazines and other military establishments; 15th, in case of a night march, the precautions to be taken in view of parts of the same column approaching each other and the provision of signals. MOVEMENTS OF CAVALRY.—In orders relating to the movement of cavalry, to avoid sending it out before daylight, having regard to rest, feeding and cleaning the horses. To avoid making the movements of the cavalry too much dependent upon that of infantry. PRECAUTIONS FOR CAVALRY.—1st, to keep it together as much as possible; 2d, to cause frequent reliefs of detached bodies, and especially those attached to the infantry; 3d, to have frequent inspections; 4th, to choose the best camping spots; 5th, to handle the cavalry to the best advantage possible, and only to fight it upon proper occasions. SIEGES.—1st, arrangements relating to the execution of the plan of the siege; 2d, establishment of the troops in camp; 3d, instructions for the laborers; 4th, employment of the cavalry; 5th, directions as to distributions; 6th, directions relative to the care of the wounded; 7th, dispositions for the assault, that should be so arranged as to permit its renewal twice or thrice if necessary; 8th, after the capture of the place, the composition of the gar-

PRINCIPAL OBJECTS.	DETAILS—REMARKS.
Special orders and supplemental instructions (continued).	rison; to be formed of the troops which have suffered most and been most distinguished; 9th, refitting the other troops; 10th, removal of prisoners and sick, and of every thing useless to the defence; 11th, instructions as to a statement of the condition of the stores and the money-chest; 12th, destruction of the siege-works, destruction or repair of the defensive works; 13th, provision of stores, munitions, &c.; 14th, if there is a capitulation after an exchange of hostages, a designation of the guards to relieve those of the besieged, receiving the arms of their troops, their departure under escort, their destination, receiving the magazines, stores, arsenals, plans, &c.
	EMBARKATION AND DEBARKATION.—1st. General arrangements of the embarkation. Every thing belonging to a division should be able to be assembled at the first signal; the corps are not divided up; the field artillery and munitions should be debarked first.
	2d. Recommend to generals of division to cause themselves to be informed of the condition of each of the boats which serve for transportation of their troops.
	3d. To chiefs of corps to assist at the embarkation of their corps, to generals to see to their own division or brigade, and to all the chiefs to send in their reports.
	4th. At the point of general assembly, giving warning to have arms in good condition; to dispose the troops in parties proportioned to the capacity of the boats.
	5th. Designation of the workmen to be attached to the elite companies to be first landed.
	6th. Recommend to generals to land

FIRST BUREAU.—GENERAL CORRESPONDENCE (CONTINUED).

PRINCIPAL OBJECTS.	DETAILS—REMARKS.
Special orders and supplemental instructions (continued).	first themselves, to regulate the movements of the troops, not to permit the first detachments to go more than 200 yards from the shore, to form in battle order on reaching land, either in close column or in line according to circumstances.
	7th. Orders relative to the distribution of provisions to be made by naval offices.
7. General orders or orders of the day, registry and numbering.	General orders indicate every thing of importance for the army to know, and a copy is sent to the minister of war.
	The orders include the general arrangements of organization of the army and such modifications as may be necessary.
	On marches the chief of staff precedes the general to the halting-place, receives his orders on his arrival, which should precede that of the troops, and writes a general order to be ready when the troops arrive. He inserts in the order, 1st, the hours of reveille, of reports of roll-calls, of guard, of meals, of tending horses, of extra duties, of giving out provisions; 2d, the place of these distributions, each article having its own place of distributions, and each corps as well as the staff its own hour of receiving; 3d, the number of men to be furnished for ordinary guards, for pickets, for orderly duty, the posts to be established; 4th, the number of officers, non-commissioned officers and privates in each division and corps to be placed at the disposal of the commandant of head-quarters; 5th, the works to be executed for establishing communications or intrenching posts, in which labors the whole army joins successively; 6th, the name of the general officer of the day, if there is one, of the superior officers of the day,

FIRST BUREAU.—GENERAL CORRESPONDENCE (CONTINUED).

PRINCIPAL OBJECTS.	DETAILS—REMARKS.
General orders or orders of the day (continued).	of pickets, of rounds, and the officer of the day of the staff;* 7th, in fortified places and cantonments, the addresses most important for troops to know, such as those of the general in chief, of the chief of staff, of the commandants of artillery and engineers, of the commandant of head-quarters, of the commissary, of the paymaster, of the post-office; 8th, the carriages, horses and servants that each may have; 9th, every thing the army should know as to the depots; 10th, the hours of inspection and issue of food, and the details relating to issue of clothing, &c.; 11th, recommendations as to discipline, hygiene, police, equipment, instruction; 12th, the composition of courts-martial, sentences, &c.; 13th, promotions and rewards, bounties to the troops.
	SIEGES.—1st. The appointment of general and other officers of the trenches.
	2d. The designation of the chief of staff of the trenches and his aids.
	3d. The guard, picket and trench duties.
	4th. The assignment of elite companies designed as special guards in the place when it has fallen, and of those points which need particular watching.
	5th. The appointment of a governor for the place.
	6th. The organization of the duties of the place, and the measures taken with reference to the local authorities.
8. List of countersigns and paroles.	Sending the countersign to those who should have it; loss of the word.
	A list should be made out and kept of those persons who are entitled to the countersign and parole.

*A list indicates, in order of seniority and by grade, all general officers who may be assigned as officers of the day, &c.

FIRST BUREAU.—GENERAL CORRESPONDENCE (CONTINUED).

PRINCIPAL OBJECTS.	DETAILS—REMARKS.
9. Rewards, proposals of promotion, &c.	
10. Disbanding an army.	Sending to the minister the archives of the staff.
	Reports as to the officers of the staff-corps.

Second Bureau.—Administration.

PRINCIPAL OBJECTS.	DETAILS—REMARKS.
1. Correspondence relative to the administration of the army, with the war department.	
2. Relations with the officers of the departments of administration.	The chiefs of staff inform the administrative departments of all the movements of the head-quarters, and of the orders of the generals. They receive from them copies of the reports of inspections of men and material, all the information which may be requisite. The chiefs of staff send to them at the end of each month a list signed and certified, containing the names, grades, employments, movements or changes of all the persons acting under their authority.
3. Relations with purveyors and contractors.	
4. Relations with the medical officers.	
5. Relations with the pay department.	The chief of staff issues orders to the paymasters for such journeys as they should make, and applications should be made to the same person when guards are needed for treasure.
	The chiefs of staff furnish them a statement of the strength of the several corps. During halts of some length, the treasure is placed in charge of some particular post, while upon marches it is guarded by a company

SECOND BUREAU.—ADMINISTRATION (CONTINUED).

PRINCIPAL OBJECTS.	DETAILS—REMARKS.
Relations with the pay department, (continued).	of grenadiers, whose commanding officer receives from the chief paymaster, when his command is relieved, a statement addressed to the chief of staff, that the duty assigned it has been efficiently and properly performed.
	The cavalry guard of the head-quarters may serve to guard the treasure.
6. Making out statements of the condition of affairs, and other statements.	Besides those special ones occasionally called for by the general in chief that he may be informed of his resources in men and means; these statements should be made after models sent by the war department or prescribed by regulations. The forms are sent to all concerned, in order to obtain uniformity. Order, clearness, conciseness, ought to be diligently striven after in making these statements.
7. Note in each corps the number of artisans of different kinds.	
8. Distributions.	Statement of the wants of the troops by arms, division, corps or detachments.
	Calculation of resources. Tariff of rations.
	Collection of food and other articles.
	Arrangements to be made relative to foraging.
	Examination of the reports of inspecting officers and improvements in the different military establishments are under the supervision of the chief of staff, and inspected by officers of the staff-corps, who send their reports to him. By comparing these reports with those of the persons immediately in charge, abuses may be corrected and improvements in administration effected.
9. Extraordinary distributions.	
10. Hospitals and ambulances.	Supervision and improvement, if possible.

Second Bureau.—Administration (continued).

PRINCIPAL OBJECTS.	DETAILS—REMARKS.
Hospitals and ambulances (continued).	Getting rid of men unfit for service. The chief of staff ought to consut the chief medical officers as to any abuses in the hospitals, as to the improvements that may be made, and the means to be taken for repressing and preventing the former, and for carrying out the latter.
11. Arrangements as to barracks in occupied towns, and the establishment of troops on the march.	
12. Management of convoys, employment of the different means of transportation.	
13. Contributions ordered, loans, requisitions.	Writing out the necessary orders. Extraordinary contributions should be proportioned to the ability of the country and individual inhabitants.
14. Demands of indemnity for losses, and reimbursement of extraordinary expenses.	
15. Special expenses of the general or division staff.	Bounties granted. Remunerations for protection and safe-conduct. Accountability for expenses thus incurred by the general-in-chief.
16. Fines imposed by the police officers, confiscations ordered, proceeds placed at the disposal of the general.	
17. Captives.	Use made of captured articles, such as horses, &c. Horses stolen, and of deserters.
18. Correspondence with the families of officers and men, or with the civil	

Second Bureau.—Administration (continued).

PRINCIPAL OBJECTS.	DETAILS—REMARKS.
authorities representing them. 19. Supervision of every thing of a civil nature pertaining to the army.	

Third Bureau.—Secret Department, Relations with the Provost-Martial, Police and Discipline.

PRINCIPAL OBJECTS.	DETAILS—REMARKS.
1. Relations with provost-martial.	The chief of staff informs him what detachments are necessary for police duty, and receives from him a daily report of his department.
2. Arrangement as to fines, confiscation of horses, wagons, effects of sutlers and traders.	The provost-martial hands to the chief of staff a list of the fines he has been authorized to impose and directed to collect.
3. Determination of the number of sutlers attached to each corps, approval of their warrants, and inspection of their wares.	Under the orders of the chief of staff, the police officers indicate to sutlers and traders the places where they may establish themselves.
4. List of civilians attached to the generals and other high officers.	
5. Appointment of wagon-master and his assistants. Guard, collection of carriages.	The instructions to be given to wagon-masters, include, 1st, The condition and kind of carriages composing the train of the head-quarters. (The wagon-master should permit the use of none of the wagons of the country without the authority of the chief of staff.) 2d, Names of all the drivers

**THIRD BUREAU.—SECRET DEPARTMENT. RELATIONS WITH THE
PROVOST-MARTIAL, POLICE AND DISCIPLINE (CONTINUED).**

PRINCIPAL OBJECTS.	DETAILS—REMARKS.
Appointm'nt of wagon-master, and his assistants. Guard, collection of carriages,(continued).	and servants attached to the carriages. 3d, All the carriages of each individual, giving his name, grade, rank and duty. 4th, Order of march of the carriages. 5th, Recommend to mark upon each cooking galley the name of the party to which it belongs, and upon all the carriages their number, taken from the list in possession of the provost-martial.
6. Organization of the service of head-quarters.	Correspondence with the commandant of head-quarters. Division of the service among the different corps.
7. Every thing relating to police and discipline. Punishments, &c.	
8. Secret part.	Everything relating to spies, to secret correspondence, to special information, to guides. Record the information collected by spies. The questions to ask them are generally suggested by the circumstances of the case, but there are some of general use, and not to be forgotten, as the following:—1st, Where are the head-quarters? 2d, Where are the generals? their names and characters? 3d, Where is the artillery park, the cavalry reserve? their composition? 4th, Names and strength of corps in each position? how many, and what kind of pieces of artillery on each point? 5th, Is the enemy concentrated or divided? 6th, What are his means of transportation, procuring provisions? 7th, How are his troops fed, clad, paid? their morale? prevailing diseases? by masses, corps or detachments? 9th, Does he expect reinforcements? whence, what and when? 10th, Is he throwing up intrenchments? on what points?

Third Bureau.—Secret Department. Relations with the Provost-Martial, Police and Discipline (continued).

PRINCIPAL OBJECTS.	DETAILS—REMARKS.
	Note.—All information obtained by the staff of a division by means of spies, is added in a separate paper to the daily report to the chief of the general staff.
9. Where to send deserters. Means of making good use of these retained.	
10. Lists giving names of prisoners taken in each affair by the different corps, and those captured by the enemy.	These lists assist in making out the reports to the war department.
11. Safe-guards.	Countersigning and registering written letters of protection. The following form may be used by safe-guards. "Every soldier and employé connected with the army is hereby warned not to injure the person or property of ——, who is placed by the commander of the forces under the protection of the army. Every one on the contrary, is expected to give him refuge and protection when needed."
12. Calling courts martial and of inquiry.	1st. List of officers eligible for such service. 2d. Preparation of the letters of appointment and assembly. 3d. Classification of the charges. 4th. Details relating to proceedings and sentences. 5th. Sending home persons sentenced to long confinements.
13. Orders relative to furloughs and leaves.	
14. In case of disbanding the army, sending to each corps certificates as to their conduct at important points.	These certificates are given by the general in chief, or in his name.

Fourth Bureau.—Historical, Statistical, Topographical.

PRINCIPAL OBJECTS.	DETAILS—REMARKS.
1. Collections of maps of roads, cantonments, winter quarters, positions, fields of battle, fortified places, forts, posts.	These maps are made in triplicate, for the war department, the general in chief, and the chief of the staff. In making them, assistance is derived from all the maps, general, special, manuscript or engraved, that can be procured. The topographical bureau makes maps of all roads used by the army, of all manœuvres executed, all ground on which combats take place. If circumstances permit, these sketches are extended to embrace ground adjacent. With this view, the officers intrusted with the duty are attached to every division and corps. When armies abide long in one place, the officers make a map of the seat of war. As a rule, a map is made for each march, and one for each affair, of which the operations are described. To this, notes are added as to the nature of the ground. In the absence of regular maps, their place is supplied by sketches and itineraries, with notes as to distances, state of roads, &c.

MODEL OF AN ITINERARY.

NAMES OF PLACES.	Distances between remarkable points.	Designation of remarkable points.	Extent of each accident of ground.	Breadth of the route.	Appearances of marked objects.	Character of the road and of the country. Details of the ground, places, and objects worthy of remark. Facilities for repairs.	General remarks as to localities, &c.

FOURTH BUREAU.—HISTORICAL, STATISTICAL, TOPOGRAPHICAL (CONTINUED).

PRINCIPAL OBJECTS.	DETAILS—REMARKS.
2. Surveys in confirmation of reports from reconnoitering officers.	To these surveys are sometimes added statistical tables, whose objects may be classed in the following order:—Population; houses; number of men that can be accommodated; number of horses that can be accommodated; carriages; boats; skiffs; wind-mills and water-mills can grind how many bushels of grain daily; ovens can bake how much bread daily; extent of ground embraced in the corporate limits; different crops, and their extent; nature of the annual harvests, and their proportions; kind and number of domestic animals; number of laborers, artificers in iron and wood, watermen, husbandmen, vine-dressers, and others.
3. Memoirs annexed to the maps of the theatre of war.	The chief objects of these memoirs are 1. PHYSICAL DESCRIPTION. Geographical position of the ground represented (limits). General configuration of this ground (general appearance). Valleys and separating ridges (mountains and valleys). Character of the soil (productive soil, quarries, mines). Hydrography (watercourses, canals, lakes, marshes). Aerography (climate, prevailing winds). 2. STATISTICAL. Political and administrative division. Population (its sum, divisions, physical qualities, manners, character). Languages, religions, public instruction, monuments, objects of art. Works of men's hands (habitations), resources for accommodating troops. Materials for building (marble, stones, bricks, pisa, wood, metals). Agriculture (execution, methods, harvests, relative production and consumption).

FOURTH BUREAU.—HISTORICAL, STATISTICAL, TOPOGRAPHICAL (CONTINUED).

PRINCIPAL OBJECTS.	DETAILS—REMARKS.
Memoirs attached to the maps of the seat of war (continued).	Woods and Forests. Animals (breeds of horses, production of barn-yard fowls, game).
	Industry (mills, factories, manufactures, tanneries, workshops, &c.).
	Commerce. NOTE.—These statistics are given in detail when the population amounts to 3,000 inhabitants.
	3. COMMUNICATIONS.
	Different roads (direction, breadth, nature, slopes, defiles, means of repair, proper for military operations).
	Railway (destination, obstacles passed).
	Canals (destination, rivers which feed them, waste-weirs, &c.).
	Navigation (harbors, docks, boats, portions navigable, rafts).
	Telegraph lines (terminal points, intermediate stations).
	Means of passing rivers.
	4. MILITARY CONSIDERATIONS.
	General considerations (lines of defence, of invasion, of operation; cross communications).
	Positions (military descriptions, advantages, communications, supports).
	5. GENERAL HISTORY.
	Political events transpired at different epochs.
	Historical monuments.
	6. MILITARY HISTORY.
	Military events.
4. Bulletins and general reports to be prepared in accordance with the reports furnished, and the observations made.	

The preceding table is given as a specimen of the manner in which the labor in the offices may be divided and indicates the principal objects to which attention should be directed. It should be the effort of the chief of staff to see that nothing essential is omitted, to have records of every thing, to collect every necessary paper. He ought to have always at hand certain memoranda, such as—

1st. The general condition and situation of the army. Names of the generals of the different corps, of the chiefs of artillery and engineers, of the commissaries, quarter-masters, &c., paymasters, governors of towns, police-officers, wagon-masters, &c., officers of the treasury department, officers of the staff, superior officers; assignments and residences of officers in cantonments; summary of instructions given to superior officers; position of different head-quarters.

2d. Daily position of the troops—Detachments.

3d. Condition of the service of the army, as to police, security, communications, &c.

4th. List, in order of seniority, of all generals and chief officers and staff officers.

5th. Orders and tours of duty for officers of the staff, for inspections, detached duties.

6th. Note of the principal orders relating to duty at head-quarters.

7th. Composition of courts-martial.

Besides the different registers, lists, files already referred to, there should be at hand cases, portfolios, or wrappers, labelled for different documents, and papers which are to be preserved.

1st. Departmental letters. 2d. Departmental decisions and circulars. 3d. Minutes of orders that the general must sign. 4th. Correspondence with generals and high officers. 5th. Correspondence with the administrative departments. 6th. With the various chiefs of the service. 7th. With the provost-marshal.

Under each head the papers should be arranged chronologically.

Portable boxes or cases are used for transporting all the materiel of the bureaus.

In each staff an officer is specially charged with the direction of the duties in the bureaus; the others assist him when necessary, but are generally employed upon active duty. To simplify the correspondence, and diminish the number of letters, use is made of a daily report from the generals of brigade to the generals of division, and from the generals of division to the general-in-chief, or the chief of the army corps; and also, sheets are made out, called "*Answers to the Reports.*" This report is made out in the following form:

NUMERICAL CONDITION.

CORPS.	Present.		Absent.		Present.		Absent.	
	Officers.	Men.	Officers.	Men.	Officers.	Men.	Officers.	Men.
Totals.								

ARMY D.

____ division. ____ brigade.

Report of the general commanding 1st brigade to the general commanding the division, at his head-quarters at ____, ____ day of ____ 186

Grand guards and posts.	
Reconnoissances and patrols.	
Papers received.	
Papers sent.	
Furloughs and leaves of absence. (Names of the officers.)	
Punishments within 24 hours (arrests, confinements, names, reasons).	Officers.
	Men.
Sick (in tents, ambulances or hospitals).	Officers.
	Men.
Applications.	
Events.	
Movements of troops.	
Distributions.	
Special notes.	

Thus arranged, the report is made out upon a large sheet, in book form, so as to leave room enough for every particular.

At the article *Papers sent*, appear all the papers, &c., accompanying the report.

At the articles *Applications, events, special notes*, add every thing which should be the cause of a special dispatch. When the report is received, the chief of staff, after having received the orders of the general, writes his own remarks, if necessary, upon each article, and adds the initials of the officer of the staff, who shall give his attention to each. These officers go over the report in succession, each preparing his own part of the sheet, styled *Answer to the report.*— This answer, prepared in this way by several hands, is made simply and briefly. It is signed by the chief of staff, who must be certain that nothing is omitted.

(The mode here indicated is that pursued at the army of Lyons.)

ART. 10.—Active Duty of Officers of French Staff-Corps.

This duty is interior or daily, exterior or detached.

The in-door duty is in charge of the officer of the day. He has a bureau duty, which consists in the reception of every thing sent to the staff, in recording letters and orders issued, in verification of things sent, in observing the times of receipt and issue of orders, &c., superintendence of clerks.

His active duty includes every thing relating to inspections of the guards, detachments and posts under the charge of the staff, in the supervision of every thing relating to the general police arrangements, to the discipline and employment of the troops.

ART. 11.—Interior duties of Staff-Corps (French).

This duty lasts twenty-four hours. For every important package of orders, &c., a receipt is prepared, numbered and recorded, upon which is written a description of the package, the day and hour of sending, the name of the person to whom sent; when the receipt is returned, it is preserved until no longer of use.

For every thing sent by mail, a memorandum is made of the matter intrusted to each courier, and these memoranda are signed by the postmaster, with an account of the day and hour of departure, as the receipts are arranged in case of matter sent by hand. These memoranda are preserved like the receipts. If the officer of the day sends the dispatches, he also receives the letters and packages, for which he gives a receipt, forwarding the letters, &c., to the chief of staff. The interior service includes also inspections of posts, magazines, hospitals, quarters, prisons, and the supervision of distributions within the lines of the army.

In order that the officer of the day, who has to attend to receiving and sending off dispatches, may not be out of the way, it is a good plan to instruct another officer with inspections.

An inspecting officer gives his attention to the following points:—

1st. If the matter in question is a store-house—to the quantity and quality of articles, to the condition and arrangement of the house, to the proper precautions for preserving the articles stored, to the vigilance of the guard.

2d. As to quarters—their subdivision and assignment, cleanliness, arrangement of effects in chambers, of bedding, matters of hygiene, condition of arms and equipments, messes, kitchens, store-rooms, stables (in cavalry), infirmaries.

3d. As to hospitals—the condition of the personnel, state of the registers, of the apothecary's branch, of the diet, expense, quantity and quality of provisions, state of the kitchens and cooking, sick-rooms, complaints and requests, lighting, stores of military articles put off by the sick.

4th. Prisons—Hygiene and support of prisoners, their requests, suitableness of localities, furniture, cleanliness, lists made.

5th. Distributions—weight and quality of food, requests.

In the interior duties may also be included the command of the head-quarters, which is given to an officer of the staff-corps. This officer is specially in charge of the accommodation and lodging of head-quarters; he establishes the posts and, guards, and in concert with the chief police-officer, makes suitable arrangements for the police and good order of the head-quarters.

ART. 12.—Exterior Duties of Officers of French Staff-Corps.

These include, specially, the choice of positions, supervision of the duties of the grand guards, and visiting the advanced posts, special discoveries and reconnoissances, posts and detachments, establishing camps and cantonments, topographical operations, direction of works to cover camps and cantonments, communications to open between the head-quarters, directing and opening marches, placing bridges, repairing roads, placing parks and batteries, choosing localities suitable for the ambulances and munitions, collecting provisions to be furnished by the towns, information to be collected respecting the numbers and movements of the enemy, duty connected with conferences and truces, service on the battle-field.

ART. 13.—Service on the field of battle of Officers of French Staff-Corps.

In every action the chiefs of staff, with all the officers of the staff-corps, remain near the generals, to receive their orders and cause them to be carried. They perform every duty he may impose.

The battle being over, the staff assist in reforming the troops, recall detachments from pursuit, establish the line of bivouacs and see to burying the dead, caring for the wounded, removing captured and dismounted cannon or carriages, collecting prisoners and sending them to the rear, escorted and guarded, to the points indicated by the general.

In sieges, the chief of staff makes constant visits to the trenches, to assure himself that the duty is well done, that every man is at his post, that the works proceed vigorously, that no munitions and implements are wanting, that the wounded are properly removed and cared for, that men remain in hospital no longer than necessary.

When a work is taken from the enemy, the chief of staff has it inspected, or inspects it himself, that he may report its condition.

He accompanies the general when visiting the trenches, as upon the field of battle. Officers of the staff-corps are especially placed at the disposal of the general or chief officer, in the trenches, and a high officer is usually placed on duty, as chief of staff in the trenches. This officer makes out a duplicate report daily, for the general of artillery and for the chief of staff.

ART. 14.—Bureau duty of the Officers of French Staff-Corps at head-quarters of Geographical Military Departments.

After having gone into the details of the bureau duties of officers of the staff-corps in the field, a few words as to their peace duties may not be out of place.

In spite of the analogy between the two sets of duties regarded as wholes, the details are by no means the same, on account of the differences of circumstances in the two cases. The requirements of peace are not those of war.

The bureaus of the staff-corps in the several geographical military departments, are organized in a manner which has been sanctioned by time, and is susceptible of but little modification.

The labors include the correspondence with the minister of war; with the generals commanding portions of the department; with the administrative officers; with the chiefs of artillery and engineers; with the chiefs of police, inspector-generals, judge-advocates, and civil officers. This correspondence includes sending to the minister of war all statements; reports and returns required by the regulations concerning troops stationed in the department; it comprises, also, recommendations for retiring officers and soldiers, pensions for widows, distribution of aid to old soldiers, admission into the hotel of invalids, applications for rewards and permissions to marry, forwarding official letters, operations of recruiting, orders for drafts, and authorization of voluntary enlistments in certain corps specified by the minister, transmission of orders for moving troops; their execution, giving warning of movements to civil and military authorities; sending itineraries on which the route to be pursued is marked; writing out and forwarding orders of the day; keeping registers of orders; communicating countersigns, paroles, &c.; sending leaves of absence for sickness or other cause; affairs relating to discipline and military justice; details for courts-martial and of inquiry; their assembling; orders of approval or disapproval of sentences.

The duties of the first military division are the most extended, and may serve well as a type.

There are five bureaus—1st. General correspondence. 2d. Recruiting. 3d. Relating to the *personnel*. 4th. Leaves granted to soldiers, and aid distributed. 5th. Military justice.

The registers and lists are:

First Bureau.

Register for the orders of the day of the division.

" for the correspondence with the minister.

" for the correspondence with civil and military authorities.

" for recording movements of the division.

" for recording countersigns, paroles, &c.

2d Bureau.
{ Register for correspondence.
"   for keeping an account of the horses of officers of the staff-corps.
"   for keeping an account of blanks issued to the different corps. }

3d Bureau.
{ Register of leaves of absence granted to officers.
"   for recording the names of officers coming to Paris on leave.
"   of the *personnel* of the division, (officers of the staff-corps.)
"   for correspondence. }

4th Bureau.
{ Register of furloughs granted to non-commissioned officers and privates.
"   of aid rendered.
"   for correspondence. }

5th Bureau.
{ Register for correspondence with the minister.
"   for correspondence with civil and military authorities.
"   for correspondence with courts of inquiry and courts-martial.
"   for recording sentences, &c. }

This bureau duty of the officers of the staff-corps at the head-quarters of military departments, consists chiefly in the daily application to current events of the military rules, regulations, laws, decisions, and circulars for the department of war.

When the general of division is making a tour of inspection through his division, he still holds the command, and there is no commander ad interim.

The chief of staff signs orders relating to ordinary current affairs, as by the order of the general, but he cannot take this responsibility in cases of military justice, when the signature of the general of division is indispensable. Neither can he sign for him in pressing cases of great importance, but the general of brigade signs under such circumstances, and is responsible for his action to the general of division.

ART. 15.—Active duties in Military Departments of French Staff-Corps.

The officers employed on the staff of military departments, besides bureau duty, reconnoitre the ground when the general assembles the troops of his division for exercises in the field; they also establish cantonments in large movements of troops; they make tours of inspection to military posts and establishments, and carry the general orders in manœuvres at review and public pageants.

ART. 16.—Duty as Aides-de-Camp.

The aides are the most active agents in the command. Attached to the person of the general, they received orders only from him. Their duties are difficult and delicate. Often possessing the entire confidence of the generals, informed of all their plans, they ought to comprehend them thoroughly, foresee their results, and especially be discreet. In the army their special duties are:—to know the places of the troops and the different head-quarters, the principal positions, roads, posts, composition of columns, names of generals, orders of battle.

On the field of battle they watch the manœuvres of

the enemy, and, if necessary, call the general's attention to them: their duty consists specially in carrying
orders, but this is not purely a mechanical duty, for
an order badly transmitted, or incorrectly interpret-
ed, may entail the most fatal consequences. An aide-
de-camp should therefore not only recollect the
words of the order, but take the spirit and intent also;
he should observe the execution of it, and if he sees
this execution answering to the letter, perhaps, but
not to the spirit, he should be firm enough to have it
rectified in the name of the general, assuming, so to
say, the whole responsibility. If an order which he
carries is not opportune, he ought to return, if time
permits, for new instructions.

Off the battle-field and in the midst of grand movements, the aides are employed, according to the
degree of confidence they deserve, upon secret missions, and upon all occasions where the general
wishes to be represented by another self.

ART. 17.—Duty when attached to Embassies.

When on such duty, they are occupied in special
diplomatic missions, the study of the military system
and laws of foreign powers, and striving to collect all
the information desirable for the better organization
of their own army.

NOTE.—It results from this exposé of the duties of
the staff-corps that its officers are the prime agents,
the messengers, and sometimes even the interpreters
of the generals; that they ought to be informed of military operations, of plans of campaigns, of the main
dispositions for battles; that they are intrusted with

the execution of these; that they should consequently be familiar with the mechanism and the spirit of the organization and movements of armies; should never lose sight of the properties of each arm of the service, so as to form correct conclusions for their use on occasions.

For these reasons, it has seemed logical, and even necessary, to add further on a summary of the most common and acknowledged principles of the art of war, as well as a comparison of the manœuvres of the three arms.

ART. 18.—Staff of the United States Army.

There is in this army no corps identical in functions with the *staff-corps* of the French army, which have been pointed out above.

Colonel Scott, in his Military Dictionary (a valuable work recently published, which should be in the hands of every officer of the army), remarks, that the staff of an army may be properly distinguished under three heads:

1. The general staff, consisting of adjutants-general and assistant adjutants-general, aides-de-camp, inspectors-general, and assistant inspectors-general. The functions of these officers consist not merely in distributing the orders of commanding generals, but also in regulating camps, directing the march of columns, and furnishing to the commanding general all necessary details for the exercise of his authority. Their duties embrace the whole range of the service of the troops, and they are hence properly styled general staff officers.

2. Staff-corps, or staff departments. These are

special corps or departments, whose duties are confined to distinct branches of the service. The engineer corps and topographical engineers are such staff-corps. The ordnance, quarter-masters, subsistence, medical, and pay departments are such staff departments.

3. The regimental staff embraces regimental officers and non-commissioned officers charged with functions, within their respective regiments, assimilated to the duties of adjutant-generals, quarters-masters, and commissaries. Each regiment should have a regimental adjutant and a regimental quarter-master.

ART. 19.—Composition of General Staff, Staff-Corps, and Staff Departments of United States Army.

The adjutant-general's department consists of the following officers:

1 brigadier-general, .	adjutant-general.
1 colonel, . . .	assistant adjutant-general.
2 lieutenant-colonels, .	" "
4 majors, . . .	" "
12 captains, . . .	" "

The inspector-general's department contains the following officers:

2 colonels, . . .	inspector-generals.
5 majors, . . .	assistant inspector-generals.

The quartermaster-general's department contains the following officers:

1 brigadier-general, .	quartermaster-general.
3 colonels, . . .	ass't quartermaster-generals.
4 lieutenant-colonels,	deputy "

8 majors,   .   .   .   quarter-masters.
48 captains,   .   .   assistant quarter-masters.

The subsistence department contains the following officers:

1 colonel, . . commissary-general of subsistence.
1 lieut.-colonel, ass't   "   "
6 majors, . . commissaries of subsistence.
16 captains,   .   "   "

The medical department is composed as follows:

1 colonel,   .   .   .   surgeon-general.
40 majors,   .   .   .   surgeons.
104 captains and lieutenants, assistant-surgeons.
Cadets in number not exceeding 50.

The pay department is composed as follows:

1 colonel,   .   .   .   paymaster-general.
2 lieutenant-colonels, .   deputy   "
25 majors,   .   .   .   paymasters.

The corps of engineers contains the following officers:

1 colonel,
4 lieutenant-colonels,
8 majors,
12 captains,
15 1st lieutenants,
15 2d lieutenants; 12 brevet 2d lieutenants may be
    attached.

The corps of topographical engineers contains the following officers:

1 colonel,
3 lieutenant-colonels,
8 majors,
10 captains,
13 1st lieutenants,
13 2d lieutenants; 10 brevet lieutenants may be
attached.

The ordnance department contains the following
officers:

1 brigadier-general,
2 colonels,
2 lieutenant-colonels,
4 majors,
12 captains,
12 1st lieutenants,
12 2d lieutenants; 12 brevet 2d lieutenants may be
attached.

ART. 20.—Duties of Adjutant-Generals.

The bureau duties of adjutant-generals and assistants are: publishing orders in writing; making up
written instructions and transmitting them; reception
of reports and returns; disposing of them; forming
tables, showing the state and position of corps; regulating details of service; corresponding with the
administrative departments relative to the wants of
troops; the methodical arrangement and care of the
records and papers of the office.

The active duties of adjutant-generals consist in
establishing camps; visiting guards and outposts;
mustering and inspecting troops; inspecting guards
and detachments; forming parades and lines of battle;

the conduct and control of deserters and prisoners; making reconnoissances; and in general, discharging such other active duties as may be assigned them.

ART. 21.—Aides-de-Camp.

These are ex-officio assistant adjutant-generals (Act March 2, 1821). They are confidential officers selected by general officers to assist them in their military duties. A lieutenant-general appoints not exceeding four in time of war, and two in peace, with the rank of lieutenant-colonel. A major-general appoints two, and a brigadier-general one. The act of August 5, 1861, enacts that "during the existing insurrection," the president may appoint aides-de-camp at will, with the rank of captains, majors, lieutenant-colonels, or colonels, upon the recommendation of the lieutenant-general, or of a major-general commanding an army in the field. These appointments to be recalled whenever the president thinks proper.

Aides-de-camp are attached to the person of the general, and receive orders only from him. Their functions are difficult and delicate. Often enjoying the full confidence of the general, they are employed in representing him, *in writing orders*, in carrying them in person if necessary, in communicating them verbally upon battle-fields and fields of manœuvre. It is important that aides-de-camp should know well the positions of troops, routes, posts, quarters of generals, composition of columns, and orders of corps; facility in the use of the pen should be joined with exactness of expression; upon fields of battle they watch the movements of the enemy; not only grand manœuvres but special tactics should be familiar to them. It is necessary that their knowledge be sufficiently comprehensive to understand the object and purpose of all orders, and also to judge, in the varying circumstances of a battle-field, whether it is not necessary to modify an order when carried in person, or if there be time to return for new instructions.

ART. 22.—Books to be kept at Head-quarters of an Army, Regiment, &c.

The following rules for keeping books at the head-quarters of the army, and in the adjutant-general's office, may, with modifications that will readily occur, be used with armies in the field, at the head-quarters of divisions, departments, regiments, &c.

1. *Letters Received.*—All official communications received will be entered in this book, excepting only such letters of mere transmittal of orders, returns, certificates of disability, requisitions, &c., as need not be preserved. The orders, returns, certificates, requisition, &c., will be themselves appropriately entered in other books specially provided for the purpose.

Preliminary to being entered, every letter will be folded and indorsed. Letter paper will be folded in three equal folds, *cap* paper in four. The indorsement will give the place and date of letter, name and rank of writer, and a summary of contents, and if other papers accompany the letter, the number transmitted will also be noted on the back in red ink. Each enclosure will be numbered, and bear the same *office marks* as the letter transmitting it. Figures A, B, C exemplify the manner of indorsing.

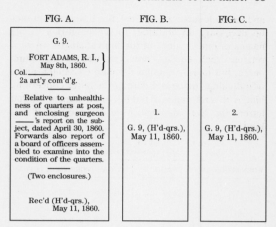

FIG. A.

G. 9.

FORT ADAMS, R. I., }
    May 8th, 1860.
Col. ———,
2a art'y com'd'g.

Relative to unhealthi-
ness of quarters at post,
and enclosing surgeon
———'s report on the sub-
ject, dated April 30, 1860.
Forwards also report of
a board of officers assembled to examine into the
condition of the quarters.

(Two enclosures.)

Rec'd (H'd-qrs.),
   May 11, 1860.

FIG. B.

1.

G. 9, (H'd-qrs.),
May 11, 1860.

FIG. C.

2.

G. 9, (H'd-qrs.),
May 11, 1860.

Every letter required to be preserved will be entered *alphabetically*, and numbered, the series of numbers beginning and terminating with the year, and including all letters *dated* (whether received or not) within the year. Only one number will be given to each letter received with its enclosures, so that the sum of the numbers under each alphabetical entry in the book of "Letters received," during any year, will show the number of letters received in that year.

As a general rule every letter will be entered in the name of its writer; but there are cases where it is preferable, for convenience of reference, to enter it in the name of the person who forms the subject of the letter, and not in that of the writer. Applications from citizens for the discharge of soldiers, &c., are of this character. Usually a single entry of each letter and its enclosures will suffice, but it may sometimes be necessary, in addition, to make entries in the names of one or more of the individuals to whom it relates. Such entries, however, will not be numbered, but merely contain the date of receipt, name of individual, place and date of the letter concerning him, with a reference in red ink to the number of that letter. Fig. E is an illustration of an entry of this kind.

FIG. E.

S. 1860.   LETTERS RECEIVED.

WHEN RECEIVED.	NAME.	DATE AND PURPORT OF LETTER.
May 11th	(Surgeon _____.)	Fort Adams, R. I., May 8, 1860. See No. 9, Letter G.

FIG. D.
LETTERS RECEIVED.

1860.   G.

WHEN RECEIVED.	NAME.	DATE AND PURPORT OF LETTER.
May 11 . . . . 9.	Col. _____ 2d art'ly com'dg.	FORT ADAMS, R. I., May 8, 1860. Relative to unhealthiness of quarters at the post, and enclosing surgeon _____'s report on the subject, dated April 30, 1860: forwards also copy of a report, dated Aug. 16, 1858, of a board of officers assembled to examine into the condition of the quarters.

The book of "Letters received" will contain a *side*

index extending throughout, and will be divided among the several letters of the alphabet according to the probable space required for entries under each letter. The book will be paged, and each page divided into three columns, headed "When received," "Name," "Date and purport of letter," respectively, as shown by Fig. D, which also exhibits the entry in the book of the letter represented by Fig. A. Each entry will be separated from the one preceding it by a red ink line; and where two or three letters relate to the same subject, they will either be filed together, or made to refer to each other by their numbers, and the filing or reference be noted in the book as well as on the letters themselves.

Letters from the executive and staff departments, and other public offices in Washington, will be entered alphabetically in the names of the departments or offices themselves, but the entry will always exhibit the writer's name likewise; thus, communications from the war department would be entered in the letter W, as follows: "War, Secy. of (Hon. ——), &c."

Communications from the President will be entered in the letter P; from the state department, in S; treasury, T; war, W; navy and its bureaus, N; post-office and its bureaus, P; interior, I; attorney-general, Q; subsistence department, S; surgeon-general, S; paymaster-general, P; engineer department, E; topographical engineers, E; ordnance, O; recruiting service, superintendent of, R; pension office, P; comptrollers of the treasury, C; auditors of the treasury, A; treasurer, U.S., T; Indian affairs, commissioner of, I; land office, L; patent office, P.

Communications from governors of states will be entered in the names of the states, the entry showing likewise the governor's names; thus, a letter from the governor of New York would be entered in the letter N, as follows: "New York, Governor of, (His Excellency ——)," &c.

Letters from the staff officers, written by direction of their generals, will be entered in the name of the generals themselves; thus, a communication from General K——'s staff officer would be entered in the letter K, as follows:

"Bvt. Maj. Genl. ——, comdg. western division,
(by Asst. Adjt. Genl. ——)."

Communications addressed to the war department or adjutant-general's office, and thence referred, without an accompanying letter, to head-quarters, for report or to be disposed of, will be entered in the ordinary way, in the names of their writers, a note (in red ink) being simply made in the second column of the book, to show the fact of reference, thus— "(from A. G. O.)"

Where letters are referred from the office for report, &c., a note of the fact must be made (in red ink) in this book, with a citation of the page (or number of the letter) in the "indorsement" or "letter book," where the reference is recorded, thus—"Ref'd for report to comdg. officer, Fort T., May 11 see book of 'indorsements,' p. 3," or, "see letter No. 7, vol. 1st." When the communication is returned, a memorandum to this effect will be made in the book, "Returned with the report, May 25th."

Should the portion of this book, appropriated to

any particular letter of the alphabet, prove insufficient for entries under that letter, they will be transferred to a few of the last leaves allotted to some other letter of the alphabet, where there is more space than will be probably required for that letter. The fact of transfer will be noted in large characters (in red ink) at the bottom of the page from which transferred, and at the top of the page to which carried, as follows: "transferred to page 250," and "brought from page 60."

2. *Letter Book.*—Every letter recorded in this book is numbered (in red ink), the numbers commencing and terminating with the year, and each letter is separated from the one which follows it by a red line.

The address of all letters should be at the top, the *surname* being written conspicuously in the margin, followed by the official title (if any) and Christian name, thus—Bvt. Maj. Genl. —.

Comdg., &c., &c., &c.,

Or Esq., Samuel H.

Each letter should be signed in the record-book by its writer.

Whenever copies of letters are furnished, the names of the persons to whom they are sent should be noted in red ink in the margin, with the date, when the last differs from the date of the letter itself. In like manner, when a letter is addressed to one officer, under cover to his commander, &c., this fact should also be noted in red ink on the margin.

The name of every person to whom a letter is addressed is indexed alphabetically, in black ink, and the names of the individuals whom it principally concerns, in red ink. A red ink line is drawn in the body

of the letter, under the names so indexed, to facilitate
a reference to them. In the margin, immediately under
the name of the person to whom a letter is addressed,
there are two references, above and below a short red
line, the one above (in red) indicates the last preceding letter to the same individual, and the one below
(in black) the next following. A detached index is
used until the record-book is full, when the names are
arranged under the letters as in city directories, and
thus classified, they are transferred to the permanent
index attached to the record-book.

3. *General Orders.*—Every order recorded in this
book shall be signed by the staff officer whose signature was attached to the originals sent from the
office, and each order should be separated from the
one following by a red line.

The mode of numbering, distribution, and general
form of orders, are prescribed by the regulations.
The distribution in each particular care should be
noted with red ink in the margin, to show that the
regulations have been complied with; and where
orders are sent to one officer, under cover to his
commander (which course ought always to be pursued), or furnished at a date subsequent to the issue
of the orders, these facts should likewise be added;
where the order has been printed, it will be sufficient
to write the word "printed" in red ink in the margin,
to indicate that the widest circulation has been given
to it.

There are two indexes attached to the book, one of
names, the other of *subjects*; every order will be
indexed in the latter immediately upon being copied.
For *names*, a detached index will first be used until

the record-book is full, and then they will be arranged under each letter, as in city directories, and thus classified, transferred to the permanent alphabetical index attached to the record-book. Every proper name will be indexed, and a red line drawn in the body of the order under it, to facilitate a reference to it.

4. *Special Orders.*—(All the directions under the last head of "General Orders" are applicable to this class of orders.)

5. *Indorsements and Memoranda.*—Every indorsement made on letters or other communications sent from the office will be copied in this book, and be *signed* by the staff officer whose signature was attached to the indorsement itself. A brief description of the communication sent out (the name of its writer, date, subject, and *office marks*), should precede the record of the indorsement, to render the latter intelligible; and where such communication has been entered in the book of "letters received," the disposition made of it should also be noted in that book, with a citation of the page where the indorsement is recorded. Should the communication be returned to head-quarters, a memorandum will be made to that effect, with the date when received back, in all the books where the fact of the reference from the office may have been noted.

In the case of such papers as proceedings of general courts-martial, certificates of disability for the discharge of soldiers, requisitions for ordnance, &c., which are not filed at head-quarters, but forwarded thence for deposit in other offices, it will generally suffice to make a brief memorandum of the general-in-chief's action upon them, instead of copying the indorsements. Where the indorsement, however, settles any rule or principle, it ought, of course, to be copied in full.

The name and address of every officer to whom a communication is referred, will be written in the margin, and all proper names, no matter in what connection employed, must be indexed.

The name of the person to whom a communication is sent, will be indexed in black ink, and the names mentioned in the description prefixed to the indorsement on the communication, as well as in the indorsement itself, will be indexed in red ink. To facilitate a reference to these last names, a red line will be drawn under them. In the margin, immediately under the name of the person to whom a communication is addressed, there are two references, above and below a short red line; the one above (in red) indicates the last preceding reference to the same individual, and the one below (in black) the next following.

6. *Book of Returns*.

ART. 23.—The Books for a Regiment are the following:

1. General order book, to contain all orders and circulars from general, department, division, or brigade head-quarters, with an index.

2. Regimental order book, to contain regimental orders, with an index.

3. Letter book, to contain the correspondence of the commanding officer on regimental subjects, with an index.

4. An index of letters required to be kept on file.

5. Descriptive book, to contain a list of all the offi-

cers of the regiment, with their rank, date of appointment and promotion; transfers, leaves of absence, places and dates of birth. Also, the names of all enlisted men, entered according to priority of enlistment, giving their description, the dates and periods of their reenlistments; and under the head of remarks, the cause of discharge, character, death, desertion, transfer; in short, every thing relating to their military history. This book should be indexed.

One copy of the monthly returns to be filed.

ART. 24.—Post Books. Company Books.

The following books should be kept at each post: a morning report book, a guard report book, an order book, a letter book; also copies of the monthly post returns.

One descriptive book, one clothing book, one order book, one morning report book. One page of the descriptive book will be appropriated to the list of officers; two to the non-commissioned officers; two to the register of men transferred; four to register of men discharged; two to register of deaths; four to register of deserters; the remainder to the company description list.

ART. 25.—Orders and Correspondence.

The orders of commanders of armies, division, brigades, regiments, are denominated orders of such army, division, &c., and are either general or special. They are numbered, both general and special, in separate series, each beginning with the year.

General orders announce whatever it may be important to make known to the whole command.

Special orders are such as do not concern the troops in general, and need not be published to the whole command; such as relate to the march of some particular corps, the establishment of some post, the detaching of individuals, granting requests, &c., &c.

A general order, and an important special order, must be read and approved by the officer whose order it is, before it is issued by the staff officer.

An order should state at the head, the source, place, and date; and at the foot, the name of the commander who gives it, as for example:

Head-quarters of the First Brigade, Second Division.

Camp at——, 1st June, 1860.

General Orders,
  No.—. }

By command of Brigadier-General——.

——, Asst. Adjt. Genl.

Orders may be put in the form of letters, but generally in the strict military form, through the office of the adjutant or adjutant-general of the command.

Orders are transmitted through all the intermediate commanders in the order of rank. When an intermediate commander is omitted, the officer who gives the order should inform him, and he who receives it should report it to his immediate superior.

All communications on public service should be marked on the cover, "Official business."

ART. 26.—Quarter-Master's Department.

This department provides the quarters and transportation of the army; storage and transportation for all army supplies; army clothing, camp and garrison equipage; cavalry and artillery horses; fuel; forage; straw; stationery.

The incidental expenses paid through this department include per diem to extra-duty men; postage on public service; expenses of courts-martial, of the pursuit and apprehension of deserters, of the burials of officers and soldiers, of hired escorts, of expresses, interpreters, spies, and guides, of veterinary surgeons and medicines for horses, and of supplying posts with water; and generally the proper and authorized expenses for the movements and operations of an army not expressly assigned to any other department.

ART. 27.—Engineers.

The engineers are charged with planning, constructing, and repairing all fortifications and other defensive works; with planning and constructing such civil works of the government as may be assigned to them. In time of war they present plans for the attack and defence of military works; lay out and construct field defences, redoubts, intrenchments, roads, and military bridges, &c.; form a part of the vanguard to remove obstructions; and in retreat, form a part of the rear-guard, to erect obstacles, destroy roads, bridges, &c., so as to retard an enemy's pursuit.

ART. 28.—Topographical Engineers.

The duties of the corps consist in surveys for the defence of the frontiers, and of positions for fortifications, in reconnoissances of the country through which an army is to pass or to operate; in the examination of routes of communication by land or by water, both for supplies and for military movements; in the construction of military roads; and the construction of such civil works as may be placed in their charge.

ART. 29.—Ordnance Department.

The ordnance department has charge of the arsenals and armories, and furnishes all ordnance and ordnance stores for the military service.

The general denomination, "Ordnance and Ordnance Stores," includes all cannon and artillery carriages and equipments; apparatus and machines for the service and manœuvres of artillery; all small arms and accoutrements and horse equipments; all ammunition; and all tools and materials for the ordnance service.

PART SECOND.

ART. 30.—Tactical Units and Formations.

The tactical units, which are the elements of armies, are the battalion, squadron, and battery. The battalion, in the French army, consists of eight companies, of 90 to 120 men each, in two ranks. In the United States service (Hardee's tactics), a regiment is composed of ten companies; in all exercises and manœuvres every regiment, or part of a regiment, composed of two or more companies, will be designated as a battalion.

A late act of Congress added to the regular army nine *regiments* of infantry, and declared that each should consist of not less than two, nor more than three *battalions*, each battalion to consist of eight companies, and each company not to contain more than eighty-two privates. The front of a battalion is equal to the number of files multiplied by twenty inches, which is the front allowed to a man. The depth of a column depends, 1st, upon the space occupied from front to rear by a man, viz., nineteen inches; 2d, the interval of thirteen inches between the ranks, and 3d, upon the variable interval between the subdivisions of the column. The depth of a column of eight companies, closed *en masse* by division, is thirteen yards. The intervals between deployed battalions is about twenty-four paces.

Between battalions in column the interval is about twenty-four paces, plus the front of a subdivision; if it is a closed column, the interval is reduced to nine paces.

A brigade is composed of two, three, or even four regiments; a division of two or three brigades. Brigades are separated by intervals of thirty paces; divisions by intervals of fifty or sixty paces. The squadron is formed of four platoons, each of twelve to sixteen files. The front of a squadron in line is as many yards as the number of files. The depth in column is derived 1st, from the space occupied by the horse in the rank from front to rear, viz., ten feet; 2d, the space of two feet between the ranks; and 3d, the variable interval between the subdivisions of the column. Between squadrons in line there is an interval of thirteen yards, and between squadrons in column, the same distance of thirteen yards increased by the front of a subdivision. If it is a closed column by squadrons, the interval is thirteen yards only. Squadrons are formed into regiments of several squadrons; regiments into brigades, and brigades into divisions. The distance between regiments in line of battle is sixteen yards; for brigades and divisions, the intervals are the same as for infantry.

Field artillery is divided into two parts, horse artillery and mounted artillery. Horse artillery is generally attached to and manœuvres with cavalry, and cannoneers being mounted on horseback. Mounted artillery is generally attached to and manœuvres with the infantry, and cannoneers marching at the sides of the pieces, or, when necessary, mounting the ammunition chests. The artillery reserves are composed of horse and mounted batteries in such proportions as the nature of the service requires.

The calibre and description of the pieces now in use in the service of the United States, are the six-pounder and twelve-pounder gun, the twelve-pounder, twenty-four pounder, and thirty-two pounder howitzer, and the twelve-pounder *light* gun, or, as it is sometimes called, *gun-howitzer*. (Rifled guns of different calibres are also now introduced into field batteries.) These guns are assembled in batteries of six or eight pieces, on the war establishment, of which four or six are guns, and two are howitzers; and of four pieces on the peace establishment, of which three are guns, and one a howitzer. The twelve-pounder guns and the twenty-four pounder or thirty-two pounder howitzer are associated together in the same batteries, which are called *twelve-pounder batteries*; and the six-pounder guns and twelve-pounder howitzers are associated together in like manner, and called six-pounder batteries. The twelve-pounder light guns are assembled in batteries by themselves.

On the war establishment, or when ordered to march, each carriage of the six-pounder and light twelve-pounder batteries is drawn by six horses. On the peace establishment, only four horses are required. When twelve-pounder batteries are in the field, each piece and caisson of the battery of manœuvre requires eight horses, the other carriages six horses each.

The number of men required for the service of a battery, including non-commissioned officers and artificers, varies from twenty to thirty per piece, according to circumstances; the number for field service should never be less than twenty-five, even in six-pounder batteries. They should be intelligent, active, muscular, well developed, and not less than five feet seven inches high; a large proportion should, if possible, be mechanics. The number of officers varies from four to six, depending on the number of pieces in the battery.

Organization of a Six-pounder mounted Battery for War. Six pieces.

	Officers.	Men.	Horses.	
Captain	1			Comd'g sections and caissons.
Lieutenants ...	4			1st serg't and qr. mr. sergt.
Staff Sergeants		2	2	Chiefs of pieces.
Sergeants		6	6	Gunners and chiefs of caissons.
Corporals		12		
Artificers		6	6	
Buglers		2	2	
Drivers		52	84	
Cannoneers ...		70		
Spare			10	
	5	150	110	

In batteries of horse artillery, two men and twelve horses per piece (one house spare) are required in addition to the numbers in the table above.

COMPOSITION AND EQUIPMENT OF A BATTERY FOR WAR.

The battery is supposed to consist of six pieces. In batteries of eight pieces there are two additional guns, with the material required for their service.

			12-pdr. battery.	12-pdr. (light).	6-pdr. battery.
Pieces and Caissons.	Guns	12-pounder, mounted	4		
		12-pounder, (light) mounted		6	
		6-pounder, mounted.			4
	Howitzers	24-pd., mounted	2		
		12-pd., mounted			2
	Total number of pieces		6	6	6
	Caissons	for guns	8	12	4
		for howitzers	4		2
	Total number of caissons		12	12	6
	Travelling forge		1	1	1
	Battery wagon		1	1	1
Ammunition for	Whole number of carriages		20	20	14
	Guns	shot	560	504	400
		spherical case	224	504	320
		shells		168	
		canisters	112	168	80
	Howitzers	spherical case	112		160
		shells	168		120
		canisters	42		32
	Total number of rounds with a battery		1218	1344	1112

For two thirty-two-pounder howitzer carriages and four caissons, the number of rounds of ammunition would be eighty-four spherical cases, one hundred and twelve shells, fourteen canisters, two hundred and ten in all. The number of friction primers is fifty percent greater than the number of rounds furnished the battery. To provide for contingencies, a small supply of port-fires and slow match is also furnished with the ammunition.

The campaign allowance of ammunition is double what has been here prescribed, or about four hundred rounds *per piece*, of which above two hundred rounds per piece accompany the battery, the remainder being with the reserve parks.

For mountain artillery service, a howitzer is used, which is a twelve-pounder, weighing two hundred and twenty pounds. For transporting one piece, its carriage, and ammunition, three mules are required. One mule will carry the *portable forge*. (See Gibbon's Manual of Artillery.)

Roads should be at least seven feet wide for the passage of artillery carriages.

A piece of artillery, or a caisson, drawn by six horses, takes a depth of fourteen yards and a front of two.

	Mounted Battery.		Horse Artillery.	
	DEPTH.	FRONT.	DEPTH.	FRONT.
	Yds.	Yds.	Yds.	Yds.
Column of sections	94	18	115	21
Line of battle	30	82	37	97
Line of battery	47	82	47	97
Section in line	30	18	37	21
Section in battery	47	18	47	21

The four companies of engineer soldiers in the United States service are composed each of ten ser-

geants or master workmen, ten corporals or over-
seers, two musicians, sixty-four first-class privates or
artificers, sixty-four second-class privates, in all one
hundred and fifty men each. There is also one
company attached to the corps of topographical
engineers.

ART. 31.—Action and Effect of the different Arms.

The dependence of infantry is upon its fire and the
bayonet; that of cavalry upon its charge, its fire being
generally of little effect; that of artillery upon its fire.

The foot soldier in ranks can fire three times a
minute. The fire of the ordinary musket is uncertain
beyond 200 yards. When troops are in masses, the
fire is still very effective beyond that distance. At 650
yards the musket ball is still deadly, and instances
have been known where men have been killed or
wounded at greater distances. The effective range of
the rifled spherical ball is over 400 yards. The oblong
rifle ball is effective at 1,000 yards. In forming a good
marksman, the first and one of the most important
steps is to instruct him how to estimate distances. On
a clear day and with ordinary light, at from 190 to
200 yards, every part of a man's body can be seen.
From 400 to 480 yards, the face can no longer be
distinguished, but the head, body, arms, and
movements, as well as the uniforms and muskets
can. At 600 yards the head, and upper and lower
parts of the body can be made out; and of the
uniform, the accoutrements and white pantaloons
only can be seen. From 750 to 800 yards, the body
appears of an elongated form. Extended arms can
be seen in profile, as also the legs of men in motion.

The uniform can no longer be distinguished at 900 yards; but the files can still be seen, as well as the movement of troops, and the dust thrown up by a projectile ricocheting on dry ground. From 1,100 to 1,200 yards, the files can be scarcely distinguished, and the troops appear like solid masses, the movements of which can still be followed.

A foot soldier travels in one minute—

in common time,	90 steps =	70 yards,
in quick time,	110 " =	86 "
in double quick time,	140 " =	109 "

We may deduce from these facts the number of discharges of a body of infantry which is charging another body of infantry before it reaches it.

In the same way we may calculate the number of discharges by cavalry while charging. The horse walking passes over 100 yards in one minute; at a trot, 200 yards; at a gallop, 400 yards.

Artillery should not fire at infantry beyond 1,000 yards, not at cavalry beyond 1,200, unless the ground is suitable for ricochet firing, and the enemy's troops are in dense masses. On favorable ground, solid shot from field guns will range as high as 1,600 or 1,800 yards or more. The probability of striking an object is the greatest possible at 500 yards. Firing should be slow at long distances, and more rapid as the effect produced is the greater, or as the enemy advances more rapidly.

A soldier should always keep his arms in good order, if he has any regard for his life and safety. A blunt point, a notched edge, or a gun that will not go off, are not worth so much as a stick. A pistol unless

fired at very close quarters, misses ninety-nine times
out of one hundred; the muzzle of the barrel should
not however touch the object aimed at, lest it should
burst. It is better to fire only one shot in ten minutes,
and that carefully, than ten in one minute, without
aiming at all. Aim is taken by raising the musket from
the ground upward, because the bullet has a tenden-
cy to rise, and if it goes off too soon, it may take
effect if at ordinary range. The trigger should be
pulled slowly, as any sudden jerk produces shock
which entirely deranges the aim. A man on foot ought
always to aim first at the horse of his adversary,
and a horseman will have nine chances to ten if he
do the same.

EMPLOYMENT OF INFANTRY.

Infantry is employed to skirmish at the beginning of
an engagement, then as soon as the enemy is shaken,
it rushes to the attack with fixed bayonets either in
line or column. Lines offer many inconveniences.
They waver during the march, they are often obliged
to break their original order, on account of the obstacles of the ground, thereby losing time and occasion-
ing confusion, they stop to fire, which checks their
ardor, and, finally, if they are forced and routed at a
point, all the rest is compromised; be, therefore,
sparing of marches in lines. Columns have none of
the above inconveniences, and if they are light and
not deep, they possess many advantages. They ought
always to be preceded by skirmishers (that protect
them more or less from the projectiles, and prevent
them from stopping to fire, inasmuch as they would
fire on their own party), which, at the moment of the

shock, close, mask the interval, and protect the flanks of the parallel masses. If a battalion has only three divisions, the first should be deployed, and the two others should place themselves in column by subdivisions behind its wings.

Infantry particularly attacks steep positions, villages, and intrenchments, When a battalion charges either in column or in line, its chief must from that moment act for himself, because the colonel or general, from whom he should have orders to receive, may not give any, being killed, wounded, or diverted by events not connected with this very battalion. Three cases may occur: 1st, the enemy gives way and takes to flight; 2d, the enemy stands without flinching, and awaits you boldly, or marches unhesitatingly to encounter you; 3d, your troops stop or turn back with more or less panic and confusion.

If the enemy runs away before you reach him, he will run quicker than yourself, and you could not overtake him. You must therefore send out one of your extreme companies as skirmishers against him, for the purpose of harassing him by a sharp fire, and you follow closely with the remaining companies, watching carefully both your flanks, lest they be turned, or lose the support of the adjoining battalions less successful than yours. Let your advance be prudent, and always take precautions against any charge of the cavalry of the second line, or of the reserves of the enemy. Before sending out your skirmishers, you may sometimes order the front of your column to fire a volley.

If the enemy awaits, or marches also to meet you, excite your men, surpass your adversary in ardor, and enter head foremost into the opposing mass; once the shock given, re-establish order by quickly rallying at a few paces in front; lastly, renew the shock or pursue, as in the former instance, with a company of skirmishers, according as the enemy resists or turns away.

If your men stop in spite of your energetic exhortations and efforts, if they give way, do not try to keep them near the enemy when their courage fails, draw them back behind a shelter, or behind other troops, and when the danger has become less, and you hope that your authority and the voice of duty will be obeyed, rally them, and act according to circumstances, either bringing them forward, or taking in flank some corps of the enemy that may have compromised itself.

It is not advisable for infantry in mass to attack artillery for the purpose of carrying it. Let it only send riflemen, more expert than numerous, who kill first the horses, and then the men; the horses once destroyed, the guns will certainly be the prey of the victorious; but as soon as they are reduced to immobility, they are not much to be feared.

A body of well-tried infantry might, in certain cases, and as an exception, await, standing still, the opposing infantry, and let it charge; for instance, when the men can be relied on, and when the enemy, marching through a difficult ground, is shaken by the fire of the skirmishers, you let him advance nearly to the muzzle of your muskets, make a discharge from your whole front, and rush upon him, with fixed bayonets and without reloading.

If infantry ought always to assume the offensive

against infantry or positions, and should act effica-
ciously at a distance with its riflemen against artillery,
it is generally reduced to the defensive before cavalry
either good or tolerably so; and the defensive almost
entirely consists in its fire. When threatened by cavalry, infantry will, therefore, quickly adopt the formation in square, in order to be in condition to open fire
on all sides. Squares formed by single battalions are
the best. A square or column should be sparing of its
fire in presence of cavalry, for it is its chief resource.
The best fire is that of a whole front. If one or more
horsemen enter the squares, the non-commissioned
officers must at once bayonet the horses.

EMPLOYMENT OF CAVALRY.

Cavalry fights as skirmishers, as foragers, in lines,
or in columns. The skirmisher are more or less
advanced, and more or less a part of the main body
according to circumstances. The engagement as foragers is useful against skirmishers rather of infantry
than of cavalry, against an enemy that has received a
check, to prevent him from rallying, and against
artillery. This sort of engagement is more fit to
deceive, or to mask another and more serious attack.
than to occasion heavy losses, except when cutting
down infantry skirmishers, or routed infantry escap-
ing through a plain. It must always be supported by
troops in good order, behind which the rallying may
be safely effected, otherwise the scattered horsemen
would be much endangered. When foragers are sent
against artillery, they begin attacking at 500 or 600
yards, gallop at once, diverging from the centre to the
wings, and threaten to turn the flanks of the battery.

This is a means of drawing the fire of the guns on scattered men, and of marching columns of squadrons, that rapidly fall on the support of the artillery, to overwhelm them and take the guns in rear.

The attacks in line are those which it is fit to employ against cavalry, in order to have more sabres at disposal, to occupy a larger front, and to threaten to outflank and turn the enemy. Employ the continuous lines against an irregular cavalry individually formidable, or when the ground being entirely favorable, the distance to clear short, and your men well trained, you have before you an enemy whom you must upset by all means, since you thus prevent your squadrons facing to the rear. But if your squadrons are not well trained, and the gallop long, the line breaks, and becomes much exposed. The line with intervals is favorable with good troops inferior in numbers to their opponents; it is then better to have large intervals, and present a front at least equal to that of the enemy than to be outflanked. Should any of his squadrons pass through the intervals, your second line is there to turn them off. The order with small intervals is that most generally employed, as having most of the advantages of the two former and none of their inconveniences. The order in column would not be bad to cut an opening in a line through which we must make our way, but in every other case, a column, especially if it is deep, is not good.

The charge of cavalry against cavalry once begun, the utmost latitude should be left to the chief of every squadron; he should not rely much on the orders of his commander, who may be killed or overthrown, &c. The essential point is to act with ensemble, and to conform to the movements of the adjoining squadrons unless they take to flight.

Five cases may present themselves in a charge: 1st, the enemy runs away before he is reached; 2d, the enemy stops and hesitates; 3d, the enemy passes through your formation, and you through his; 4th both of you stop; 5th, your men turn back. 1st, the enemy runs away before he is reached: then, as he is some distance in advance of you, it would be useless to pursue; stop, rectify the dressing by placing yourself a few paces in front, and be ready to gallop up to charge the second line when it issues through the first that is flying. If you see great disorder, and if no one comes to oppose you, send out your first or fourth division as skirmishers, and follow trotting. 2d, the enemy stops and hesitates—increase your speed, and fall upon him at the risk of blowing your horses, but as soon as he is broken, stop short, rally quickly, and if your horses are too much out of breath to begin a new charge, let the columns of support of your wings form themselves in your front to pursue the line defeated, or to repulse a fresh one. 3d, the enemy passes through your formation, and you through his; you are then in great disorder, and most probably out of condition to sustain the shock of the second line; stop short, rally quickly, and face about to the rear, to charge on the rear of the enemy that has passed, keep behind, and give full play to your flank columns and reserves; the former take the dispositions required by circumstances, either inwardly or outwardly, becoming first line, the reserves becoming second line, and forming flank columns, and the troops that have charged form the reserve in their turn. 4th, both the enemy and you stop: immediately start on at full gallop; the success is yours if you are the first to take the offensive; the enemy will certainly give way, and then you will proceed as in the first case. 5th, your men run away. Let them run a little, for it would be useless to attempt to stop them in the first moment of fright, and then you would waste your breath and your energies. You were in front of your troops before they turned, and, of course, now find yourself behind: follow them closely, calling near your subalterns and best men, in order to draw them away from the flying mass and to form a nucleus for rallying; then as soon as you find any accident of ground, or any thing favorable for rallying, increase your speed, push on before your men, face them, and give the command to halt, employing both voice and gesture to be obeyed.

As soon as the first line gives way, the columns on the flanks must take the necessary measures to charge the enemy should he venture to pursue, or to detain him until the reserve comes up.

When engaging, the chief of the first line must recollect that evolutions are dangerous in presence of the enemy, and he must abstain from them unless they are very simple, as gaining ground on a flank, retreating, breaking into small parallel columns to pass over difficult ground, &c., &c. A change of front might often be fatal; and rather than attempt such a movement for the purpose of attacking the flank of forces advancing resolutely to the encounter, and before which one fears to give way, it is better to face to the rear by a general command, retreat rapidly, and let the columns on the wing punish this audacity should the enemy venture between them after the line that is retiring.

Unless cavalry surprises infantry on the march, or in the middle of some evolutions, it should not attack it in front without its having been previously shaken by an effective fire of musketry, or of artillery. Bad infantry should be charged without hesitation, in whatever order it happens to be, if it is not protected by material obstacles. Cavalry that is not aware of the moral value of infantry in position, must first test it. To that effect, they pass in front, and threaten it at 400 or 500 yards, sending out against it a few horsemen, who fire, gallop, and raise dust; if the infantry instead of standing firm, begins to fire, it is lost. Let the cavalry immediately charge it vigorously in column, or in line, without waiting any longer. If on the contrary, the infantry keeps a bold face, is not intimidated, retains its fire, and merely sends a few marksmen out, it is not prudent to attack it at once. You must follow it up, observe it, and endeavor to find it at fault, or bring some artillery to break it.

When infantry in position does not stir, and has some guns, if you must overthrow it at all costs, repair to the extremities of its lines of squares. Two squadrons well led will have a great chance of breaking through a battalion by the following plan:

Both squadrons (Fig. 1.) are formed in close column, perpendicularly to the capital of the salient to be attacked, and out of range: a dozen skirmishers deploy, who fire and gallop to the right and left so as not to advance too far, and to mask what is going on behind them especially on the capital. The first

FIG. 1.

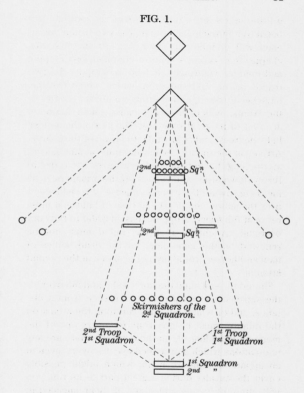

squadron divides into two parts, one going to the right, the other to the left, to menace the fronts of the square, and trot to the encounter. The second squadron, having allowed these two parts to advance a little, starts in its turn, at a trot, as soon as they begin to approach each other. The two fronts threatened will undoubtedly open fire. At the first discharge, the second squadron commences galloping and charges vigorously. It has for support the two troops of the first squadron, which whilst trotting, have been passed, and continue to attract the fire of the fronts, which does not cause much harm on account of its great obliquity. The skirmishers close in by degrees, and at last take the head of the charge. Arrived at the square, the cavalry must at all risks cut an opening; having succeeded, it gives the order to throw down arms, and carries off the prisoners, driving them toward the reserve; in case of resistance, it uses the sabre mercilessly. In case of failure, it must retire at full speed, stopping loss, in order to rally out of range. A charge that has failed must not be renewed on the same side, for the dead bodies of men and horses would break the shock at the second attempt.

Should the soil sink, the horses slip and fall over, or the skirmishers signal objects not seen from a distance, and of which you may run foul, the attack on the infantry must be given up, for every one of the men would be lost. If, on the contrary, there are any undulations which a practiced eye discovers, even in an apparently smooth plain, which might possibly cover the cavalry during a great part of its run, you will often, by taking advantage of them, succeed in overthrowing the best infantry. In general, ascending slopes, when not too steep, are favorable to cavalry against infantry, the latter almost always aiming too high; it is, therefore, an error on the part of this army to select almost exclusively very elevated positions. Those with gentle slopes are far preferable.

CAVALRY OPPOSED TO ARTILLERY.

Cavalry should never attack artillery in a direct manner; foragers ought to harass it in front whilst it endeavors to overcome the supports by falling on their rear. Having taken the guns, it is useless to carry them away, for it causes a delay and an encumbrance often fatal; cut the traces, kill the horses, if there is any fear of the enemy retaking them, and above all destroy the ammunition. The main point is to insure the victory: with it you remain master of all the material left on the field of battle; without it, the material is more cumbersome than useful.

EMPLOYMENT OF ARTILLERY.

Artillery if scattered indiscriminately, two or three guns together, will produce but little effect, being much in the way of the movements of the troops it is attached to, and will sometimes clumsily expose them to a fire it draws upon them. Employ it, therefore, in batteries tolerably strong, for from a distance it can do without supports, near enough to suffer from the projectile destined for it; and at close quarters, its grape-shot soon causes such mischief that it will be able to protect itself if it makes timely manœuvres. Let it above all avoid encumbering the ground on which other arms are moving, for it is only an accessory: it is, therefore, better to do without it than to let it cause pernicious delays and hindrances on a field of battle, where good order and time are every thing.

Howitzer shells are most useful to set fire to, or shower shells upon any shelter behind which the enemy is protected. With cannon-balls, the material obstacles found in front can be destroyed, or troops out of reach of an attack, for instance, behind a river, can be attacked. Canisters, especially several at a time, produce disastrous results, if fired at 200 or 300 yards against lines of columns, particularly on a dry and hard soil.

ART. 32.—Duties of Artillery.

In the field, the artillery has charge of the service of their pieces. The horse artillery manœuvres with the cavalry, having more lightness and mobility than mounted artillery, of which the weight is increased by that of the cannoneers: the latter is generally attached to the infantry. The foot or reserve artillery is for service in the attack and defence of places, and whenever it can be safely brought into action.

ART. 33.—Duties of Ordnance Department.

The ordnance department has charge of the arsenals and armories, and furnishes all ordnance and ordnance stores for the military service, also equipments for the mounted troops.

ART. 34.—Duties of Engineers.

The duties of engineers relate to the construction of permanent and field fortifications; works for the attack and defence of places; for the passage of rivers; for the movements and operations of armies in the field, and such reconnaissances and surveys as may be required for these objects, or for any other duty which may be assigned to them. By special direction of the President of the United States, officers of engineers may be employed on any other duty whatsoever.

ART. 35.—Proportion of different Troops in Armies.

The mass of an army should be composed on infantry. The cavalry should range from one quarter to one-sixth of the infantry, and not more than one-tenth in a mountainous country. The artillery should be in the proportion of two, three or four pieces to 1,000 men, or two or three batteries to a division, and in reserve a battery for every division. The engineer troops should be about one-thirtieth or one-fortieth of the infantry, furnishing one company to every division of infantry, accompanied by its wagon of tools. Several companies should be in the general reserve. When an army numbers fifty or sixty thousand men, it is sometimes divided into corps of from two to four divisions, each having four distinct parts, a centre, two wings, and a reserve.

ART. 36.—Rank, &c., of the different Arms.

The arrangement of the troops on parade and in order of battle is, 1st, the light infantry; 2d, infantry of the line; 3d, light cavalry; 4th, cavalry of the line; 5th, heavy cavalry. The troops of the artillery and engineers are in the centres of the brigades, divisions or corps to which they are attached; marines take the left of other infantry; volunteers and militia take the left of regular troops of the same arm, and among themselves, regiments of volunteers or militia of the same arm take place by lot. This arrangement is varied by the general-in chief as the circumstances of war render expedient. Brigades in divisions, and divisions in the army, are numbered from right to left; but in reports of military operations, brigades and divisions are designated by the name of the general commanding them.

ART. 37.—Assemblage of Armies.

To assemble an army, choose a great highway for the principal line. Let this be traversed by a corps d'armée, or by divisions distant a day's march from each other, and let the remaining troops follow the side roads in a similar manner, so that the distance from the centre to the wings shall not be too great.

An army is assembled in successive portions when it is desired not to encumber the roads, and not to overburden the population of the country; it may be assembled simultaneously to surprise an enemy, or to keep secret its destination. When an army is operating, an advanced guard is usually formed of a mixed division, that is to say, one composed of all arms.

ART. 38.—Definitions relating to Strategy.

By the *strategic line* upon which an army operates, we understand a surface of country in the direction of a communication to the rear, which it wishes to cover, or toward an obstacle to the front, which it wishes to remove or take. A strategic line connects two strategic points. When parallel to the point of positions occupied by an army, strategic lines are *bases of operations*; when perpendicular, they are lines of operations. The strategic triangle formed by the base of operations, and the converging lines of operations, ought to be as nearly as possible equilateral; the successive bases rest upon fortified points, or points of supply.

A front of operations seldom extends more than forty or fifty miles, in order that the forces may be assembled in five or six hours. In this extent are comprised the detachments, at several miles' distance from the flanks. In 1809, after the fall of Ratisbon, Napoleon operating with 90,000 men upon the right bank of the Danube, marched toward Vienna in the following order:—Bessières and Lannes at the centre of Bavaria; on the right, the Bavarians were skirting the foot of the Tyrolean Alps; on the left, Massena in front, Davoust in rear, were descending the river, followed by Dupas and Bernadotte. The army thus occupied a front of sixty or seventy miles, which was constantly diminishing, because the valley contracted toward Vienna, and this was the point to which all the columns were directed.

ART. 39.—Transportation.

This is in charge of the quarter-master's department, which provides transportation for the army, and all its supplies.

When troops are moved, or officers travel with escorts or stores, the means of transport provided should be for the whole command. The baggage to be transported should be limited to camp and garrison equipage and officers' baggage. Officers' baggage should not exceed (mess-chests and all personal effects included) as follows:—

	IN THE FIELD.	CHANGING STATIONS.
General Officers,	125 pounds.	1000 pounds.
Field "	100 "	800 "
Captains "	80 "	700 "
Subalterns "	80 "	600 "

These amounts should be reduced by the commanding officer when necessary.

The regimental and company desk should be transported; also for staff-officers, the books, papers, and instruments necessary to their duties; and for medical offices, their medical chest. The sick should be transported, on the application of the medical officers. The wagons for transportation march either in rear or on the flank of the column. When carriages cannot be used, as, for example, in a mountainous country, mules and horses should be used, and each may carry from 175 to 300 lbs.

If the war is active, and the troops distant, it may be well to use the system of requisitions. A quarter-master then, under the orders of the general, keeps himself several days in advance of the army, collects wagons in the country, establishes them in temporary depots, and uses them for four or five days.

ART. 40.—Supplies.

Supplies of food are calculated in proportion to the strength of the army, the kind of war, and the resources of the country. Large stores should be collected upon the lines and bases of operations; stores are also collected in smaller quantities nearer the enemy, for a few days' supply, and reserve stores further to the rear. The following data may be useful in collecting stores in magazines:—

The ration is three quarters of a pound of pork or bacon, or one and a quarter pounds of fresh or salt beef; eighteen ounces of bread or flour, or twelve ounces of hard bread, or one and a quarter pounds of corn meal; and at the rate, to one hundred rations, or eight quarts of peas or beans, or, in lieu thereof, ten pounds rice, six pounds coffee, twelve pounds sugar, four quarts vinegar, one and a half pounds tallow, or one and a quarter pounds adamantine, or one pound sperm candles; four pounds soap and two quarts salt. The act of August 3, 1861, sec. 13, provides "that the army ration shall be increased as follows, viz.: twenty-two ounces of bread or flour, or one pound of hard bread, instead of the present issue; fresh beef shall be issued as often as the commanding officer of any detachment or regiment shall require it, when practicable, in place of salt meat; beans and rice, or hominy, shall be issued in the same ration, in the proportions now provided by the regulation, and one pound of potatoes per man shall be issued at least three times a week, if practicable; and when these articles cannot be issued in these proportions, an equivalent in value shall be issued in some proper food, and a ration of tea may be substituted for a ration of coffee, upon the requisition of the proper officer; provided, that after the present insurrection shall cease, the ration shall be as previously provided by law and regulations."

On a campaign, or on marches, or on transport ships, the ration of hard bread is one pound. Loaf bread will keep four or five days in warm weather, and seven or eight in cold weather. Biscuit or crackers will keep much longer. One gallon of water per day per man for all purposes, and four gallons per day for each horse, are sufficient.

An ordinary sized beef will furnish about 500 rations; a mutton about forty.

1 bushel of wheat weighs 60 lbs., or 48 1-4 lbs. to the cubic foot.
1 bushel of oats weighs 40 lbs., or 32 1-6 lbs. to the cubic foot.
1 bushel of rye weighs 58 lbs.
1   "   barley "   54 "

A cubic yard of grain contains about twenty bushels. Hay well pressed weighs eleven pounds to the cubic foot, or 225 pounds to the cubic yard. One cubic yard of straw weighs 145 pounds. Oats in store, in large quantities, will spoil, if not turned over at least twice a week. Musty and new-mown hay is highly injurious to horses. In southern countries, hay is scarce; straw is generally given chopped, and is more nourishing than in northern countries. Barley requires great precautions, as it is apt to prove injurious. Green fodder is better than new hay—when the grass is of some height it is better. Green rice is the next best of the indigestible green fodders. Clover in large quantities is injurious, but when dried is much improved. Clover cut in the evening seldom causes sickness.

To provide food by requisitions, the people of the country should be paid. The requisition should not exceed one ration for every three inhabitants in a low country, nor one for six in mountainous regions. This must, however, be regulated by the number of troops, and their time of stay, or rapidity of movement. In fertile and populous countries, their resources will suffice to support the army, and it is then only necessary to exercise proper foresight in collecting stores; in a sterile country, the army must not go too far from its magazines, and reserve supplies must be collected. When the inhabitants of the country destroy every thing, great care must be exercised to have regular and secure magazines.

Effects and baggage of every kind should be collected in depots or fortified towns: in the same places, and always upon the great lines of communication, are collected parks of artillery, spare supplies, articles of clothing and equipment. The supplies necessary for a siege should be collected upon the same principle.

ART. 41.—Ammunition.

A good allowance is 100 rounds to each infantry soldier, forty in the cartridge boxes, fifty in the artillery wagons, ten in barrels; for the cavalry, ten cartridges in the boxes; for the artillery, 400 rounds to each piece, of which 200 are with the reserve parks.

In mountain warfare, it is well to organize mule trains to carry cartridges at the rate of twenty to each man, besides what he carries in his box. These may be packed in boxes containing 2,000 rounds for the infantry, and eight for the mountain howitzer. One mule can carry two of these boxes.

ART. 42.—Marches Executed to Assemble Armies.

To assemble armies, *route marches* are executed.

Generally these are made by battalions, distant one day's march from each other; the cavalry the most of the time proceeding by the side roads, usually the less direct, but it is difficult to make a numerous cavalry corps march together during a whole campaign without interfering with the rapidity of its movements, and without great difficulty of subsisting it; this corps should not exceed 6,000 horses. The artillery follows the cavalry, or, if it has a very long train, it may proceed by itself on a separate road.

The troops begin their concentration on the base of operations: when operations are beginning, the successive bodies draw toward each other, and the army encamps in lines a day's march from each other; upon getting near the enemy, columns are formed, especially if the country presents parallel roads of debouche. It is always advantageous to march a corps d'armée by several roads, its divisions at distances apart suitable for deployment, and in order of battle; but if there is but one communication, distances of 200 yards should be left between the different arms, and the cavalry more in rear of the column.

In these marches, when a defile is to be passed, the order in which the troops shall successively pass, should be arranged beforehand, and made known. The general rule is never to pile up the troops in such a manner that their movements shall be difficult, and their action paralyzed; but they must be kept sufficiently near, so that the enemy may not by a rapid movement fall upon isolated bodies and beat them in detail.

To arrive at the point of general concentration, which is always selected out of the reach of the enemy, too short as well as too long marches are to be avoided. A mean average of twenty miles is the proper measure to adopt, remembering that cavalry can, from time to time, clear as much as thirty miles, and that infantry ought never to march less than fifteen miles. For both infantry and cavalry one day of rest is sufficient after six or eight days of consecutive marching. It is of importance, when far from the enemy, not to regulate the march of the cavalry by that of infantry, for it would be prematurely injuring the former. The departure should take place neither too early nor too late. One hour between the reveille and the assembling of the troops will enable every one to make easily all the preparations for departure. The men eat their soup and keep the meat for the halt. The horses take a feed of oats. A guide, either civil or military, well acquainted with all the particulars of the road, accompanies the commander of the troop, if he is not himself familiar with them. Let us now suppose a march of twenty miles to be made, and see how cavalry and infantry will perform it.

Cavalry.—Departure at six o'clock, march of forty-five minutes, halt of ten minutes, reckoned from the moment when the last division has closed up to its distance (the troops forming, when halting, whatever may be the order adopted for the march) to the trumpet's call. The vanguard stops at the same time as the head of the column; and the rear-guard keeps at the proper distance from the rear. During the halt the horses have their girths tightened and their feet looked to. Some two and a half miles having been passed over in this first period of the march, the de-

tachment will clear six or seven miles without any
new halt, alternately walking and trotting, in about
100 minutes; then it will halt in a proper situation in
close column, if possible, and half an hour will be
allowed the men to breakfast on the meat kept for
that purpose. The second half of the distance will be
performed in two intervals of time, divided by a rest
of five or six minutes, alternately walking and trotting, so as to make five miles an hour. The destination will thus be reached at eleven o'clock in the
forenoon, five hours after departure. If the distance
be more or less than twenty miles, the halts would
almost always be the same in number and length as
above mentioned, but the duration of each march
would be lengthened or shortened by a few minutes.
If the cavalry has any baggage, this should start so as
to arrive, at the latest, one hour after the column.

A horse or mule carries 200 pounds, harness included; two-wheeled one-house carriages (the only sort
that should be tolerated) can receive a load of 800
pounds. Above these limits it is impossible to depend
on a regular speed of two and a half miles an hour, at
a walk, halt included, an average which should be
obtained.

Infantry.—Departure at six o'clock. After forty-five
minutes, a halt of ten minutes, reckoned from the
moment when the rear subdivision has closed up (the
companies forming as they halt) to the moment of
resuming the march. Afterward a halt of five minutes
for every hour of march. When half the distance,
rather more than less, is accomplished, the men
rest thirty minutes, to eat the morning's meat, and
the march is resumed, halting for a short time

every hour. An hour is the limit of an uninterrupted march, unless by continuing for a few minutes more, the destination, or the place of the great halt can be reached, but this increase should not exceed twelve minutes. Reckoning two and a half miles per hour, short halts included, as is ordinarily done, it is found that a column of infantry starting in the morning at six o'clock, will arrive at two in the afternoon, which allows sufficient time for resting until the next day. Should the infantry have any baggage, this should start at the same time, and both will arrive together. A detachment that might be obliged to go and seek for beds or stables at a distance, on the right or left of the direction to be followed next day, would do better to bivouac near the corps to which it belongs, especially if the weather is fine. It would thus avoid useless fatigues, and accustom itself to the necessities of war; besides it is sometimes far better to sleep on straw in a barn than two in a bad bed.

Sometimes the assembling is performed very near the enemy: it becomes necessary in such cases to calculate accurately the distances to be passed over, and to combine the marches in such a way that the columns arrive together at the point of assembly. In this case, special use is made of forced marches, and hastening some of the troops by transporting them in carriages, or otherwise—railroads will be much employed for this purpose in war, and will have a great influence upon the art. In forced marches, the number of halts is sometimes doubled, and then a half ration is served out at each alternate halt; cavalry does not generally make more than thirty miles a day when the march is to be long.

A train of 250 wagons takes, at the rate of twelve yards to a carriage, a space of 3,000 yards in a file, and may transport from 2,000 to 2,500 men in a body. When the troops are moved partly on foot and partly by carriage, care should be taken that while those on foot are passing over a given space between two halts, those in the carriage shall pass over twice as much. The same carriages do not pass over the entire route travelled, fresh relays of vehicles being provided at intervals of two or three days. When an army is assembling, the generals of divisions send forward to the rendezvous, in advance, a staff officer to receive the corps; the brigades and isolated regiments also each send an officer to the same point. These officers form the troops upon the ground in compact order ready for battle, and according to rank.

ART. 43.—Service of Subsistence during Route Marches.

During the different marches, the troops are subsisted: 1st, by issuing rations at the halts when it can be so arranged; 2d, from magazines established at suitable intervals, or by provisions drawn from depots formed in advance; or 3d, by the system of requisitions.

ART. 44.—Manœuvre Marches.

On marches near the enemy, it is proposed either to attack him, or to attempt to turn him, and attack in an advantageous position, or to avoid him by retreating; these are the movements which precede or follow an action, and are called manœuvre marches. They are executed either by the front or flank.

ART. 45.—Forward Movements.

Always march in column, and in several columns, if they can be near enough to each other to be held well in hand by the chief, and to be ready to afford mutual assistance in time of need. The distances between them should not be more than those necessary for deployment.

In these marches, the principle is always to march toward the sound of the cannon. Upon different roads, the heads of columns endeavor to keep as nearly as possible equally advanced; bodies of troops are placed so as to keep up the connection between the columns. They march moreover in the order in which they are usually brought into battle. The distance between the divisions of a corps d'armée should not exceed a few hours' march; between the corps d'armée, not more than one day's march. A corps d'armée, while formed in columns, will also be organized by lines; thus it may form three or four columns, each nearly in the following order: a battalion or several squadrons, a whole or half battery, a brigade of infantry, a battery, a second brigade; at the last, the reserve, then the head-quarters.

In country somewhat broken and obstructed, the mass of the cavalry is generally kept in the centre with infantry supports; in an open country on the wings. The heads of columns in open country are also formed of squadrons escorted by horse artillery.

As it is nearly impossible to find three parallel roads at such distances apart as suit the strength of the columns of a corps d'armée, and as it is moreover necessary to make use of the travelled roads, the columns will not always be separated by suitable intervals; then the proper distances should be taken when near the field of battle by opening, if need be, new debouches. With this view, each column is, as far as possible, preceded by a detachment of engineer soldiers, or other pioneers, whose duty it is to remove all obstacles which might retard the march. The sappers are assisted, if necessary, by the people of the country, or by infantry soldiers. The detachment should be formed into two sections: at the first obstacle, the first section stops, and the other goes forward: an officer of engineers, or of the staff, directs the work. The road is marked out by guide posts or otherwise. When they get near the field of battle, the lines approach each other, to within 300 or 400 yards for the battle corps. Columns are multiplied, avoiding hollow roads, as well as separations resulting from obstacles difficult to cross. Further on will be seen the dispositions for deployments.

Every column in marching is preceded by an advanced guard, and protected by flankers, whose duty it is to cover the head of the column and the deployments. The moving skirmishers are usually relieved every time such an obstacle presents itself upon the front that they are obliged to use the same road for passing it as the column.

Besides the advanced guards attached to each corps and each column, there is usually a general advanced guard which keeps at a distance of five to ten miles, or sometimes falls back to within one mile. Its strength and composition, as well as those of the special advanced guards are dependent upon the character of the ground and the relative positions of the different bodies of troops as to the enemy.

Advanced guards are chiefly formed of light troops, but of all arms, in order to be able to act on all ground. When necessary, detachments of engineer troops may be attached to advanced guards. They should have also skirmishers in front and flank, and these supported at intervals by small detachments, who occasionally relieve them, and who explore suspicious points.

The figure (2) gives an example of an advanced guard of six squadrons, two battalions, and a half battery, marching in a plain, with small patrols of three horsemen upon the flanks, to which are added small detachments not shown in the figure.

In a mountainous country, this arrangement would be modified by placing the infantry at the head of the column; that arm would then be called upon to

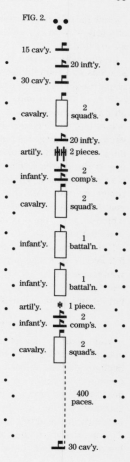

FIG. 2.

15 cav'y.

20 inft'y.

30 cav'y.

cavalry.   2 squad's.

20 inft'y.

artil'y.   2 pieces.

infant'y.   2 comp's.

cavalry.   2 squad's.

infant'y.   1 battal'n.

infant'y.   1 battal'n.

artil'y.   1 piece.

infant'y.   2 comp's.

cavalry.   2 squad's.

400 paces.

30 cav'y.

furnish patrols and skirmishers, the artillery and cavalry following in rear of the infantry, patrolling as far as possible.

In wooded countries, the arrangement is nearly the same as in a mountainous: sometimes a double line of patrols is formed, of which the cavalry furnishes one. In broken ground, infantry is mingled with cavalry. The advanced guards of the different columns in manœuvre-marches advance at the same rate as the heads of columns, keeping up a constant intercommunication by the patrols; those of the wings keep an eye to the extreme flanks of the march. If in these marches bridges, villages, ravines, and deep-cut roads are met with, the infantry of the advanced guard examines them; it also occupies the defiles which may be found upon the route passed over or upon the flanks.

The wagons of the columns on a manœuvre-march follow at 5 or 6,000 yards in rear of the centre, and with an escort.

In forward movements, there is also a rear-guard, but its duties are chiefly to collect stragglers.

ART. 46.—Retrograde Movements.

When an army passes from an offensive march to a march in retreat, it is necessary, especially at the beginning of the retreat, to increase the number of columns, in order to hasten the movement and deceive the enemy: a general rendezvous should be assigned to the columns. The second line then becomes the head of column.

In open country, the cavalry marches at the head, but most usually is between the two lines, or at the rear, and in the latter case, the artillery takes its place between the cavalry and the infantry.

The wagons are placed in front one day's march.

There is always an advanced guard, but it serves hardly any other purpose than to remove accidental obstacles. The important duty falls to the rear-guard, which in a woody country keeps distant a half-day's march, being strong in infantry and artillery, and composed especially of the best light troops. The chief of the rear-guard ought particularly to try to choose the best positions for holding the enemy in check.

A rear-guard, composed of eight squadrons, three battalions, and one battery, in a plain country, may march in the following order:

At the head of the column, in the direction of the main body to which the rear-guard is attached, three squadrons, preceded by a small advanced guard, then a half-battery, two battalions, two squadrons, a half-battery, two companies of infantry, two squadrons, and the remainder of the cavalry; a chain of patrollers surrounds the flanks and rear of the column.

It would be proper, even in a plain, to keep the greater part of the cavalry at the tail of the column; in a mountainous country the infantry alone remains at the tail, with a small detachment of light cavalry. The partial rear-guards keep up the same kind of a connection with each other as the advanced guards.

ART. 47.—Flank Marches.

Flank marches are to be executed only when they may be concealed either by accidents of the ground, or by impassable obstacles, or may be accomplished at night. When none of these means of concealment offer, the march must be made under cover of a detached corps composed of all arms, which occupies the enemy on the exposed side, and prevents him from attacking the flank of the column.

Flank marches are executed by lines and by battalions, or regiments en masse, leaving between them proper intervals to permit forming to the right or left, and placing partial advanced and rear-guards, which keep quite near each other. A portion of the artillery keeps opposite the centre of the columns, to protect accidental and lateral deployments; portions are also kept at the head and tail of the column, protected by squadrons or battalions, in order to cover formations in line of battle perpendicular to the fronts, if necessary.

The cavalry is placed upon the exposed flank, at the extremities of the lines, and sometimes also between the first two lines; the wagons are on the safe flank, and keep as close as possible to their respective divisions. Impassable obstacles are left on the exposed flank; practicable obstacles, such as woods, villages on either flank, are carefully examined, and, as far as possible, the march is so directed as to leave them on the safe flank.

The advanced guard covers the march in front or flank, according to the position of the enemy. It should be formed as usual.

ART. 48.—Arrangements for all Marches.

The chief of staff always prepares a description of the march, indicating the real or apparent object of the operation, the composition of the columns—that of the advanced guard, rear-guard, and flankers; it contains special instructions for each column, and defines the position each should hold the evening preceding each day's march, the dates, halting-places, &c.; it comprises instructions as to camps and bivouacs, as to the course to be pursued in the event of retreat, of the advanced guard, and its supports in case of attack; it indicates the successive locations of the head-quarters.

MARCHES IN THE VICINITY OF THE ENEMY.

These cannot be performed by separate detachments of the same arm, each advancing at its own peculiar speed. It is generally necessary to unite troops of cavalry and of infantry, which ought not to lose the support of one another, and consequently those that are accustomed to move the quickest, must regulate their speed by that of those that move more slowly. The distances to be accomplished in a day cannot be so long as when marching at a distance from the enemy, and the rules to be observed for the departure, halting, speed, &c., depend on a great many variable circumstances. It is considered very good work, if a considerable corps travels ten or twelve miles a-day. If it attempts more, it loses many men, and forced marches soon become as murderous as a battle, especially with young troops.

The principles to be observed are as follows:—To give always in writing the order of march, and communicate it to all the chiefs on detachments and adjutants. To secure as many guides as there are detachments marching on parallel directions likely to lose sight of each other. To acquire the most intimate knowledge of all that concerns the direction to be followed. To regulate the time of departure according to the distance and the difficulties to be overcome during the day. To make the halts as numerous and as long as may be necessary, so as to arrive in a mass, with the least possible loss and fatigue. To have in every column a detachment of pioneers (mounted), provided with tools, and marching with the vanguard, to clear or repair the way whenever necessary.

FIG. 3.

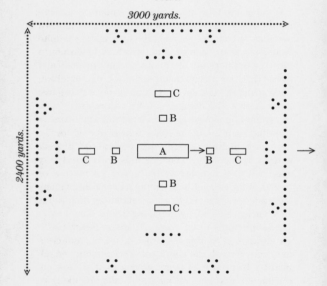

A. Principal corps. B. Reserve of the detached portions.
C. Main body of the detached portions.

To surround the main body (Fig. 3.) with detached corps, vanguard, rear-guard, and flankers, in such manner that the principal body cannot be attached without having had time to prepare itself. With respect to this, it should be observed that the new rifle is more dangerous at 600 yards, than the old musket was at 300; that an enterprising cavalry is to be dreaded as soon as it is within 1,500 yards (five or six minutes); that in full march, at least ten minutes are required by a deep column to put itself into readiness to repulse an enemy suddenly announced.— March the baggage apart from the troops, at the rear of each column, in front of the rear-guard. For a rapid march, organize this baggage into one or more convoys having each a sufficient escort, and following at a distance, or having an ulterior rendezvous.

It results from these considerations, that a corps must be guarded all round for some distance, this distance being increased for a more numerous corps, as it requires more time to put itself on the defensive, however good may be the order observed during the march. If ten minutes are required by the main body to make its preparations when the enemy is signalled, the main body of every detached portion must be within twenty minutes of the centre of the column. The detached parts sought to be in all a third, a fourth, a fifth, or a sixth of the chief corps, according as it is strong or weak; when strong, it has greater difficulties to cover itself on account of the nature of ground; when weak, it has less trouble to do so.

If there is as much danger in front as in rear, on

the right as on the left, four detachments of equal strength should be formed, viz.: one in advance, one behind, and one on each flank. The strength of one of these should be reduced, if reconnoitring is easy on its side; and that of another, having more fatigue and danger to incur, should be increased; and lastly, a detachment of no use should be suppressed, as, for instance, the one on the right flank of the column, if there happen to be on that side a frontier or a river belonging to the army. Each detached fragment again subdivides itself into several parts: the *point* nearest to the enemy especially intrusted with the care of scouring the country, and composed of scouts and flankers, with their supports; the *main body* destined to support the point; the *reserve* serving as a link between the main body and the principal corps. The first is about one-sixth of the detachment.

The scouts and flankers that surround the column have not only to cover it, and to reconnoitre all that may be of interest, but also to prevent desertion, and to see that the enemy's spies do not come near the corps in march to ascertain its composition, direction, intentions, &c. The detached subdivisions, either cavalry or infantry, dispose themselves and act in the same manner; but as a horseman, on account of his elevation, can see farther, and on account of his speed, can go over a larger and wider tract of ground, the strength of a detachment of infantry to cover the side of a corps in march must be at least double, and sometimes treble that of a detachment of cavalry capable of fulfilling the same duty. Thus the scouts and flankers of infantry should be two or three times as numerous, and half or one-third less distant from each other than those of cavalry, if they wish to scour the country well.

It will be difficult in practice to adopt the precautions indicated in the preceding diagram, which represents the dispositions above indicated. It is deplorable that troops on a march are usually overconfident, and will neither scour thoroughly, nor far enough; but a commander possessing the prudence which is to be expected from him, will neglect none of the measures described. It is useless of course to expect from the scouts and flankers the correct dressing figured in the diagram, since it is rendered impracticable by the accidents both of the march and of the ground.

Some generals march their forces, in the proximity of the enemy, in close columns, in order that the rear may be quickly enabled to support the front; but this formation is only advantageous when the columns are numerous and not deep. If they are heavy and deep, they are much exposed to the projectiles of the enemy; they cannot deploy without disorder, and extend considerably when passing through defiles, or over bad roads. The last subdivisions, especially with infantry, have then to run to join the first. The order in open columns must be assumed, whenever the foregoing drawbacks acquire weight according to the size of the masses.

As many parallel columns as possible must be formed, without telling off under a battalion or a squadron. On halting, the companies form, and leave between themselves as little distance as possible; they must not form into line, if there is no danger

compelling them to do so, lest precious time should
be wasted.

If the passage of a defile, or of a bad road, or, if
some accident, such as a storm, a flood, &c., stop the
rear of a column, the advance must wait until the
cause of the stoppage has ceased, for every break in
a column may have evil consequences. If several
roads cross each other, somebody must be left at
each crossing, to point out to the last subdivisions of
the column the way they have to follow. Avoid marching in tall grass and corn, as nothing is more detri-
mental to men and horses. Always stop *beyond*, not
before defiles you have to pass, and near which the
march is to terminate. Contrive so as to arrive by day-
light, and at least two hours before dark, at the place
where night is to be passed, as nothing is more
tedious or so difficult as to establish yourself in a
cantonment, camp, or bivouac, when no longer guid-
ed by the light of the sun. Consider well before
undertaking a night march, which offers few advantages and great inconveniences, inasmuch as it is
very slow, the men are much fatigued, and individuals, as well as the whole corps, are likely to be lost, if
they wander; and as the least attack of the enemy
would cause the greatest confusion, the cavalry
would then be utterly useless, and the infantry would
be exposed to the risk of firing at and destroying one
another.

BEFORE STARTING.

Privates should carry only what is strictly necessary. They should not load themselves with useless
objects. Many a horse and many a man have been left

behind, for the mere overload of a pound. A pair of pants, a coat, a great-coat, two pairs of shoes, two collars, three shirts, two pairs of drawers, three pocket-handkerchiefs, two flannel waistcoats, two caps, one for extra duty and one for usual wear, are sufficient for every one, officer or private, on horseback or on foot. All these must be new, full, and well made. A fortnight of march wears out tightly fitting clothes, which would have lasted six months if made fuller. Generals should take timely precautions for replacing every object, and bear in mind that the same article which would last a twelvemonth in garrison, requires to be replaced much sooner in the field. The regulation time can no longer be adhered to, as soon as the soldier leaves the ordinary routine of garrison life; and to maintain him healthy, strong, and able-bodied, his outfit must be kept up carefully, and replaced as soon as it becomes insufficient, whatever be the expense. Contrive therefore, cost what it may, to have everywhere and always sufficient stores, and to place the home magazines in a condition to forward in proper time all the necessaries to the smaller depots, which keep removing further and further, as the military operations proceed.

Two great problems in war are to find harness that will not hurt the horse, and shoes that will not hurt the feet. Cavalry should bestow great attention on adjusting the saddle and bridle, always keeping for each house four spare shoes, with as many nails as are necessary to fix them, and half as many more. Infantry should have light and easy shoes. When good shoes are not to be had, the best substitute for them consists in binding around the foot linen rags wrapped up, in a piece of skin freshly cut off, and laced with strips of the same.

GUIDES.

It is indispensably necessary in the proximity of the enemy, to have guides. They are selected as carefully as possible, and compelled by force, if they do not come willingly. A guide taken against his will, must always be treated with consideration, lest the desire of revenge for some bad treatment should become stronger than the apprehension of the death which, he is given to understand, awaits him, should he prove treacherous. Every guide precedes the head of the column a few paces; he must rely upon a handsome reward if he is useful, even if he serves unwillingly. Punishments are only spoken of when there are grounds for distrusting him. He marches free when there is no doubt entertained of his good intentions; otherwise, he is tied round the waist by a rope held by a picked man, and another picked man watches him with a loaded musket. When fastened, he is made to understand that such a measure is resorted to with regret, but that it is necessary, lest, if left free, he should attempt to run away and be killed. A trustworthy guide ought to be carefully watched if any danger occurs, because fear might induce him to make his escape. Two other safe and intelligent men are to be placed around him, who, without any apparent intention, keep him forcibly among themselves. Although possessing guides, a commander must avail himself of all possible information respecting the position and particulars of the road, in order to know it well, and to be in a condition to take a decision immediately, should some difficulty occur suddenly. He must know exactly the distance between the chief points of the way and those that are in its vicinity, and obstacles to be met with, the crossings, &c. The same information should be communicated, whenever it can be done, to the commanders of the detached subdivision, and of the various parallel columns, if the march is accomplished by several columns.

SCOUTS AND FLANKERS.

The scouts and flankers are the men disposed as skirmishers in front, in rear, and on the flanks of a corps in motion, so as to form all around it a chain of vedettes or moveable sentries, that guard it during its march. These are subject, in their general movements, to the regulations for skirmishers, for what relates to the manner of deploying, marching, closing, opening, fighting and retreating. All the corporals, instead of keeping in the same line with the men, remain nearer to the principal corps, and have with them two or three men, thus forming small troops of support for the parts of the line most distant or most exposed. The scouts and flankers reconnoitre and scour attentively all the exterior ground; they investigate every indication, and impart the result of their observations to their immediate chief, who reports to his officer, and he in his turn informs all whom it may concern. If a scout or flanker fulfills a temporary duty, as, for instance, searching a hollow, accompanying a traveller, &c., he is replaced by a man sent by the nearest corporal. A flanker who meets with a defile or a road opening on the direction followed by the column, guards it till the arrival of the flanker next behind him; this one stops in his turn, and so on to the rear, each flanker rapidly gaining his distance. They arrest and send to their chief every individual coming from the exterior, and all soldiers coming from the interior without permission or an order. The skirmishers scattered behind the rear-guard oblige the loiterers to join the main body, and carry to the ambulances those whom weakness or pain has compelled to stop. If a village is met with on the front or flank of a march, a scout enters it, and questions an inhabitant; if the information he receives implies no danger, he advances further in, stops some important person, and brings him to his chief. After these precautions, and after the assurance given by that person that there is no danger, he passes through the village, and stops outside of it, so as to discover and be ready to announce the approach of the enemy by the report of his musket. At the same time a few other scouts go round the village on both sides, scour its hedges and gardens, and join at the other end the rest of the detachment, passing quickly through afterward. A wood and thicket are searched in the same manner: one man first goes across, and two go round on both flanks. A vanguard in war, beside the duty of scouting the march of the principal corps, has a perfectly defined object, as for instance, to arrive at a certain point, and to await there the principal corps, which will take up a position under its protection, or another less clearly defined purpose, which is to follow and seek for the enemy. In order to effect the first, the officer commanding the vanguard taking the proper precautions, advances resolutely in the given direction. He takes note on his way of all indications and information likely to interest the commander of the main body, and according to its importance, makes his report at once, or after the arrival. If the enemy presents himself with the view of attacking, he reconnoitres, tries him first, then overthrows or resists him, according as he is weak or strong, so as not to delay the principal corps, or to give it time to take the measures dictated by the circumstances.

If the order is given to follow a retreating force, the vanguard follows close, and harasses it, scouring the country to discover its ulterior designs, ascertain its strength, its physical and moral conditions, and its intended direction, in order to cut it off, or arrive before it if possible. The duty of every commander of a vanguard arriving at the place where the night is to be passed, is to prepare the encampment of the corps he precedes, to collect resources of all kinds for the lodgement and food of men and horses, and to place himself in a condition to facilitate ulterior operations, by attending to all necessary details, such as securing guides, sending spies, opening letters, translating documents, reconnoitring fords, passages, defiles, positions, &c.

DETACHMENTS PLACED ON THE FLANKS OF A COLUMN.

A detachment placed on the flank of a column has only to watch for the safety of the principal corps that has sent it out. It regulates its march by that of this corps, covering it, repulsing attacks, but never venturing on a pursuit. The part performed by such a detachment is naturally much more passive than that of a vanguard, yet it becomes very similar while a flank march is performing.

REAR-GUARD.

In an offensive movement the rear-guard is on the look-out to prevent hostile detachments from stealthily approaching the rear of the column, to cause disorder and delay by sudden attack, especially at the passage of a defile. It follows near enough not to be cut off itself, nor to be too long in coming up, if the commander of the main force has occasion to mass all his troops. It avoids carefully all serious engagements that would check the advance of the whole army, by forcing it to come to its rescue. In a retreat, the rear-guard has recourse to every measure for stopping the enemy, avails itself of every opportunity of making protracted counter attacks, and while retreating, opposes all physical and tactical obstacles likely to delay pursuit. In mountainous districts, where culminating positions and defiles abound, one of the best dispositions to adopt to cover a retreat, is that of a series of echelons, formed beforehand, and retiring successively. The echelons nearest to the enemy begin the manœuvre, under the protection of those behind, between which they pass, to stop again at the extreme rear, and so on. The position of each echelon is selected according to the facility the ground affords to enable them to support the nearest ones, when in their turn these go to the rear.

ART. 49.—Calculation of the Time of Marches.

It is often important to calculate exactly the time necessary to execute a given march. This calculation is based upon the following facts. A column of infantry passes over about two and a half miles in an hour, at the route step, including halts; a column of cavalry alternately walking and trotting will get over six miles an hour. Let D be the distance to be passed over; d, the distance passed over in one minute by the troops composing the column, including halts; l, the length of the column, r, the approximate time of delay, occasioned by obstacles: $t = \dfrac{l}{d}$ will be the time of the column's passing a distance equal to its length, of the time necessary to bring the rear of the column into line; the formula $T = t + r + \dfrac{D}{d}$ will give the time sought. One of the elements of r is due to the elongation l' of the column in a defile; it may be taken account of by introducing $\dfrac{l'}{d}$ into the formula; r is also dependent upon the state of the troops whether fresh or not, and upon the delays occasioned by marching across fields. All these elements should be calculated and introduced into the formula. In route marching, the interval between the ranks of infantry and cavalry, between pieces and carriages may be one yard. A division of infantry of twelve battalions, of 700 to 800 men each, marching in close column by company and at route step, will occupy a space in length of 700 or 800 yards. Two batteries of artillery, with their caissons, marching in double file, will occupy about 350 to 400 yards.

A corps of 25,000 men in similar order, will occupy a space of about two and a half miles in length, will take a little over one hour to deploy by either flank, and about half an hour to deploy on the centre.

A division of cavalry of twenty-four squadrons of forty-eight files each, marching by platoons, will make a length of about 1,300 yards; it can deploy by either flank in eight minutes, at a trot; in four minutes on the centre, in ground free from obstacles.

ART. 50.—Camps.

Camp is the place where troops are established in tents, in huts, or in bivouac. Cantonments are the inhabited places which troops occupy for shelter when not put in barracks. The camping party is a detachment detailed to prepare a camp.

Reconnaissances should precede the establishment of the camp. For a camp of troops on the march, it is only necessary to look to the health and comfort of the troops, the facility of the communications, the convenience of wood and water, and the resources in provisions and forage. The ground for an intrenched camp, or a camp to cover a country, or one designed to deceive the enemy as to the strength of the army, must be selected and the camp arranged for the object in view.

The camping-party of a regiment consists of the regimental quarter-master and quarter-master-sergeant, and a corporal and two men per company. The general decides whether the regiments camp separately or together, and whether the police guard shall accompany the camping-party, or a larger escort shall be sent.

Neither baggage nor led horses are permitted to move with the camping-party.

When the general can send in advance to prepare the camp, he gives his instructions to the chief of the quarter-master's department, who calls on the regiments for their camping-parties, and is accompanied, if necessary, by an engineer to propose the defenses and communications.

The watering places are examined, and signals placed at those that are dangerous. Any work required to make them of easier access is done by the police guard, or quarter-master's men. Sentinels, to be relieved by the guards of the regiment when they come up, are placed by the camping-party over the water, if it is scarce, and over the houses and stores of provisions and forage in the vicinity.

If the camping-party does not precede the regiment, the quarter-master attends to these things as soon as the regiment reaches the ground.

On reaching the ground, the infantry form on the color front, the cavalry in rear of its camp.

The generals establish the troops in camp as rapidly as possible, particularly after long, fatiguing marches.

The number of men to be furnished for guards, pickets, and orderlies; the fatigue parties to be sent for supplies; the work to be done, and the strength of the working parties; the time and place for issues; the hour of marching, &c., are then announced by the brigadier-generals to the colonels, and by them to the field-officers—the adjutants and captains formed in front of the regiment, the first sergeants taking post behind their captains. The adjutant then makes the details, and the first sergeants name the men. The regimental officer of the day forms the picket, and sends the guards to their posts. The colors are then planted at the centre of the color line, and the arms are stacked on the line; the fatigue parties to procure supplies, and the working parties form in rear of the arms; the men not on detail to pitch the tents.

If the camp is near the enemy, the picket remains under arms until the return of the fatigue parties, and, if necessary, is reinforced by details from each company.

In the cavalry, each troop moves a little in rear of the point, at which its horses are to be secured, and forms in one rank; the men then dismount; a detail is made to hold the horses; the rest stack their arms and fix the picket ropes; after the horses are attended to, the tents are pitched, and each horseman places his carbine at the side from the weather, and hangs his sabre and bridle on it.

The standard is then carried to the tent of the colonel.

The terms front, flank, right, left, file, and rank, have the same meaning when applied to camps as in the order of battle. The front of the camp is usually equal to the front of the troops. The tents are arranged in ranks and files. The number of ranks varies with the strength of the companies and the size of the tents.

No officer should be allowed to occupy a house, although vacant and on the ground of his camp, except by permission of the commander of the brigade, who should report it to the commander of the division. The staff-officer charged with establishing the camp should designate the place for the shambles. The offal should be buried.

ART. 51.—Infantry Camp.

Each company has its tents in two files, facing on a street perpendicular to the color line. The width of the street depends on the front of the camp, but should not be less than five paces. The interval

FIG. 4.

CAMP OF A REGIMENT OF INFANTRY.

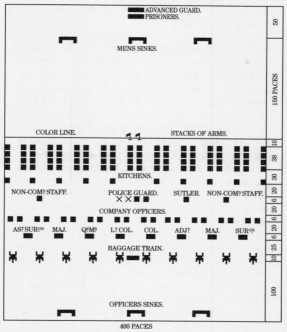

400 PACES

between the ranks of tents is two paces; between the files of tents of adjacent companies, two paces; between regiments, twenty-two paces.

The color line is ten paces in front of the front rank of tents. The kitchens are twenty paces behind the rear rank of company tents; the non-commissioned staff and sutler twenty paces in rear of the kitchens; the company officers, twenty paces farther in rear; and the field and staff, twenty paces in rear of the company officers.

The company officers are in rear of their respective companies, the captains on the right. The colonel and lieutenant-colonel are near the centre of the line of field and staff-officers; the adjutant, a major, and surgeon on the right; the quarter-master, a major, and assistant surgeon on the left. The police guard is at the centre of the line of the non-commissioned staff, the tents facing to the front, the stacks of arms on the left. The advanced post of the police guard is about 200 paces in front of the color line, and opposite the centre of the regiment, or on the best ground; the prisoners' tent about four paces in rear. In a regiment of the second line, the advanced post of the police guard is 200 paces in rear of the line of its field and staff.

The horses of the staff-officers and of the baggage train are twenty-five paces in rear of the tents of the field and staff; the wagons are parked on the same line, and the men of the train camped near them.

The sinks of the men are 150 paces in front of the color line; those of the officers 100 paces in rear of the train; both are concealed by bushes. When convenient, the sinks of the men may be placed in rear or on a flank. A portion of the earth dug out for sinks to be thrown back occasionally.

The front of the camp of a regiment of 1,000 men in the ranks will be 400 paces, or one-fifth less paces than the number of files, if the camp is to have the same front as the troops in order of battle. But the front may be reduced to 190 paces by narrowing the company streets to five paces; and if it be desirable to reduce the front still more, the tents of companies may be pitched in single file—those of a division facing on the same street.

ART. 52.—Cavalry Camp.

In the cavalry, each company has one file of tents; the tents opening on the street facing the left of the camp. The horses of each company are placed in single file, facing the opening of the tents, and are fastened to pickets planted firmly in the ground, from three to six paces from the tents of the troop.

The interval between the files of tents should be such that the regiment being broken into columns of companies (as indicated in plate), each company should be on the extension of the line on which the horses are to be picketed.

The streets separating the squadrons are wider than those between the companies by the interval separating squadrons in line; these intervals are kept free from any obstruction throughout the camp.

The horses of the rear rank are placed on the left of those of their file-leaders.

The horses of the lieutenants are placed on the right of their platoons; those of the captains on the right of the company.

Each horse occupies a space of about two paces. The number of horses in the company fixes the depth of the camp, and the distance between the files, of tents; the forage is placed between the tents.

FIG. 5.

CAMP OF A REGIMENT OF FIVE SQUADRONS OF CAVALRY.

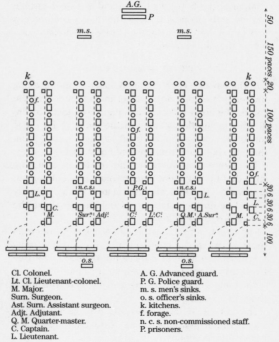

Cl. Colonel.	A. G. Advanced guard.
Lt. Cl. Lieutenant-colonel.	P. G. Police guard.
M. Major.	m. s. men's sinks.
Surn. Surgeon.	o. s. officer's sinks.
Ast. Surn. Assistant surgeon.	k. kitchens.
Adjt. Adjutant.	f. forage.
Q. M. Quarter-master.	n. c. s. non-commissioned staff.
C. Captain.	P. prisoners.
L. Lieutenant.	

The kitchens are twenty paces in front of each file of tents.

The non-commissioned officers are in the tents of the front rank. Camp-followers, teamsters, &c., are in the tents of the rear rank. The police guard in the rear rank, near the centre of the regiment.

The tents of the lieutenants are thirty paces in rear of the file of their company; those of the captains thirty paces in rear of the lieutenants.

The colonel's tent thirty paces in rear of the captain's, near the centre of the regiment; the lieutenant-colonel on his right; the adjutant on his left; the majors on the same line, opposite the second company, on the right and left; the surgeon on the left of the adjutant.

The field and staff have their horses on the left of their tents, on the same line with the company horses; sick horses are placed in one line on the right or left of the camp. The men who attend them have a separate file of tents; the forges and wagons in rear of this file. The horses of the train and of camp-followers are in one or more files extending to the rear, behind the right or left squadron. The advanced post of the police guard is 200 paces in front opposite centre of regiment; the horses in one or two files.

The sinks for the men are 150 paces in front, those for officers 100 paces in rear of the camp.

ART. 53.—Artillery Camp.

The artillery is encamped near the troops to which it is attached, so as to be protected from attack, and to contribute to the defence of the camp. Sentinels for the park are furnished by the artillery, and, when necessary, by other troops. For a battery of six pieces the tents are in three files, one for each section; distance between the ranks of tents, fifteen paces; tents opening to the front. The horses of each section are picketed in one file, ten paces to the left of the file of tents. In horse artillery, or if the number of horses makes it necessary, the horses are in two files on the right and left of the file of tents. The kitchens are twenty-five paces in front of the front rank of tents. The tents of the officers are in the outside files of company tents, twenty-five paces in rear of the rear rank—the captain on the right, the lieutenants on the left. The teams of a peace and its caisson should be together, and the horses of the chiefs of pieces with their appropriate teams.

The park is opposite the centre of the camp, forty paces in rear of the officers' tents. The carriages in files four paces apart; distance between ranks of carriages sufficient for the horses when harnessed to them; the park guard is twenty-five paces in rear of the park. The sinks for the men 150 paces in front; for the officer, 100 paces in rear. The harness is in the tents of the men.

ART. 54.—Bivouacs.

Bivouacs are solely resorted to to enable the men to refresh and rest themselves. Fatigue ruins and destroys an army more rapidly than battles do; therefore, all that can alleviate the extra duties required for the feeding of men and horses, and facilitate their temporary encampment, all that can diminish the service and increase the security of the mass, will constitute the essential qualities of a well selected bivouac. In the first place, water is sought for; it should be abundant, good, and near at hand. After water come provisions and forage. Care should afterward be taken that fuel be in close proximity and plentiful, especially if the weather is cold and bad. In warm and dry weather the quantity strictly necessary in preparing the food need only be sought. A soil dry and sloping, which cannot be inundated suddenly, or become muddy after a storm or a flood, should be looked for. If the season is inclement or damp, facilities for obtaining a quick and comfortable shelter, as well as for obtaining fuel in abundance will be of great importance. Positions where the enemy could arrive without obstacles, and from which you could not rapidly march off, must be avoided, and a preference should be given to those that command the neighborhood, where you cannot be seen, and from which the country around is easily overlooked. It is better to make a longer march to obtain all these desirable advantages than to stop too soon, and be badly placed far from every thing. The bivouac is reconnoitred and examined beforehand as much as possible. Every corps on arriving should immediately be informed of the place it is to occupy, and of the picket it must furnish, in order that no time may be lost in waiting, and that not one should uselessly take up a wrong position. The orders regulating the hours of distributions, of collecting fuel, of foraging, of watering horses, of grooming, of inspection, of retiring for the night, of departure, &c., are given immediately after arrival. As soon as a troop knows the site reserved for it, it establishes itself thereon. The infantry pile up muskets and prepare shelter. The cavalry fasten their horses and place their arms each behind his own horse; so that they may not run any risk of being broken should the animal roll, and the harness should be placed near them after unsaddling, to avoid, in case of alarm during the night, the confusion which would result from a careless or irregular arrangement. While they are taking up their respective quarters, the officer intrusted with the service of external safety, goes to place the grand guard and the outposts. Lastly, by a skillful foresight of every thing, and a judicious division of duties, the moment of repose can be hastened, and rest be given to the greatest number. The order in which the march is to be performed the following day, the direction to follow, especially for a departure before daybreak, are the causes for determining the relative places of the different arms, for the less the difficulty of marching off at the appointed time, the longer will the men rest.

A regiment of cavalry being in order of battle, in rear of the ground to be occupied, the colonel breaks it by platoons to the right. The horses of each platoon are placed in a single row, and fastened as prescribed for camps; near the enemy, they remain saddled all night, with slackened girths. The arms are at first stacked in rear of each row of horses; the sabres with the bridles hung on them, are placed against the stacks.

The forage is placed on the right of each row of horses. Two stable-guards for each platoon watch the horses.

A fire for each platoon is made near the color line,

twenty paces to the left of the row of horses. A shelter is made for the men around the fire, if possible, and each man then stands his arms and bridle against the shelter.

The fires and shelters for the officers are placed in rear of the line of those for the men.

The interval between the squadrons must be without obstruction throughout the whole depth of the bivouac.

The interval between the shelters should be such that the platoons can take up a line of battle freely to the front or rear.

The distance from the enemy decides the manner in which the horses are to be fed and led to water. When it is permitted to unsaddle, the saddles are placed in the rear of the horses.

In infantry, the fires are made in rear of the color line, on the ground that would be occupied by the tents in camp. The companies are placed around them, and, if possible, construct shelters. When liable to surprise, the infantry should stand to arms at daybreak, and the cavalry mount until the return of the reconnoitring parties. If the arms are to be taken apart to clean, it must be done by detachments successively.

Troops should bivouac when the enemy is near, and when there is a wish to engage him also in pursuit, and retreats, and generally whenever on a march houses enough for shelter cannot be found in a proper place. Dry and sheltered positions should be chosen for bivouacs.

ART. 55.—Cantonments.

The cavalry should be placed under shelter whenever the distance from the enemy and from the ground where the troops are to form for battle, permit it—taverns and farmhouses, with large stalls and free access, are selected for quartering them.

The colonel indicates the place of assembling in case of alarm. It should generally be outside the cantonment; the egress from it should be free; the retreat upon the other positions secure, and roads leading to it on the side of the enemy obstructed.

The necessary orders being given, as in establishing a camp, the picket and grand guards are posted. A sentinel may be posted in a steeple or high house, and then the troops are marched to the quarters. The men sleep in the stables, if it is thought necessary.

The above applies in the main to infantry. Near the enemy, companies or platoons should be collected as much as possible in the same houses. If companies must be separated, they should be divided by platoons or squads. All take arms at daybreak. When cavalry and infantry canton together, the latter furnish the guards by night, and the former by day.

Troops cantoned in presence of the enemy should be covered by advanced guards and natural or artificial obstacles. Cantonments taken during a cessation of hostilities should be established in rear of a line of defence, and in front of the point on which the troops would concentrate to receive an attack. The general commanding in chief assigns the limits of their cantonments to the divisions, the commanders of divisions to brigades, and the commanders of brigades post their regiments. The position for each corps in case of attack is carefully pointed out by the generals.

At a distance from an enemy, a battalion of 800 men would occupy a village of 100 or 120 houses; but closer quartering is proper when an attack is apprehended.

The order of battle is preserved as far as possible as in camps. The number of regiments is marked on the doors. A corps of 25,000 or 30,000 men ought to be able to assemble in one day, and therefore should not spread over more than twenty-five or thirty miles.

When a cantonment for several days is formed, place a cordon of advanced posts, and if necessary, throw out light troops in front of the covering obstacles.

ART. 56.—Grand Guards.

The approaches of a camp or cantonment are covered by grand guards.

It is in the service of its outposts that a corps encamped for a time must particularly seek for the security it requires in order to rest. This service is of such high importance and requires such concentration and such an intimate connection between all its various parts, that it is necessary to place it under the direction of one man alone. Every chief of corps may be intrusted with the care of establishing provisionally the detachment destined to watch for the safety of the corps under his immediate command, but a general rectification will always be necessary to bring a perfect harmony between all the particular dispositions taken for regiments, brigades, divisions, &c. As soon as a body arrives at its proper place, its commander sends out without delay the number of men which a previous order has fixed as his contribution for the outposts. The chief of this body will bring it in the given direction acting conformably to the instructions he has received, which will be sometimes to take preliminary dispositions on a specified ground, sometimes to wait at a given point, until the officer especially appointed for these functions comes to place and subdivide his troop.

An encampment cannot be said to be well guarded unless the watch is kept for a considerable distance around it, and unless it is maintained so effectively that the enemy cannot glide unseen through the chain of the outposts. A mistake often made by the chief of a detachment destined to guard a numerous body at a great distance, consists in taking all the steps necessary to avoid a surprise to himself, while he leaves behind him a considerable space in which a hostile party can form an ambush, to fall on the rear of the guard, at the moment when attacked in front by superior forces he fancies he can easily retreat upon the main body: the guard is then carried off, leaving the surface it was intrusted to occupy unguarded. It is to avoid a mistake of this kind that all the outposts must constitute a combined system, with the view if covering the principal corps even in what related to the posting of sentries and vedettes.

The general of a division is assisted by his staff officers in supervising the placing in position and the duties of the grand guards; but as this detached duty should be methodically performed in each brigade, in order to have regularity and a proper responsibility, these staff officers just mentioned restrict themselves to making reports to the general of division and give no orders except in cases of emergency, when no high officer of the brigade is present who is engaged in this duty.

One of the high officers of each brigade should be designed to take command of the grand guards, when the strength and composition of the troops make it necessary: he established himself at the point indicated by the general, unless there is an approach which must be specially observed or defended.

Grand guards are placed in some open spot, elevated if possible. They should not be with a forest just in rear: in the day time placed near or in sight of the enemy, at dark they are drawn back; they are also drawn in near or in obstructed, hilly or wooded localities, especially when the inhabitants favor the enemy. If it is necessary to push them out to a distance, there must be intermediate posts furnished by the main body; the commander of a grand guard makes a reconnaissance which enables him to determine for himself the proper strength and positions for the smaller advanced posts.

The grand guards receive their countersigns from the general officers and from the chief of staff of the division; the commanders of grand guards should communicate their countersigns, &c., to the staff officers of the army or of the division, and should moreover furnish to these officers all the information their position enables them to give.

Usually the advanced posts are in a straight or curved line: their extremities should rest upon ob-

stacles—infantry grand guards may be thrown out
from 2,000 to 4,000 yards when they belong to a
large body of troops; those of cavalry may be farther.
The grand guard duty will take about one-tenth of
the troops furnishing them. A single grand guard
ought not to exceed 150 men; each infantry
grand guard should have with it two or three mounted men.

The officer commanding a grand guard, after
reconnoitring the ground distributes his small posts
and sentinels, taking with him only one-half or one-
third of his men. At the small posts thirty men may be
placed; they should not be more than 600 or 700
yards apart; their chains of sentinels thrown out 100
or 200 yards. When grand guards are supported by
artillery, only one-ninth of the main body is assigned
to the duty.

A perfect analogy exists between the outposts that
cover a force at rest and the detachments that surround a corps in march. The strength of both may
vary from one-third to one-sixth of the total amount
according as the latter is weak or strong. The chief
object of the outposts is to insure complete security
on their rear and to delay the attack of the enemy
should he come. Their secondary object is to observe
all that happens on the outskirts and to report upon
it. The principal corps cannot be in complete security unless it has time to be informed of danger and
to place itself in readiness to resist it. An encamped
force requires, according to its numerical strength,
from ten to thirty minutes to take up arms, mount
on horseback, and be ready to accept or decline
battle. If it requires to be informed ten or thirty

minutes in advance, it must be granted that the officers commanding the grand guards will employ as
much time to ascertain thoroughly the intention of
the enemy and to transmit their information: these
guards should therefore be placed at from twenty to
sixty minutes, viz., at from a mile to two and a half
miles from the centre of the corps they have to cover.
In a plain this distance will be increased, whilst in
uneven ground it may be diminished, since the enemy
can then be stopped by positions, obstacles, ambush-
es, &c., which compel him to be cautious. A considerable army, the front of which is of great extent,
should guard itself in such a manner as to be able to
concentrate in a proper place in front, in rear, on the
right, or on the left, according to circumstances and
ulterior views.

PLACING THE GRAND GUARDS.

Every commander of a grand guard having brought
his detachment to its appointed station, subdivides it
into three equal portions numbered one, two, three.
The first rests, but in such a way as to be ready at the
first signal; the second remains under arms in front
of the first (in some stances the cavalry may alight
and the infantry pile up muskets); the third is destined to furnish the pickets, sentries and vedettes,
and provisionally places itself in front of the second.
After these preliminary dispositions, the officer
intrusted with the duty of establishing the exterior
chain, advances with the portion three, stops at the
place where the central post is to be set, plants its
sentries or vedettes, composing that picket of a chief
and of twice as many as are on duty. Thus for four

sentries the chief of the post will have with him eight men. After the establishment of the central picket, the officer moves to the right with all the disposable men formed into three files, the exterior file giving the sentries or vedettes, the two others giving the men for the picket. Having set the post on the extreme right he returns toward the centre, rectifying if need be what he has just done. This operation completed, if any men remain, they are distributed among the most important posts. It is usually the officer commanding the grand guard who performs the duty above explained: he gives every one his particular countersign. As for himself, he has previously received his instructions, viz.; whether his flanks are uncovered or are protected by adjoining posts; about what extent of ground he must watch; whether he will have support or find no intermediate detachment between his own and the principal corps, &c. The general outline of a grand guard and of its exterior parts ought to have the form of a fan, as represented in the annexed diagram. (Fig. 6.)

The portion No. 2 of the grand guard, and the small posts have, properly speaking, no sentry; yet as many men as may be needed are, by turns, intrusted with watching the pickets, or sentries, or vedettes placed in from, in order to know what they are doing, and to mark all their signals. In like manner a man of each grand guard has to direct his attention to and keep in view the adjoining grand guards, to report upon what is happening in them. The most important thing is to detect at once any serious attack, therefore every chief of a grand guard plants near the party No. 1, a pole with a truss of damp straw

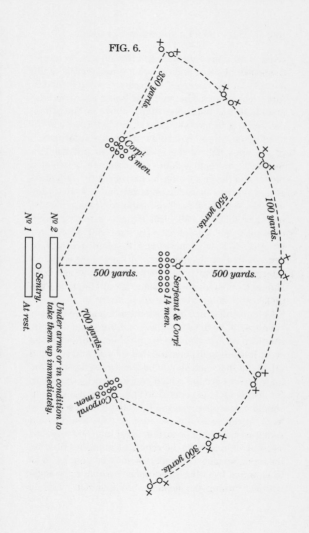

FIG. 6.

350 yards.

Corp! 8 men.

550 yards.

100 yards.

500 yards.   Serjeant & Corp! 14 men.   500 yards.

700 yards.

Corporal 8 men.

300 yards.

Nº 1   Nº 2

○ Sentry.   Under arms or in condition to take them up immediately.

At rest.

fixed at its extremity, and sets this on fire, to advise the principal corps and the other grand guards of the advance of the enemy, if he comes resolutely, and in force. The distance between the grand guard and the main body has been determined above on the principal that the former shall cover the latter for a sufficient distance, to give it time to receive information of the approach of the enemy, and to put itself in readiness to repulse him. The distance between a picket and the grand guard, also that between a picket and sentries or vedettes, is regulated so that they may see one another. This distance, however, must not exceed 700 or 800 yards (from two to three minutes at a gallop) for cavalry, and 250 to 300 for infantry. If it were necessary to plant a sentry or vedette that could not be seen from the picket, an intermediate sentry or vedette that could see both should be posted; and the same should be done for a picket not visible from the grand guard.

As for the distance between the adjoining sentries or vedettes, it is fixed by the condition, that nothing should pass between or before them without being seen. It is not indispensable that they should see each other, but that each should be able to see a part of the intermediate ground which is also seen by the other; for instance, if the vedette A (Fig. 7) does not see B, it should at lease see as far as C, whilst B must see as far as D. At the same time, even in a plain, sentries and vedettes should not be farther apart than 800 yards, so as to be able to hear the report of a musket fired by the next. Sentries and vedettes must be double, so as to embrace from the same point a whole right angle without turning the head, as in K and L. (Fig. 7.)

FIG. 7.

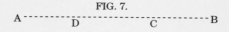

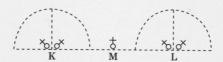

If, however, from K to L the ground is well explored, except a narrow strip in front of M, a single sentry or vedette will be sufficient to watch over it. Yet if there are men enough to double everywhere the sentries and vedettes, it should be done, inasmuch as one can go to make a report, bring a deserter, &c., whilst the other remains on the look-out.

Where from some particular circumstances (as, for example, if it is important to guard a defile through which the army has to pass next day) a grand guard is placed very far from the main body, and forms a point in its front, it would become liable to be cut off by any hostile detachment that should creep in and form an ambush on its line of retreat; in that case it must be supported by a special force, which constitutes an intermediate grand guard. Fig. 8 shows the disposition to be adopted in such a case.

The line of retreat of sentries and vedettes on their pickets, that of small posts on their grand guard, and lastly that of the grand guard on the principal corps, must be free from obstacles, either insurmountable or even difficult to pass, such as marshes, rivers, rivulets with high embankments, &c. If separating two de-

FIG. 8.

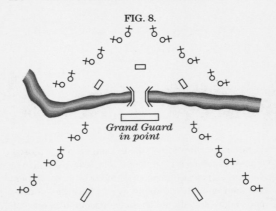

Grand Guard in point

Support of the Grand Guard

Principal Corps.

pendent portions of a system of outposts by a defile (bridge, hollow, rod, ravine, &c.) cannot be avoided, this defile should be guarded by an intermediate picket, lest the enemy, after having suddenly overcome one of these portions, should, by an oblique movement, occupy the defile, and arrive at it before the troops which must pass through it in order to retire. We must as much as possible avoid placing sentries and vedettes within range of obstacles, behind which a rifleman of the enemy could conceal himself for the purpose of killing them. Now-a-days, with a good rifle, a sentry may be killed at such a distance (700 yards for instance) that the report cannot be heard nor the smoke seen. These obstacles must be enclosed within the circle; if not, they should be left out of range. The grand guard, as well as its pickets and their sentries or vedettes, being placed, the time should be divided into three intervals nearly equal. The length of service of a grand guard should not exceed twenty-four hours. After the first interval the pickets, sentries and vedettes constituting party No. 3, are relieved by party No. 2, and take the place of party No. 1, in order to rest, and No. 1 will replace No. 2. At the end of the second interval of time No. 2 is replaced by No. 1, and goes to rest; No. 3 repairs to the point just left by No. 1, and remains from that time on the watch. Sentries or vedettes should be relieved every hour, or every two hours, according to circumstances.

NIGHT POSITION.

As sentries and vedettes cannot overlook in the dark a piece of ground so extensive as they can in the day, and as consequently they must be much nearer to each other, the circumference occupied by the system of outposts is narrowed at night-fall, in order not to be obliged to increase the detachments, a measure which keeps too large a force up all night, and thus fatigues the troops. The enemy being thus obliged to be cautious and slow in his movements whilst it is dark, it is not necessary to extend the watch to so great a distance, and thus the narrowing above alluded to cannot be attended with danger. The position to be occupied at night is reconnoitred by the chief of the grand guard as soon as the posts for the day have been established. We should continue as much as possible to occupy that site at the moment when portion No. 2 has to relieve No. 3; in that manner the same portion has not to move after it has once begun to be on the look-out. Let us suppose that the army has arrived at the bivouac at two o'clock in the afternoon, that the departure is fixed for six next morning, and that it is completely dark at 8 P. M. The portion No. 3 will form the exterior circle from he moment of arrival until 8 P. M., and will then retire on the site indicated, passing through the chain of sentries, vedettes and pickets, actually forming on the site for the night by party No. 2; No. 1 having finished at the same time its period of rest, will repair to the place assigned to it, and will go at midnight to relieve No. 2. If the departure is fixed for next morning, the positions of the day will not be retaken, but if the army is to stay or depart late, these positions will be again occupied at daybreak, when, if possible, No. 1 has to relieve No. 2. If we suppose the arrival to have taken place at 12 o'clock, and that next day will be a day of rest, No. 3 will retire at 8 P. M., No. 2 will form the exterior circle from 8 P. M. to 5 A. M., and No. 1 will at 5 A. M. establish itself on the ground occupied at first by No. 3, to remain there until 12, at which time the whole grand guard will be retired. Before reoccupying the day posts patrols should be sent all round, to see if the enemy may not have prepared some ambush. At night sentries or vedettes need not be numerous, since they can hear sounds at a great distance, and the enemy, for fear of wandering, is almost compelled to follow roads and paths. It is only necessary to watch these for a continuance, and as for the rest of the ground, it is sufficiently secured if the service of rounds and patrols is well performed. The outposts once established must not be disturbed; if any modification in their position is to be made, this must be done at the moment when one portion relieves another. A general must never take an escort or a detachment from the outposts, but take the men that he requires from the principal corps. The outposts at the time of departure overtake the column to which they belong only at the precise time appointed for that purpose. They often are employed to form the rear-guard.

SENTRIES AND VEDETTES.

These observe all that happens on the outskirts, and report upon it, either verbally or by signals, to their pickets, which transmit the information to the grand guard; they give warning of the approach or retreat of the enemy, of his flank movements, of any reinforcements or convoys he may receive, and of the detachments he sends out; they stop all men that come to parley, deserters, travellers, and suspicious individuals, coming from outside or inside, and execute the orders they have received concerning persons of that description.

ROUNDS.

The object of rounds is to ascertain if they are on the look-out at the outposts, if the countersigns are

well executed, and if every one performs his duty.
The commander of the principal corps dispatches to
these outposts some officers, who return and give
him an account of what is going on; the chief of a
grand guard inspects, or causes to be inspected, his
pickets, sentries and vedettes; the chief of a picket
visits, or causes to be visited his sentries or vedettes.
The man whose duty it is to go the rounds, is alone or
is accompanied by 1, 2, 3, 4, or 5 men, according to
his rank and the nature and extent of ground to be
inspected. He can go either from post to post, or from
a post to a sentry or vedette, or from a sentry or
vedette to a sentry or vedette. His mission is to exercise an especial control, but at the same time he
observes all around him, particularly in the direction
of the enemy. The grand guards and pickets are visited three or four times during the service, and the
sentries or vedettes at least once during their duty.
The person on duty must either be familiar with his
route or have a guide, so as not to wander or remain
too long absent. He places himself in the centre of his
men, who scour the march in the same manner as
that hereafter indicated for patrols.

ART. 57.—Positions.

Troops take position to make or receive an attack;
a position is a portion of ground offering some
advantage either for attack or defence; it is usually
an elongated rectangle or a succession of rectangles
in a broken line.

The principal conditions a position should fulfil are
the following:

1st. A development in proportion to the troops oc-

cupying it, calculating it so as to give 300 yards
between the lines and 200 yards from the first line to
the front; a usual allowance is 120 yards front to
1,000 men of all arms and a total depth of 600 yards.

2d. Free communications in every direction.

3d. No separation by obstacles.

4th. Several debouches for retreat if necessary.

5th. Wood and water within reach, if the position is
to be long held, and healthy localities should be
selected under the same circumstances.

Positions are *offensive* or *defensive*. The special
conditions of offensive positions are: 1st, an unob-
structed front; 2d, debouches for all arms; 3d, wings
supported; 4th, roads in front penetrating the invad-
ed territory; 5th, if the surrounding ground presents
commanding points, occupy them with a few troops
as detached posts.

The special conditions of a defensive position are:
1st, a front protected by an obstacle which should
not be impassable; 2d, wings supported; 3d, debouches to the front for offensive returns; 4th, not to be
commanded by high ground within extreme range of
cannon; 5th, the obstacles in front to be under fire of
the position.

The longer the enemy is under fire before arriving
upon the position, the more perilous will his advance
be; and this is the reason why the obstacles should
not be absolutely impassable except on the flanks: it
is very advantageous for the defence if the ground
slopes away gradually in front and also if there are
salient points which can be made to receive the first
shock of the attack.

The enemy should never be able to pass by or turn

a defensive position without exposing his own flanks or communications; and the position should be such that its own communications to the rear are perfectly secure and its supplies of food, &c., at convenient positions not more than ten or fifteen miles distant.

A position should be strengthened by intrenchments when there are no natural obstacles and when time permits; an army of reserve or of observation at twenty-five or thirty miles distance from the active army should intrench itself when the latter does not cover well its line of retreat. The key of a position is the point the possession of which controls the whole.

To guard positions, advanced posts are formed which should be relieved every day; sometimes also detached posts are formed which are left to their own defence, but guarded from a sudden attack; for example, a village may be guarded by an isolated brigade.

ART. 58.—Special Reconnoissances.

The choice of routes, of the points to be occupied by camps, of positions, &c., give occasion to certain preparatory operations called special reconnoissances.

They are made to gain a knowledge of the topography of the country, to get an idea of distances, the state of the roads, the routes that are necessary, the positions the ground offers for receiving attacks or effecting retreats, the position and strength of the principal posts of the enemy, the outline of his position, its artificial defenses, its difficult points and the means of approaching it; finally, to estimate his strength at every point. These duties in the French service are performed by officers of the *staff* or état-major, who receive their instructions from the general: in the United States army, these duties appertain to the engineers. The reconnoitring offices communicate their instructions to the generals of brigade whose advanced posts they must pass: these generals furnish such information to the reconnoitring officers as their special knowledge of the dispositions of the enemy enable them to give; they provide troops to act as his escort, and these should be taken from the men who are to compose the advanced guard, that they may gain a knowledge of the ground upon which they are to act. If it is necessary to drive off the enemy's men from any point, the officer previously asks the consent of the general of brigade, and should not undertake any such operation without obtaining it. His report should be accompanied by a sketch, usually made upon a sheet traced in advance from a map of the country. These reports are generally divided into four parts; 1st, the physical description; 2d, the statistical; 3d, the communications; 4th, military considerations. In examining the ground the following points should receive special attention.

Woods and Forests.—Their respective position, extent, thickness, trees; are there tall trees or undergrowth? Are there clear spaces? Their extent? Are there thickets? In which direction? May they be turned? Where is the most clear space? Is the ground of the forest flat or hilly? Where do the roads come from and go to? Their condition? Must they be widened? The necessity, the facilities for opening new roads, the directions to give them that their flanks may not be liable to attack. The means of intrenching the forest, making abatis, taking advantage of thickets; the character of the ground in the vicinity of the forest. Does it give good positions? The cultivated fields, the meadows, ravines, of which the direction and depth must be noted. The little streams, marshes, springs, country houses, villages.

To reconnoitre a forest well, it is necessary to go round it, examine the routes which lead out of it, see where they go to and where from; make the same observations as to streams and ravines.

If they are of some size, to follow them to their sources, note the roads crossing them, and the marshy places they cross.

Heaths, Hedges.—For what troops practicable? The kind of thickets or brushwood, the ravines, small streams, roads? Character of the hedges. Heaths on high ground are practicable at all times; in low ground they are likely to be boggy. When the sand of heaths is of the ordinary color, the roads are always good—if the sand is blackish or mixed with fine white sand, the roads will be next to impassable in winter and even in a wet summer.

Canals.—See the article *river*. Their connection, the character of the earth in which they are made, the means of emptying them, of turning them aside. The dams; the means of destroying or preserving them; the means of interdicting or interfering with the navigation.

Country Houses and Mansions.—Their position and extent; their connection with towns in the vicinity; their object; their arrangement; their existing de-

2

2

fenses, if any; those which may be added; their defensive relations to the country or towns around; their underground vaults, if any; their strength.

Roads.—The direction, their terminus, their breadth, whether constant or variable; the nature of the soil; whether paved, firm, or beaten; what ascents and descents, with time of their passage in hours of march; in what seasons practicable; lined with trees, hedges, ditches; what country, rivers, cities, they pass; roads intersecting them, their extent, the heights over looking them, embankments, dangerous defiles, the repairs necessary for the passage of artillery; their length, and note the extent of country in sight on either hand. If the road under consideration is the only one in that direction, see whether others can be opened in connection with it for other columns, and mark out the route of those columns. The only roads which are always good are those whose foundation is coarse sand, gravel or rock. Those passing through tenacious soils, which are embanked, enclosed by plank fences or hedges, are certainly bad in rainy weather. Sometimes a road of this kind on a height is kept dry by the wind and it is good in the autumn, but these are almost always new roads, little known, little travelled; they must be marked out: by-paths must not be neglected; the country people often think them impassable for troops on account of ditches and other obstacles crossing them, when they may be made good roads with little trouble. Hollow roads are dangerous because they are easily chocked by the breaking down perhaps of a single wagon and thus a column may be checked.

Climate.—Physical causes, which may influence

the health; quality of the air, whether cold, warm, dry, moist; seasons and length of unhealthy terms, means of protection, practice of the inhabitants in this respect.

Hills and Passes.—Whether practicable for infantry, cavalry, carriages; their direct communication; communications by means of the crests or summits; means of guarding them; the time necessary to reach the greatest altitude by the ordinary roads; may new ones be opened.

Coasts.—Their character, whether bordered by downs, covered with rocks, rendering them more or less dangerous, or so precipitous as to make access to them impossible; what parts are of sufficient extent and openness for descents; the re-entering portions making coves and harbors; the projecting points and capes suitable for fortifications and batteries, to defend the accessible points, the neighboring islands to serve as advanced works, to form barriers to the enemy's attempts; the creeks, inlets, bays, roadsteads, harbors; the nature of the winds necessary for ingress and egress of these harbors, of which the relative advantages and inconveniences must be pointed out; the different batteries established for the defence of anchorages, entrances, &c.; the intrenchments in those parts where an attempt may be made to land; the camps, posts, &c., which should cover the principal establishments and the interior of the country; indicate every thing as to the accessible points, the dangers to be met, the obstacles to be surmounted, the means of increasing them; the times when the tides favor the approach of those places; indicate the points most advantageous for the means of defence, and the positions to be defended; the actual condition of the forts which protect the coast, of the batteries, of the coast-guards, and of all the pieces of artillery to be found there; analyze the system of defence adopted, improve it or make a new one if possible; calculate the troops necessary to furnish in a moment of surprise the cannoneers and coast guard, while the troops ordered up from such and such points can arrive at the point of attack; if there are rivers having mouths on the coast, the tides have an effect upon these, and this influence must be carefully observed and noted.

Defiles.—Their gorges, whether more or less closed, their length, the posts to occupy in covering a retreat, the character of the ground at the outlet; how to arrange a certain number of troops of different arms either for the attack or defence.

Marshes, Ponds, Bogs.—Their cause. Is the soil moist? Are they fed by springs? Are they formed by a river overflowing firm ground; their position; how cross them? Are there causeways through them, or can such be built? How defend these causeways to prevent or effect the passage of columns? Are there clumps of trees? What kind of ground joins them? During what periods are they unhealthy? When passable? Are they turfed? Are there mists and fogs?

In sandy and healthy localities there are often marshes covered with water in winter and nearly dry in summer. Often old marks of wagon wheels are found, which must be followed up and examined. Marshy prairies, which sometimes in summer seem quite passable, may not bear a column of cavalry;

they must be carefully examined, and those parts should be doubted where the grass is high and thick, as they are usually impassable for cavalry, and even for infantry in rainy weather.

Wells, Springs.—Quality of the water; ease of drawing; quantity they can furnish; relative position to the camp. Have you control of the stream?

Fortifications.—Permanent or temporary, low or high; if reveted with stone, brick, or sods; natural, artificial, old or new; is the surrounding ground favorable or not? Their position with reference to the debouche by which an enemy might penetrate; the defence of which they are capable.

Fords.—Banks, their shape, character, level at entrance and exit; their position in bends, elbows, &c.; the signs indicating them; the points in the neighborhood which may mislead the enemy; their bottom, entrance, outlet; depth of water, velocity; their direction, breadth. Means of breaking them up.

A ford for cavalry should not be more than four feet deep; for infantry not more than three or four feet; for artillery with safety to the ammunition not more than two and a half feet deep. The fords will be indicated by roads leading to the river banks. In hilly countries fords are often obstructed by large stones, rendering them inconvenient for horses, and impassable to carriages; fords with hard gravel bottoms are the best, and these are almost always found in low cultivated localities. In sandy and healthy countries the bottom is usually shifting sand or fine gravel, and is dangerous, because if a great number of horses pass such a ford, the sand gets mixed with water, the ford deepens, and the last passers must swim.

If large bodies of troops are to pass a ford, the infantry should go first, the artillery next, and the cavalry last, and the bottom may not be cut up by the horses' feet. To break up a ford, put into the water farm harrows, with the points up, keeping the harrows in position with pickets or rocks; or cut down trees and throw them into the ford, with their tops toward the opposite bank, filling up the entire width. If the water is rapid, throw the tops obliquely up the current. Dig a ditch across the ford, which is the best way. Place no confidence in reports of common people as to fords. When in seasons of low water a river flows rapidly between banks of sand, have it sounded. Although there may not be a travelled ford, or one known to the country people, it is rare that a river may not be forded under such circumstances.

The best method of reconnoitring for a ford is to descend the river in a skiff, to which is fastened a lead hung by a cord of proper length. The lead will give notice of the proper depth being beneath you by striking the bottom. Mark out the direction, length, breadth, quality, &c., of the ford. Mark the depth of water as soon as the ford is found, and plant a stake by which you may observe whether the water rises or falls, as it often happens that because of rains or certain winds a river may rise a foot or more in a short time, and render the ford impassable.

The best way of marking a ford is to put two rows of stakes at the sides of the ford to show its width, and to stretch a cord along the stakes. Use torches at night.

Hamlets.—The arrangement of the farms, the ground they occupy, the manner in which they are built, the assistance they can procure.

Inundations.—Their ordinary level, the play of the sluices; do they produce their effect rapidly? How soon can the inundation be made? How gain possession of the sluices, or how defend them? How prevent or delay their use? How drain the inundation, or if necessary how erect dykes to increase its safety?

Mountains.—Roads over high mountains are very rare, the valleys only being inhabited and passable. Therefore, in having a good knowledge of these valleys, their entrances, their outlets, the hills and the passes, it will be unnecessary to traverse the mountains otherwise than by the roads and paths.

Mark out the principal chains which form a main defence for the country, the different branches which prevent or favor exit, the relative height of their different parts. If the chains are sufficiently extensive to form a place of defence, point out the communications, the abatis, the places suitable for redoubts, the roads to be destroyed, and the other means of arresting an enemy.

Position, slopes; means of reaching the summit; nature of the ground; its configuration. Are they covered with timber, with bare rocks; their fertility, pasturage, forage, dwelling-houses, cities, towns, mansions, rods, paths; positions suitable for troops.

Mountains, which are but elevated plains, are more difficult of observation, because the configuration of the country is less marked.

Hilly Country.—A hilly country, partly under cultivation and partly wooded, is not difficult of examination. Commence the reconnaissance with the highest part, whence proceed the ravines and watercourses in every direction, of which the origin must be noted before entering upon further details; follow the principal ravines, brooks, and rivers as far as possible, observing carefully the number and position of all the ravines and tributary streams, to the right and left of the one under observation.

As to the roads, it is to be observed that there are valleys cut up by so many sinuosities, with so many streams winding from one side of the valley to the other, that they may be rendered impracticable for troops, on account of the great number of bridges which may be necessary. There are few mountain crests where there are not roads throughout their length, which are often little used and little known, but may be extremely useful.

In country of elevated plains, when two valleys or two rivers run parallel to each other, and distant six or ten miles, the intervening ground is usually quite high, with its side slopes furrowed with hollows and ravines, while the crest is practicable throughout its entire length. Such a crest should be carefully examined to the junction of the valleys, as it will afford a better road than the sides.

There are sometimes ravines whose debouches are easy, and the bottom a gentle and dry slope, at least in summer. Such ravines make an excellent road for a column. They must be well examined, the work estimated to make them practicable for troops of different kinds, and a note made of the roads they intersect. The outlets of such ravines must be carefully guarded against the enemy.

Flat Countries.—Such ground, when fertile, is very much cut up. Note the hedges, ditches, villages, houses, brooks, canals, marshes, rods, rivers, bridges, open ground for camps, their extent.

Plains.—Open plains, rivers, rivulets, cities, towns, principal rods, positions; every thing which can be an obstacle.

Plains wooded, and partly in cultivation. More details; heavy or small timber, quality; extent of woods.

Hilly Plains.—Note with care the roads, generally hollow at the approaches to town, cities, &c.

Bridges.—Their position, use, connection, dimensions; their materials, whether wooden, stone, &c.; strength, whether they can bear artillery. The means of destroying them, of rebuilding them most advantageously; considering the banks, the current, width, embankment; fords, and rods leading there; how fortify the head of the bridge; which bank is highest. For bridges in towns and cities, note the streets in different directions, their entrance, their outlet, the country beyond.

Profiles.—In the profiles of ground whose details are examined, observe what parts will hide infantry, cavalry, and artillery; note the ascents and descents estimated in hours of march.

Ravines.—Nature of the ground, whether in rocks, earth, rolling pebbles, sand; may the steep slopes be rendered more gentle? are rain storms like to leave bad results? snow storms; cavings in.

Rivers.—Whence come they, whither go, the nature of the country they water; is it ours or the enemy's? what use can be made of it before or during war? quality of the water, their bed, their banks, current and velocity. By throwing into the water a floating body, exposing but little surface to the action of the wind, by observing when it has attained a uniform motion, and with a watch noting the time required to pass by a certain measured distance upon the bank, the velocity may be deduced. By stretching from bank to bank a cord, divided properly, and taking a sounding at each point of division by means of a skiff, the depth and profile may be learned. See whether the bottom is muddy, gravelly, &c. Does the river freeze? will the ice bear? The thickness of ice to bear infantry, passing even by small detachments, must be three inches; for cavalry and light pieces of artillery, from four to seven inches; and for heavy carriages, at least from eight to eleven or twelve inches. Point out the mills, bridges, ferries, fords, times and height of freshets, inundations. At points of passage the breadth, depth, banks, rods, paths.

Rivers which divide into several arms, and form islands, are subject to changes in the principal bed at every freshet, which may from year to year make reconnoissances useless.

Rivers which run from high mountains where the snow does not melt all at once near midsummer, generally have two freshets a year, the first in March or April, at the melting of the mass of the snow, and the second in July or August, when the remainder of the snow is melted by the great heat.

Rivers whose source and course are in a level and low country, have great freshets only in winter, and generally in times of heavy rains.

Are they navigable? This requires a depth of at least three feet. Limits of navigation, the size of boats which may be used, those in use, the number that may be collected.

Islands: inhabited, wooded, cultivated, size, elevation, as compared with banks.

Elbows, curves, form of peninsulas; adaptability to bridging; mountains, hills, ridges in the neighborhood; their elevations, slopes, forms, distances. Ravines debouching at the river; arms or branches of other rivers which may be near and above the points where bridges may be built.

The positions the ground may offer to an army resting parallel, or by the flank toward the river.

ART. 59.—Reconnoissances of Rivers for Offensive Movements.

Bridges are best established generally at the most re-entering points of curves. A position of this sort must be carefully examined as to its suitableness. Upon the sides of the elbow batteries should be placed to protect the passage, and the further forward from the point of the elbow the better do they attain the enemy; but care must be taken lest they are themselves commanded, taken in flank, or reverse.

If there is no bend, a favorable position for throwing a bridge and passing the river, is one where the bank from which the passage is made commands the other. If the banks are of the same height, take a point where the opposite bank will be most exposed to the action of your artillery.

If, in a position suitable for a bridge, the opposite bank is obstructed by hedges, clumps of wood, &c., these covers may be favorable to the construction of the bridge, provided the bank from which the passage is made decidedly commands the opposite bank, and there is nothing to interfere with the fire of the artillery. In these covers your infantry may be concealed, but they should not be too much extended, nor difficult of passage. The country upon which the army debouches after passage, should not be cut up with marshes, forests, &c. The neighborhood of tributary streams, entering the main river upon the side from which the passage is to be made, is very favorable for the construction of bridges.

The breadth of a river may be calculated without crossing it, in the following way: take $bc=bd$, ba being very nearly perpendicular to the banks; then taking e on the prolongation of ac, make $bf=be$; join

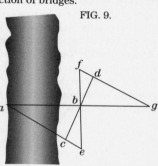

FIG. 9.

fd, and prolong it to meet ab at g, then $bg=ba$. If we take $bd=\frac{1}{2}\,bc$, we find $bg=\frac{1}{2}\,ba$. These elements are necessary for the determination of the kind and dimensions, as well as the quantities of the supports necessary to effect the passage. In constructing bridges, pontons and boats may be used, also rafts of casks or trunks of trees, also trestles and piles. Ponton bridges are seldom used, if the river is more than 150 or 200 feet wide. Raft bridges answer best when the velocity of the current is not very great. For bridges of trestles the bottom should be firm and smooth, the depth of water not more than six or seven feet, and the velocity not great; as the velocity diminishes, the bridge may be constructed in deeper water. Pile bridges need a solid bottom, and little depth of water; they are usually built to keep up communication after an army has passed.

Other means of passing rivers are also used, such as flying bridges and ferry-boats, manœuvred either by the use of a rope stretched from bank to bank, or by poles or oars. The flying-bridge answers well for rapid streams, when the passage need not be continuous. The ferry-boats attached to a rope stretched across, may be used also upon rapid streams, and of moderate width. The ordinary flat-bottomed, shallow ferry-boat, only answers upon rivers with quite a gentle current. When the banks are steep, and not more than fifty yards apart, a bridge of rope may be constructed. Streams of moderate width may often

FIG. 10.

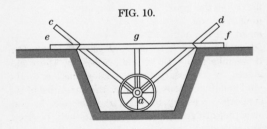

be crossed rapidly with means collected in the neighborhood. A portion of a carriage may thus serve as a trestle in a canal from four to six feet deep. Two pieces, ac and ad, fixed to an axle a, which joins two wheels, and attached also to beams ef, which are supported in their middle by two uprights, ag, and covered with light boards, form a bridge that may be put together at a distance, and rolled up to and into the ditch.

FIG. 11.

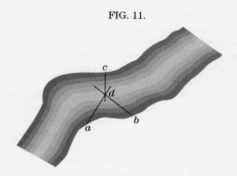

Three trees may serve as supports on a rapid stream in the following manner (Fig. 11): two trees, *a* and *b*, are bound together at *d*, one quarter the length of *a*, and thrown into the water while still attached to the bank; the third tree is slid along the tree *b*, and its top, abandoned to the current, will rest at *c*.

To pass a broken arch, trees may also be used, if they can be procured, reaching across the void. If the span is too great for the length of the timbers, an intermediate point of support may be a raft or boat, or a trestle, or struts abutting against the piers, if standing.

ART. 60.—Reconnoissances for Defensive Purposes.

Rivers.—Indicate the means the enemy has for passing the river by fords and otherwise, and the advantages of the bank he occupies; the nature of the country he must traverse after the passage of the river; the means of guarding our own bank. Indicate the positions an army may take up to guard the greatest possible length of a river; examine the roads the patrols pass over in going from one post to another. They should be as near the bank as possible. Break up fords. If the ground is difficult, and presents but few points suitable for throwing up bridges, secure those points by redoubts and batteries.

Smaller streams, as brooks, runs, creeks.—These require nearly as many details as large rivers. It is necessary to examine in even more detail as to depth of water by sounding these, than the larger streams. As runs and brooks serve to cover the flank and front of an army, all the usual and practicable points of passage must be well known, their direction, bed, quality and quantity of water, high and low states, the meadows and marshes they traverse, the mills on their banks, the breadth of their valleys, the hills and crests near them; on which side are the commanding heights; the tributary streams with high banks; the intersecting ravines, their distance apart, in order to see if they will form good points of support for the flanks.

Mills often control the fordableness of rivers, by their dams being open or shut. Ascertain the state of the water when the sluice-gates are open or shut, the time the water takes to run out if the gates are open.

Lands.—Cultivated or not; their products, fertility, time of different harvests, quantities of wheat, rye, corn, barley, oats, hay, &c., produced, after deducting the consumption of the inhabitants.

Orchards.—Their products; are they thick set? are they enclosed by hedges, ditches, or walls? are they in grass, &c.?

Vineyards.—Nature of their soil; are they planted in furrows? their depth; are the vines propped, or supported on trees? are they surrounded with hedges, ditches, &c.?

Villages.—Their situation, number of houses, character of the ground, quality and quantity of the crops in the neighborhood; the markets; the country around attending the markets; beasts of burden, flocks, herds, fowls, ovens; the quality of the water, the style of building of houses, barns, sheep-folds; the position of the church, cemetery; is it enclosed with walls? are there clumps of trees, ditches, water-mills or windmills? may the village be advantageously intrenched?

Fortified Cities.—The connection of the places with the movements of troops. The relative positions of several cities, whether in the first or second line; the assistance they may afford each other in case of threatened attack or actual siege; the means of moving up those succors in the direction of the attack; the aid in provisions, the means of bringing them up; may an important depot be established? hospitals. The rivers, the fortifications, the strength in each direction; the environs within cannon range. The form of the investment; the posts to connect with the lines of circumvallation; the means of fortifying the lines, having reference to the ground, the positions occupied, and the means at hand. The safest communications and the means of cutting them. The advantages the ground from the foot of the glacis to the lines offers for opposition to the advance of the besieger.

Open Cities.—Their situation, construction, population, commerce; the provisions in them; the assistance that may be drawn from them in men, horses, &c.; the parks, large buildings, the defence of which they are susceptible, the walls surrounding them; do the walls come in contact with the houses? are there towers; ditches, either dry, marshy, of full of water? the number of outlets; the gardens in the neighborhood; the roads centering there. The report of an officer intrusted with a reconnoissance, is rendered complete by the addition of statistical information as to the resources of the country, which is generally embodied in a table indicating the following particulars:—the total population of cities, towns and villages; number of houses, whether in a body or isolated; the number of horses and men they can accommodate; the quantity of grains, hay, straw, oxen, cows, calves, sheep, hogs; mills, their grinding power in twenty-four hours; wells and springs; the means of transportation; carriages, boats, horses, oxen, mules; the number of farriers, wheelwrights, mechanics in wood or metal, tailors, shoemakers, saddlers; the taxes, commerce, industrial pursuits. To this may be added, remarks as to the health of the dwelling-houses, stables, the air, the water; as to resources for fuel, in metals, cloth, leather, &c.

Besides *special* reconnoissances, there are also *daily* reconnoissances, and those called offensive.

ART. 61.—Daily Reconnoissances.

Daily reconnoissances are made with a view to the safety of camps and posts; their object is to observe the movements, the preparations of the hostile army, and the changes in the positions of his advanced posts.

They are made by special detachments or by the patrols of the outposts. They should not be repeated at the same hours, and by the same roads.

These reconnoitring parties are generally composed of infantry and cavalry. However, in a hilly country, but few horsemen are necessary; whereas, in a low country, little else than cavalry are used. Small detachments are posted, or messengers dispatched to and fro, to keep up a communication with the outposts which are passed by. Skirmishes are thrown out in front and flank, who should be well mounted, and, if possible, they should keep in sight of the main detachment; they extend outward about 400 yards in daytime, and from twenty-five to fifty at night. An advanced guard marches a few hundred paces in front, and a rear-guard in the rear. The commandant should have a good general conception of the ground passed over, as well as of its details, taking notes and making sketches. He never is drawn into combat, unless he is forced to do so to gain desired information, or when his business is to check the rapid march of a hostile detachment.

ART. 62.—Offensive Reconnoissances.

These are for the purpose of examining with the greatest minuteness the general position of the enemy, or certain points of it, in order to learn exactly his strength, and his means of defence; it is thus necessary to drive in his outposts, and sometimes to engage his main lines, especially where the object is to compel a display of his whole force; these operations often open battles; they should be ordered by the general-in-chief alone; the office intrusted with such a duty should accompany his report with a field sketch.

Among the indications which give an idea of the enemy's force, &c., when in position, are the bivouac fires at night, the distance between the vedettes and advanced posts, the strength of patrols; at daybreak attend to the movements which take place in every direction, and to the dispositions that can be observed; see the number of men who go after water, fuel, provisions.

To reconnoitre a column on the march, penetrate the line of flankers. When the dust is very thick and rises very high, the column is chiefly cavalry; if the dust is irregular, the indication is of carriages; if the dust is low, of infantry. The reflections of the sunlight from the arms are to be observed also. The number of flags is an indication of the number of troops.

ART. 63.—Offensive and other Patrols.

The duty of a patrol is to reconnoitre a certain object or extent of ground; to go and seek for news of a neighboring post independent of its own; to search a village, a wood, &c.; to discover what happens on its front, rear, or flanks. When there is not a sufficient number of men to overlook completely the country by means of sentries and vedettes, this deficiency is supplied by employing patrols in constant motion.

FIG. 12.

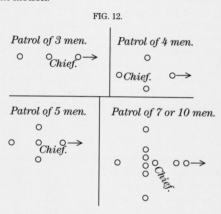

Every patrol has a chief; it is composed of at least three men, and very seldom of more than 30 or 40. (Figs. 12. and 13.) When it is strong, it is almost always formed of cavalry, whose mission it is to venture far enough to obtain news of the enemy. A single patrol follows the same rules as a numerous body, i.e., it scours its front, flank, and rear; under all circumstances it avoids noise, and any thing that might reveal its approach. In general it has not to fight; if, therefore, it can accomplish its duty without coming to an encounter, it avoids engaging either on the offensive or the defensive. The dispositions it adopts for its security are shown by the figures annexed. The distances between the chief of a patrol as a centre to its flankers, vary during the day from 10 to 60 yards, during the night from 5 to 20 yards, so as at all times to be able to see them, or to hear them speak in an under tone. Patrols, properly so called, belong to the special service of grand guards; they must not venture much out of the circle of the sentries or vedettes, because their strength being necessarily limited and small, they would be in jeopardy at great distance. They ought, so to speak, never to fight unless they are cut off, and in that case they rush impetuously through the enemy that has turned them.

RECONNOITRING PATROLS.

In order to know what happens at all points within a long radius, recourse is had to reconnoitring, or strong patrols drawn from he principal corps itself; they go beyond the outposts, and advance to a distance necessary to obtain news of the enemy, or of the neighboring corps. These patrols are under the special order of the commander of the forces, who decides whenever any are to be sent; but he may leave to his subordinates the care of composing them or of fixing the detailed particulars, when their main object and general direction have once been pointed out. It is particularly when the army is in cantonments or at rest that reconnoitring patrols must be sent. They are composed of infantry and cavalry, but they ought not to contain any strong subdivision, lest, if they were cut off, a corps might remain deprived the whole campaign of one of its component parts; as, for example a battalion of a company or a cavalry regiment of a squadron.

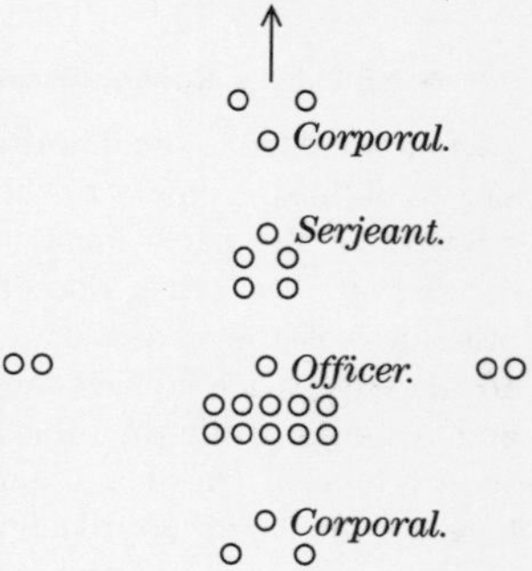

Reconnoitring patrols observe on a march the same precautions as patrols, i.e., they detach on front, flanks, and rear, scouts and flanks. The main body keeps in the centre of these skirmishers, which are immediately supported by small reserves, if the force at disposal permits it. If a patrol needs to pierce the chain of the hostile outposts, it attacks vigorously a well selected point of that chain, drives away the sentries and vedettes, skirmishes a few minutes, during which an officer or non-commissioned officer, well mounted, ventures forward to see what is to be reconnoitred, and returns, and then the reconnoitring patrol retires.

FIG. 13.
Patrol of 12 or 15 men.

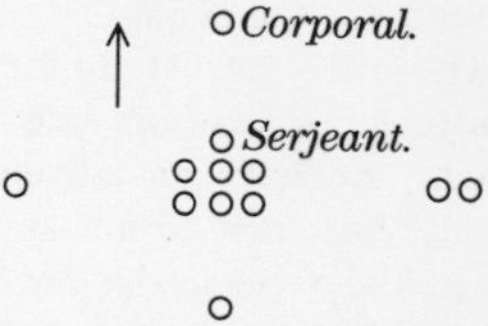

Patrol of 25 or 30 men.

Like other patrols, these must seldom fight, and then only for the purpose of opening a passage in a route they must necessarily follow. During the absence of a detachment sent out to reconnoitre, the guards should keep a more careful look-out, in order to be ready to rescue it if pursued, and to avoid all blunders on its return, such, for instance, as to mistake it for the enemy.

Offensive patrols are for the purpose of examining an enemy's position; may be composed of about 20 men, and have an advanced guard, flankers, main body, &c. They do not approach the position nearer than 400 paces in the day, but at night may approach to 30. The commander of a patrol takes notes and sketches, remaining always in sight of the troops to which he belongs.

ART. 64.—Reconnoissance of a Village.

When a village is reconnoitred a skirmish is necessary to oblige the enemy to show himself in force; the strength of the party must be ample. It should be divided into two parts, one of which acts, while the other makes the necessary observations. One part advances to twice musket range, driving in sentinels and outposts; while the other, as soon as the enemy shows himself, dashes upon him, examines him, harasses his flanks, approaches the nearest houses in order to see their interior arrangements, and then falls back upon the second portion.

ART. 65.—Reconnoissance of a Ford.

To examine a ford occupied by a hostile detachment, divide your party into two sections, one of which will remain concealed at a certain distance, while the other makes a demonstration in another direction. When it is impossible to stake out the ford, at least examine the banks.

ART. 66.—Offensive Order.

An offensive movement, it has been observed, is usually preceded by armed reconnoissances, which oblige the enemy to show himself, deploy his troops, and give battle.

In the offensive, an attack is made upon the advanced points of the enemy's line, unless there should be detached or isolated posts, or except in the case when the retired parts of the line may be attacked without uncovering the attacking troops; but in this last case, care must be taken to avoid being taken in flank. Attacks are made upon the wing, on the centre, upon both wings, a flank, the rear, in accordance with the following principles:—

Upon one Wing.—Threaten other points of the line, conceal your movements, do not let them be too much extended, do not give the enemy time to reinforce the wing attacked; choose that wing which is in proximity to the line of the enemy's operations, in order to cut his communication with his base of operations.

Upon the Centre.—Support the flanks of the attacking column by troops which may be thrown upon one wing while holding the other in check.

Upon both Wings.—Execute the double movement at the same moment. This is difficult, and requires a great superiority in numbers and mobility.

A Flank.—Combine the attack with one upon the wing in front.

The Rear.—Avoid cutting yourself off from your own communications, while striving to cut those of the enemy.

ART. 67.—Order of Battle.

A battle is a general action in which all the corps

of an army are or may be engaged. If you find yourself suddenly in presence of the enemy, attack; for in such cases, he who attacks has almost invariably the advantage, whilst he who wavers or retires suffers considerable losses. Avoid a battle if you think that the consequences of a defeat would be more serious than the advantages to be expected from a victory; if the enemy occupies an impregnable position; if you have not all your troops; and if you hope that time, fatigue, sickness, scarcity, or discord will do your work. It being once resolved upon to give a battle, be the first to attack; it is a fact that the offensive, independently of its tactical advantages, excites the courage and impulse of the men. Therefore, when you are under the necessity of fighting, unless you find yourself behind impregnable intrenchments, march to encounter the enemy, and even in your intrenchments, have always some openings through which to sally forth. A partial defensive at a point is only advantageous in so far as the force assuming such an attitude occupies a very strong position, from which it can by its artillery join in the attack by throwing projectiles on the enemy, and even then it must not be liable to become isolated or rendered useless at any time of the engagement. Let us now examine the different cases that may occur: there are three. 1st, the enemy is in position. Reconnoitre carefully his dispositions, find out his weak side, then approach him, form your troops, do not neglect to put on your side, if practicable, the advantages to be derived from the ground, the wind, the sun, and the dust; impart your plans to your generals, and, in some cases, to every one, at least in their general bearings, and point out the chief aim; foresee the case of a defeat, and point out the routes through which to retreat, and the place where to rally.

2d, the enemy advances. Ascertain the direction he follows, and if you know of any strong position in the vicinity, occupy it, but let it be such that you may act offensively as soon as the enemy comes within proper range, without awaiting him; deploy your troops beforehand, in order to begin the attack first, and to fall upon your adversary when he is making his own dispositions. Do not give him time to form.

3d, the enemy retreats. Let your vanguard be numerous; composed of your best troops, and closely supported, let it attack suddenly, whenever it finds a good opportunity, and reinforce it quickly if it meets with resistance, and for that purpose form as many parallel columns as the ground will permit. If you find a vigorous resistance, whilst you endeavor to surmount it in front, try to turn your adversary, for such is the human mind that in war men are ten times more disconcerted by danger on the flank than on the front.

So dispose your troops that every arm may act efficiently, infantry firing and charging, cavalry charging, and artillery firing. Avoid for artillery and infantry the positions that give a plunging fire. Do not accumulate masses behind one another. Extend your front. Do not fear to have large intervals, masking them with skirmishers. Take care lest a cannon ball from reverse or enfilade should carry off twenty or thirty men at a time. Three lines are generally sufficient; the first of infantry, the second of infantry or cavalry, or both mixed (the second always in small parallel columns), and a third composed of the reserves kept according to their strength and the distance in two, three or four columns. The baggage, under a sufficient escort, can occupy some hollow place in the rear of the reserve. The artillery officers dispose the guns so as to protect the troops they belong to without ever embarrassing them: it is better to fire two or three rounds less than to spoil a movement by encumbering the ground. If any cavalry is placed in the first line, it ought not to be dressed on the adjoining infantry, but should be drawn a little back, to be removed from the fire of the opposed line until an opportunity offers itself for charging. Cavalry is usually best placed at the extremities of the line, because it has there a greater scope for manœuvering than at the centre, being particularly enabled to extend outwardly in order to fall on the rear of the enemy or outflank him, which its speed permits. If your troops are good, and if, after a defeat, all is not considered lost, manage the means of retreat; if on the contrary, it is absolutely necessary that you should conquer, or if you have any doubt respecting the spirit of your men, place them in a desperate situation, as, for instance, with a river or the sea in their rear, and make them understand that their only safety is in success.

In the offensive, as in the defensive, we distinguish two general orders of battle, the *continuous* and that *with intervals*.

The former presents no such intervals as to prevent ready assistance being mutually given by the different parts of the line. In the *order with intervals*, there are, on the contrary, between the corps in action, breaks in the line, completely separating its parts; the action of the separated corps cannot be simultaneous, and this order is seldom used except in ground much wooded or broken up. It serves to deceive the enemy, but these great open spaces must be covered by obstacles, and light troops should keep up a connection between the divisions of the army. This order is employed for the defensive rather than the offensive; it is useful then to cover the debouches of the position by small posts spread over a great extent of ground, and to divide the enemy's forces and attention. A strong reserve should be kept in hand, and always have free communications. These orders may both be parallel, oblique, concave, or convex. The oblique order permits the greatest variety of combinations, and is very generally used. The concave order is applicable when the centre of the line is covered by impracticable obstacles; the convex order is used to attack the enemy's centre by a wedge-shaped formation. It is formed by throwing forward the centre and throwing back the wings, while supporting them by strong reserves; this is a useful disposition for covering bridges while the wings rest on the stream.

ART. 68.—The Defensive Order.

We must observe a distinction between the *active* and the *passive* defence. The latter consists in simply waiting for the enemy, either on account of inferiority of number, or because there are as many

or more advantages in awaiting the enemy in the
position assumed than in going to meet him: in the
active defence, we go out to meet the enemy.

From the various respective positions of armies
result offensive and defensive battles, in both of
which very varied combinations appear, depending
upon the ground, the properties of the arms used, the
resources and means of the enemy. We shall endeav-
or to explain the spirit of these combinations, indicating those most commonly used.

ART. 69.—Dispositions for Offensive Battle. Infantry.

When approaching the enemy, the army is drawn
up in four or five lines, viz., an advanced guard, a
battle corps in two lines, a reserve, and a rear-guard.
The infantry of the battle corps marches in front
with its pieces of artillery. Quite frequently, however, if the ground permits, a detachment of cavalry
is placed at the head of the column to sustain the
advanced guard and cover the deployment. The
mounted artillery does not immediately precede the
columns of infantry, but it should have but a single
battalion in front of it, for at the first signal, it
should take up its position. After the infantry
comes the mass of the cavalry and the reserve,
followed by the materiel of the battalions and the
parks; the rear-guard keeps distant about a half
march. As soon as the enemy shows himself, the
commanding general, forewarned by the advanced
guard, which is distant from the main body about a
half day's march, hastens forward to the place where
the fight will begin. The advanced guard takes a de-

fensive position, deploying its columns, in order to arrest the enemy and hold him in check by a destructive fire until the main body has taken a position for battle; the duty of the advanced guard being to act strictly on the defensive while the main body is making its dispositions for battle.

The general commanding examines the ground and the enemy when he arrives in his presence; he immediately sends his aids to the main body to direct the heads of columns, and give the generals the first instructions for entering into line of battle. The divisions quicken their pace, separating as they reach the field of battle, and move to their designated positions.

The cavalry hastens to the wings, to take its proper duties in the battle. The infantry first deploys by battalions en masse, upon two lines, 300 yards apart, a proper distance for the second line to be beyond musket range of the enemy's lines, and not to be cut up if the first line is routed, but still sufficiently near to be well in hand. It should take advantage as far as possible of all natural covers. Each division is usually in a single line.

The masses are next deployed, either to move toward the enemy in this order, preceded by the skirmishers, or to form double columns at deployment distance, a disposition always taken by the second line, the centre of its battalions being opposite the intervals of the first.

If the columns are not very deep, they may, in debouching, deploy at once, without the preliminary formation into battalions en masse. The reserve, or third line, usually forms by battalions en masse, and takes up a position to the rear, while the first two lines are engaged.

The action is begun by skirmishers, who halt as soon as they are within good range of the enemy's skirmishers, and hold them in check. The main body halts at the same time, and being soon unmasked by the skirmishers, the first line opens fire. If this is not simply a demonstration, the second line does not halt, but passes into the intervals of the first, and attacks in column with the bayonet, protected by skirmishers, which are spread along the intervals. The first line being thus passed by, ceases its fire, forms in double columns, in order to be ready in turn to succor the second line, now become first. If the latter overthrows the enemy, it reforms after the charge, and the skirmishers follow the enemy, supported by detachments; if not, the columns of the new second line again advance, and are replaced by those of the reserve, which prepares to move while the first line is retiring. There is in this way a constant passage of lines, in which consists the mechanical part of battles.

Often all the battalions of the first line are not deployed; only a part taking this formation. The battalion in column is more manageable, and on the battle-field it is found best to hold the troops as much as possible in this order.

The attack is to be made in deployed lines, or in *shallow order*, whenever we wish to come to close quarters with an enemy, whose front is well garnished with artillery, when we wish to withdraw troops as much as possible from the effects of this fire, and also where the ground is favorable to moving in ex-

tended order. The movement should always be preceded by numerous skirmishers, at a distance of
from 300 to 600 paces. Generally the order of battle is
formed by combining deployed battalions firing at
short range, with columns en masse making a simultaneous attack with the bayonet, under cover of the
fire. These columns, with skirmishers in the intervals
to harass the enemy, advance straight forward without firing, their chief placing himself at their head
to give them an example of courage, and remaining
exposed to the enemy's fire until all resistance
ceases.

ART. 70.—Skirmishers.

The skirmishers who cover the debouches of the
columns on the field of battle are accompanied by
supports equal to about one-third of their number;
and when they are thrown forward more than 300
paces, they should have strong reserves equal to half
their number. These skirmishers play a most important part, whose importance is every day increasing with the improvements in small arms. They
are employed in large bodies to attack a post or position; the columns of attack then move forward,
protected by their fire, which becomes more close
and converging as they approach the object of attack,
and the position is finally carried with the bayonet.
To get possession of hostile batteries, the skirmishers pour a murderous fire upon the cannoneers,
whom they soon render hors de combat, and charge
with the bayonet, whilst the columns which have
been previously masked, rush upon the supports of

the artillery in flank and rear; if the attack is repelled, the skirmishers cover the retreat.

Thus, by a skilful combination of skirmishers and columns, the latter attain their greatest value. Infantry burns the most of its powder as skirmishers, and in contests with cavalry.

ART. 71.—Fires.

The fire most used in war is by file, or by two ranks. being very effective against repeated attacks of cavalry. The fire by battalion is used in preference, when the battalion is covered in front by obstacles of ground, and when it is desirable to produce at the moment an imposing effect. The fire by rank, which combines the powerful effect of the one with the known advantages of the other, and is recommended by several authors, especially against cavalry, is not much used, on account of the difficulty of obtaining its proper execution, which is entirely dependent on the coolness of the men.

NOTE.—We have just seen the method of conducting an attack in front. If we wish to manœuvre upon the flanks of the enemy, in order to dislodge him from a position too strong to be attacked in front, a portion of the line is made to execute a movement by echelons, either direct or oblique; and if it is desired to mask a part of the front, the echelons may be caused to overlap by lateral movements, and formed in column by companies. Usually the echelons are in double column, and not in deployed lines. Columns threatened by cavalry form squares flanking each other, and march in this order without reforming in column, when it is only necessary to gain ground slowly by occasional movements; but the arrangement must be such that the prolongation of the line shall not be enfiladed by the enemy's artillery.

ART. 72.—Disposition in Battle for the Defensive. Infantry.

Upon the defensive, the advanced guard forms the line of advanced posts with supports, and fights in open order, while falling back by echelon or checker-wise, to join the reserve. During this time the main body has formed two lines. In a strong defensive position, the first is deployed, excepting, often at least, the battalions of the centre and the wings: it defends the borders of the position, and covers them with its fires, and often the deployed line charges with the bayonet, after delivering its fire; for example, when awaiting behind the crest of a plateau a column which is climbing the slope. Thus the line, deployed about fifty paces from the crest, with columns on the wings intended to threaten the flanks of the enemy, and pre-ceded by skirmishers who, posted half way down the hill, annoy him in his onward progress, gives him a volley as soon as he reaches the row, and then charges with the bayonet. The skirmishers, by their pursuit, will then complete the defeat. In the defen-sive, as in the offensive, the second line is in double columns. It should outflank the first line in both direc-tions, if either flank is unsupported by some natural obstacle. The reserve, deployed by battalions en masse, and covered, if possible, by obstacles, keeps in the rear, but at hand to succor the battle-corps; it should be placed toward the weaker wing.

If the enemy attacks in front, the second line

moves to assist the first with the bayonet, supported by the reserves. If he only makes a demonstration upon the front, and threatens the unsupported wing, the battalions of the second line at once proceed to succor the line attacked, while the reserves threaten the flanks of the enemy's columns. If a charge of cavalry is made, the first line forms squares, and in a plain, the second does likewise. Use then the formation of battalion squares, arranged checkerwise, at eight paces, or form in echelon squares, resting those of the head and tail upon inert obstacles, or supporting them with cavalry, artillery, and skirmishers. If a mound, or a clump of trees, occurs in the line of the squares, occupy it with infantry. In some cases, when time fails for other dispositions, oblique squares are used; they have the inconvenience of changing the front of the line, and, moreover, their angles are difficult to be fixed.

Squares of four battalions are still formed, with good reserves. Generally, however, the more numerous the squares, the more thorough is the flank defence; in all cases, the horsemen of the light cavalry, who are thrown forward in open order, are kept off by skirmishers.

In retrograde movements the first line, if time permits it to adopt that formation, retires in double columns, the second line deploying while the first passes. If not, that is to say, if the first line, being overthrown, has no time to form columns, it rallies in rear at some favorable position, reforms, and makes a stand, and thus goes on the fight until a position is found which allows the onset of the enemy to be checked, and marching columns to be reformed;

these movements are always supported by skirmishers.

To sum up—in the *passive* defence, the chief dependence is the fire, and the troops should therefore be deployed. In the *active* defence, columns are formed, covered by skirmishers, or the *mixed* order is used, consisting of deployed lines combined with columns. In the *offensive*, it is generally best to multiply columns, to have them not too deep, and well covered with skirmishers. The general rule is, to apply the principles of the *defensive* to those points of the line which are to be held defensively, and to make other dispositions on those where it is advantageous to take the offensive. In war, nothing is absolutely fixed.

ART. 73.—Disposition for Battle. Cavalry.

In the primitive order of battle, the cavalry is usually deployed a little to the rear of the wings of the infantry, especially toward that one which is least protected, or else in columns of squadrons behind the centre of the second line, that it may readily give succor in every direction. Deployed behind the wings, it does not interfere with the fire of the infantry, and is in a convenient position for a charge. In column, and forming a third line, it acts as a reserve, and allows passages of lines or movements in retreat of the infantry.

The deployed order is the fundamental one, but it has the disadvantage of very weak wings, because cavalry cannot form a crotchet to defend them; the wings of a line of cavalry should therefore be supported by infantry or natural obstacles, or by squadrons in columns of companies thrown to the rear.

A mass of cavalry arranges itself in two lines, 400 to 500 yards apart; the second follows the movements of the first, and is in readiness to cover the flanks when exposed.

When the 1st line of cavalry is formed in columns, it should be carefully masked from the enemy's view by accidents of ground until the moment of its making an onset. It is specially proper to use cavalry columns against squares, the columns being at double distance, and charging in succession upon the capital of the square, if it is large; on the short faces, if it is oblong or small; let the squadrons be in echelon, so that each may overlap the preceding one by half its front, and all attacking the same point are partly masked by each other; their movements converge to the same point, but the path of the later squadrons is not encumbered with the debris of the preceding ones. The attack of the squares is usually preceded by a great number of skirmishers, who harass the enemy, and oblige him to deliver his fire.

For a charge against lines of infantry, the extent of front of a regiment in line of battle seems most suitable, and this formation is usually adopted in such cases. The order by echelon is also used, each being composed of a regiment. This is the method of attacking the wing of a hostile corps. Against a line of cavalry the charge should be in a right line, if this line is more extended than the enemy's, but in an oblique line otherwise; in all turning manœuvres use echelons. All charges are followed by reserve squadrons, and covered on the flanks by skirmishers.

The cases in which cavalry may charge an enemy's cavalry are those where it is evidently superior in organization or experience, or in the size and strength of its horses. In a charge the second line is usually in column.

Suppose it be desired to attack in front, and by echelons, the left wing of an enemy's line; three echelons will be formed, left in front, each of a brigade; the first composed of light cavalry, will have one regiment deployed and the other thrown back in column of squadrons, for the protection of the flank if necessary; this will hold in position the enemy's right; the second echelon, composed of two regiments of reserve cavalry, in two lines, at a distance apart equal to the depth of a regiment in column of squadrons, will be prepared to charge, having a suitable distance to charge with full force; the second line may be in column by platoons, ready to form squadrons, an arrangement which prevents being drawn into the confusion of the first line, if repulsed in its charge; finally, the third echelon, formed of cavalry of the line, will be the reserve, and will form close column by squadrons. In each echelon each regiment should support its outward flank by a detached squadron, partly in column of platoons and partly in open skirmishing order, and two platoons of light cavalry should be added as an escort to each battery of horse artillery attached to the brigades.

To *turn* the enemy's left wing, echelons by the right may be formed; the first echelon will then be in close column by squadrons, and will form to the left into line of battle, when arrived at the prolongation of the enemy's flank.

Cavalry in masses is used thus to assure the victory at the decisive point, or to fill up the space left in the order of battle, when, for example, a part of the line changes front, or executes a flank movement in order to make an attack in the rear.

Some authors, when not using the formation by echelon, recommend the following: three brigades, of two regiments each, are arranged in three lines; each brigade forms one line, with its regiments in close columns, separated by the extent of one squadron; first with the left in front, and the second with the right in front. The lines are distant from each the depth of a regiment in column.

The light cavalry is in the first line; in the second the reserve cavalry; in the third, the cavalry of the line. This corps moves thus against the enemy in two twin columns proceeding at the same rate, one squadron of each regiment furnishing flankers and skirmishers. The charge is left to the reserve cavalry, which for this purpose forms in two lines, when the proper moment for charging has arrived, the first deployed, the second in column of platoons, at full distance. The light cavalry in front deploys also, but unmasks the reserve cavalry by oblique movements, and prevents the enemy charging on the flanks by throwing out numerous skirmishers. The cavalry of the line remains in reserve, deploys in turn in two lines, if the charge is repulsed, and takes the place of the second brigade.

The spirit of this manœuvre is to cover by light troops those intending to charge, to harass and annoy the enemy on the flanks of the charge while unmasking it, at the same time holding a strong reserve in rear.

Retrograde movements of cavalry in masses are made by passages of lines or by echelons. The checkerwise order is not used, because it disunites the elements of the charges, and it is difficult in retiring to keep the squadrons of the second line opposite the intervals of the first.

When cavalry attacks a system of squares in echelon, it should charge those at the head and tail. If it attacks a double line of squares arrayed checkerwise it attacks simultaneously, each with a regiment, the four squares of the outer angles, holding back a reserve to support it if necessary, and to engage the enemy's cavalry if it should charge.

Cavalry attached to the infantry divisions is usually placed in the rear of the first lines, that it may not be needlessly exposed; it should generally be kept together; it follows the infantry to complete its successes. In retreats it protects its flanks, and repels the enemy's cavalry.

On the defensive, cavalry should be established at the extremity of the battle corps, on that side where the ground is more favorable for its action, to take in flank the enemy's columns of attack.

Cavalry fights as skirmishers on advanced guard and rear-guard duty, on reconnoissances, escorts, foraging, to cover the front and flanks of masses and of deployed lines, in attacking batteries, making false attacks on infantry squares; these skirmishers repel the enemy's skirmishers by charges as foragers, and are supported by platoons in close order; they slip in open order through the infantry columns. In reconnoissances the main body is preceded by a dozen or more advanced troopers, distributed in squads of 200 paces to the front.

ART. 74.—Manœuvres. Corresponding and combined Movements of Infantry and Cavalry.

Infantry and cavalry pass from the order in line to the order in column, and the reverse in the same manner. Both break by companies or platoons and divisions, to the right and the left. Both break from the right to march to the left, and *vice versa*, either to front or rear. A line of infantry may ploy on one of its subdivisions, at full or half distance or closed en masse, with either right or left in front. Double column is also formed on the centre in the same way. Cavalry formations are upon the same principle.

A column of infantry at half distance or closed en masse may take full distance either by the head or tail of the column, or upon an intermediate division; the same may be done in cavalry tactics.

Infantry may change direction from a halt by simply facing to the right or left. Cavalry can only do the same by wheeling.

The double movements for forming line of battle with columns which have commenced to change direction, are similar in both.

Infantry retires in double column in presence of cavalry, in line before infantry.

If a first line of infantry retires deployed, a second line of cavalry, whose duty it is to present itself in front of the enemy, passes the intervals in columns of platoons, and forms squadrons while advancing with a view to deployment. If the infantry retires in double columns, the cavalry forms in close columns on the squadrons opposite the intervals of the infantry, and deploys after the passage.

If a first line of cavalry retires behind a second of infantry, it should pass through the intervals, forming column by platoons; infantry remains in line when cavalry retires before infantry, but when it retires before cavalry, the infantry forms double column and battalion squares.

A first line of cavalry may pass to the rear of a second line of infantry by moving half to the right and half to the left in columns by platoon, passing behind the wings of the second line, forming squadrons there and countermarching, so as to be ready to deploy on the wings of the infantry, or may at once form line of battle faced to the rear.

A second line of cavalry passes to the front of a first line of the same arm in columns of platoons, passing between the squadrons.

A second line of infantry passes a first of the same arm through the intervals and in double columns: it would pass in the same way, or in line to the front of a line of cavalry whose regiments would be formed in close columns.

In perpendicular changes of front, a first line of infantry executes the movement by double columns, which pass to the new line at the proper point and deploy; the cavalry in second line forms close column on the squadron, which is on the prolongation of the new line, and then forms line of battle on this squadron.

The same principles prevail in other manœuvres.

The passage of a defile in front or rear is executed in the same manner by both arms.

In dispositions against cavalry, a square of several battalions is formed perpendicular or parallel to the line of battle, according as the cavalry threatens the front or flank of the line, care being taken always to present to the enemy the longest face.

ART. 75.—Dispositions for Battle. Artillery.

Artillery, upon reaching the field of battle, separates from the columns of infantry, and marches upon their flanks to take up its positions, the reserve being left in temporary positions, that of each battery following the movements of the troops to which it belongs, keeping safe from the fire and attacks of the enemy, that of each corps d'armée being placed in some central position, from two to five miles from the troops, and under a good escort.

A few pieces may be detached to increase the effect of the skirmishers left in advance of the lines.

The object of artillery is to harass the enemy and cause disorder in his ranks at distances where musketry is useless or nearly so. It takes position on the wings in front of the line of battle, or opposite the intervals, especially while the troops of the first line are not yet deployed, but it should not go to a greater distance to the front than 150 yards, nor approach the enemy within 300 yards. If the enemy makes a decided forward movement, it retires to the neighborhood of the second line.

ART. 76.—Supports and Duties of Batteries.

It may happen that the second line cannot give the artillery immediate protection. In this case supports are provided for it, and these place themselves a little to the rear, and upon the flanks of the battery, but never behind it, especially if of cavalry, in order not to furnish a double mark for the enemy's artillery. The ground alone can determine the proper position: it should be sheltered from counter-batteries, allow the defenders to take the offensive against the columns of attack, and to be beforehand with the enemy in all his turning manœuvres. The supports are generally formed in column, except when being of infantry a favorable use may be made of their fire, and then they want to deploy; they should be surrounded and covered by skirmishers, who try to outflank the enemy's, and some of these should also occupy the intervals between the pieces.

When a battery is captured, the supports rally and endeavor to retake the offensive.

The battery usually fights with the troops to which it is attached, and in fractions, either to obtain a converging fire, or to adapt itself to the broken state of the ground.

Horse artillery follows and supports the cavalry; mounted batteries the infantry. In offensive marches or infantry, as for example, in debouching upon the field of battle, the artillery moves at the heads of the columns of attack and upon their flanks, in order to overwhelm the enemy at the moment when he is attacked. In defensive battles, the greater part of the artillery always takes position on the side of the wing which rests on obstacles of the ground: as to the batteries placed on the opposite side, they should be supported by detachments often composed of infantry and cavalry together, and arranged in columns or in echelons, according to the circumstances of the war and the locality. Artillery operating in mass ought to have the greatest possible front with skirmishers intermixed.

In retreats in checkerwise order, the artillery takes position in front of the wings of the first line, and is divided in such manner as to give protection successively to each of them.

In squares, it should be placed at the angles, the pieces outside, and firing grape.

In a system of oblique squares, it may be placed between the squares in the spaces unprotected by fire.

In a system of echelons, having every facility for free movement in the intervals of the echelons, it moves wherever it can best protect the echelon against which the enemy's efforts are chiefly directed.

Generally a portion of the artillery moves while the remainder stays in position near the wing which is refused, in order to support the movement of the troops engaged: the nature and configuration of the ground decide whether to place it on the outer wing, or upon the inner flank of the echelons; it takes position so as to converge its fire.

Changes of front are made under the protection of the batteries, one of which establishes itself as a pivot. In changes of front of cavalry, a battery moves at a gallop on the side and in front of the marching flank, supported by its escort.

Horse artillery always prepares the way for charges of cavalry. Thus, in the attack of squares, half-batteries or sections establish themselves at 300 yards distance, and break the squares or counterbatter the pieces which support them.

In a front attack executed by a double column of squadrons which moves forward and deploys in order to charge, one or two light batteries placed between the leading regiments advance to the line of skirmishers, move into battery, cover thus the deployment, crush the part of the enemy's line which is to be attacked, cease firing at the moment of the charge, break rapidly into columns of sections to unmask it, and move to position with the reserve.

In attacks of cavalry against a wing, the batteries occupy a lateral position in order to get a slant fire, and to be enabled to continue their fire to the moment of the shock.

In an attack by echelons to turn a wing, a part of the horse artillery precedes the troops destined to effect the turning movement, and goes into battery at the moment when the first squadron deploys; another part accompanies the second echelon upon one of its flanks, and opens fire at the same time with the first, so as to take the wing assailed both in front and flank. Sometimes horse artillery, without being followed by its caissons, dashes itself in the very face of the enemy, who is deluged with grape in preparation for a charge, the battery returning at a gallop, and unmasking the charging cavalry, gaining a position a little to the rear of its flank, in order to cover its retreat if repulsed.

ART. 77.—Manœuvres of Artillery.

The column of manœuvre is the column of sections.

A line of several batteries may break into column by sections either to the front, by the flank, to the right or left, or to the rear: this column may in turn be formed in line of battle to the front, to the left, to the right or rear. A line of batteries may be formed in column of sections on the centre. Columns of pieces, half-batteries, and batteries are also formed.

Batteries fire advancing and retreating like skirmishers.

The passage of obstacles is effected by breaking by sections in the same manner as in passing defiles, both under protection of a battery which keeps up its fire.

ART. 78.—Ground in its Relation to the Three Arms.

Infantry fights on all kinds of ground: when climbing hills, the depth of the column should be diminished, and lines used when necessary. Slopes of five degrees to fifteen degrees permit infantry to advance in line, in good order, and at short distances; on those of twenty to twenty-five degrees, they can fight only as skirmishers; finally, on slopes of thirty degrees, it is difficult for infantry to use their fire.

Cavalry can act with facility only on ground that is flat, smooth, and open; it may charge in an effective manner up slopes of five degrees. On those of fifteen degrees, which it cannot descend at a trot, it cannot be actively used.

The slopes suitable for artillery are those of two degrees to four degrees, considering the inclination from its own position to that of the enemy, which answers nearly to $\frac{1}{100}$.

ART. 79.—Summary as to Battles.

We may here sum up and complete the general principles regulating offensive battles; avoid in battles manœuvres from right to left; avoid moving under the fire of the enemy; after passing accidents of ground, deploy by battalions en masse; leave in the second line intervals through which the first may pass; in advance of the latter carefully examine the ground at the beginning of the action: cause intrenchments to be taken by the troops in front of whom they may be found; take up oblique positions or in echelon to refuse a part of the front.

The general principles of defensive battles are: to multiply the obstacles in the front; support the flanks which do not rest on natural obstacles, with troops; change front if attacked in flank; make counter attacks and attacks in rear; when the reserves are insufficient, weaken distant posts to strengthen the reserves; be not deceived by false attacks; have your intrenchments not continuous lines, if the defence is to be of the active kind.

ART. 80.—Position of the Generals in Battles.

The position of the generals during an action is determined and marked out by them beforehand: if they leave it, an officer should remain to give information of the direction they have taken.

ART. 81.—Calculation of Distances and Marking out Lines on the Ground for Manœuvres.

In the manœuvres of the different arms it is often useful and necessary to mark out lines and calculate distances, by approximate and rapid methods. A line may be traced from one point, or between two points in a given direction.

On one point, by an officer simply turning about on the given point as a centre, and having a marker facing toward him, whom he stops when in the right direction; a second marker, placed in its prolongation, fixes the direction of the line.

Between two points, by two markers, who face each other, and move slightly to one or the other side until they are accurately fixed each by the other on the line between the two points. When the two are on the line, a third is placed on their prolongation, as already explained.

To calculate the spaces occupied by a body of troops, we must recollect that each file of infantry is allowed 20 inches and each cavalry file one yard. A man may easily accustom himself to pace yards. The pace of a horse at a walk is about a yard, at a trot about one and one-fourth yards, at a gallop about four yards. Spaces may be also estimated by the time required to pass over them; a man in quick time will make about 100 yards a minute; in the same time a horse will walk about the same distance; at a trot about 200 yards, at a gallop about 400 yards.

Finally, the explosion of powder furnishes a means of estimating distances, by observing the time elapsing between the flash of a discharge and the arrival of the sound, as sound travels about 1100 feet a second. An ordinary watch may serve to give the seconds, as five beats are equal to two seconds. The enemy's distance may be thus known.

ART. 82.—Pursuits.

Battles are ended by pursuits or by retreats.

An enemy is followed up in columns when he retires through defiles, or goes to occupy another position a little distance to the rear; he may be outflanked by oblique echelons.

Upon open ground a pursuit may be conducted in line; the cavalry in that case makes charges sustained by infantry and the fire of artillery.

In all cases the flanks should be threatened by detachments, while the main body presses upon the rear.

Night pursuits of large bodies are improper.

Look with suspicion upon a cordon of troops, which may be intended to deceive, and mask a line of retreat.

Endeavor to intercept the columns at entrances to defiles, and continually threaten the communications of the retreating body.

ART. 83.—Retreats.

In retreats, the cavalry forming in one or more lines checks the light troops of the pursuer, and retards the march of his columns; the divisions of the army fall to the rear in echelon.

In a difficult and obstructed country, make feints of attacking: retreat by several roads toward some point of junction: occupy in advance positions where defence may be made; deceive the enemy so as to gain a march upon him; leave for a rear-guard those troops which are in the best condition from having suffered least, and always batteries of horse artillery.

ART. 84.—Mountain Warfare.

It consists, when upon the defensive, in guarding the passes by detachments while occupying a central position; observe the points where valleys intersect, and occupy them; make a stand in the middle of a

valley when you can command the side slopes: occupy the hills most advantageous for the defence; form
camps at the junctions of several passes from which
movements may be made upon an enemy: take
advantage of the crests when they are suitable for
defence; form detached posts; make artificial
defences in the gorges; fortify the debouches and the
hills bordering the level county, and put lines of
intrenchments on the slopes.

A defensive army in a mountainous country need
not be very large if well handled; the cavalry especially need not be numerous; a few light squadrons
kept in the valleys being sufficient; keep strong
reserves and an advanced guard, which should be in
front of the hills when a position is held to the rear of
the crest of a chain; but in advance of the debouches
if the position is upon the heights themselves.

In offensive operations, endeavor to turn the
enemy; place camps upon his flank and rear; force
him to take the initiative unless it be necessary to
drive him from his position: use lateral roads for taking possession of the hills which overlook the enemy.

ART. 85.—Passage of Rivers.

A passage may be effected either by surprise or by
main force. In either case detachments are thrown
upon the enemy's side, and when they are sufficiently strengthened the construction of the bridges is
begun.

By Surprise.—The troops intended to occupy the
opposite bank, pass at night in boats with the necessary artillery; several boats, in case of need, being
attached together: the troops keep the most perfect

order and silence, no matter what may be the movements of the boats. When cavalry passes, the riders sit in the boats holding the bridles of their horses, which swim alongside. The army advances in columns, with its centre thrown forward, and the wings retired; it covers its own side with light troops, places artillery in the re-enterings of the river, makes false demonstrations to deceive the enemy, and builds the bridges at the points selected, which are already occupied by detachments previously thrown over in boats.

With a vigilant adversary a passage by surprise cannot be effected without meeting serious opposition, at least toward the close of the operation, which thus generally becomes, sooner or later, a passage by force.

In passage by *main force*, the batteries open their fire upon the point on the opposite shore where a landing is first to be effected, and under their protection detachments pass over either in boats or by swimming; an advanced guard of infantry is thus formed, which takes position at the point chosen for the end of the bridge, supported by batteries on the inner bank; these detachments should avoid firing until debarked; when they are in possession of the point of landing, the construction of the bridge begins.

The most favorable moment for passing a river is daybreak.

The order of passage depends on circumstances; generally the mass of the infantry passes first, with a suitable quantity of artillery and cavalry: the remainder of the army, the reserves, parks and trains do not pass until the repulse of the enemy is complete.

A passage by main force should be always accompanied by strong demonstrations at other points.

ART. 86.—Defence of Rivers.

To dispute the passage of a river by an enemy, you must be superior to him in numbers, unless you have the means of watching the whole river, and moving rapidly and in time to any threatened point. The force should be held, if not in a single mass, certainly not in more than three or four corps, having close connection by signals and posts of warning; these corps are stationed near the stream, and in a direction nearly parallel to its banks; a reserve should occupy a central position, or near the point most favorable for the passage of the enemy, and should be principally composed of cavalry. Indeed, in the defence of rivers, cavalry plays a very important part, on account of the rapidity with which it can give warning of the approach of the enemy, learn his dispositions, and the point threatened. With the aid of horse artillery it may arrive at a point in time to arrest an enemy who has succeeded in deceiving as to the true point of passage; it charges the first columns when shattered by the fire of the batteries, while the infantry is arriving and taking position.

The passage of a river in a retreat is a case of passing a defile, and will be treated under that head.

ART. 87.—Passage of Defiles.

To pass a defile in retreat, the flanks should, as much as possible, be secured by numerous skirmishers crowning the surrounding heights, by detachments guarding the points where side roads come in:

a convex arrangement should be adopted, which keeps the assailant at a distance, and closes the mouth of the defile: the artillery occupying positions on the flanks crosses its fire in front of the defile, and the cavalry of the wings stands ready to charge the head and flanks of the enemy's columns. The mass of the army passes the defile by company, platoon, or section from the centre or the wings, and leaves a rear-guard, of which the last column retires in such a manner that each division of it, having delivered its fire, falls to the right and left, uncovering the next. The artillery and cavalry, which are not employed in defending the entrance of the defile, precede the infantry in the movement of retreat, and all the troops, as they pass, take position in a concave order, so as to converge their fire upon the columns of the enemy, as he debouches from the defile. This concave order is formed of columns and deployed lines, with many skirmishers.

To pass a defile in front, and by main force, numerous skirmishers are thrown out upon the flanks, who are directed to gain possession of the obstacles which close and overlook the entrance, and batteries are posted to throw a slant fire into the entrance. The infantry advances by echelon, on the centre, and the cavalry on the wings, to attack the enemy's cavalry in flank; as soon as the enemy seems thrown into confusion, charge him vigorously in column.

The defile being forced, keep close on the heels of the retreating enemy, and let your column, debouching in small masses, deploy rapidly in front of the defile, under the protection of numerous skirmishers, and of artillery established on the lateral heights.

ART. 88.—Sieges.

Among the most important operations in war, are the attack and defence of fortified towns.

The strength and composition of a besieging army depend upon the locality and upon the garrison of the place attacked: commonly, for a small place well arranged, ten or twelve times the garrison are thought necessary; for a place of 3,000 men, eight times; for a large city, five times; but when there is also an army of observation, the besieging army may be much less numerous.

The first thing after approaching within twelve or fifteen miles of the place, is to detach a body of 4,000 or 5,000 men, chiefly cavalry, who advance to within about three miles of the place.

These columns establish themselves thus beyond cannon range, and the small detachments, which cover their movements, drive back into the place or capture whomsoever they come across, collecting, at the same time, all the information they can. This operation is called the investment. The troops necessary for this operation are estimated at 200 men to 1,000 yards of the circle of the investment, and this will be increased as the ground is more broken. The investing circle is gradually contracted, and a strict blockade is made, which remains in force throughout the sedge, resulting in two chains of posts, the one 1,500 yards from the glacis, and the other nearer to the outworks of the place; these posts, which are established after driving in those of the place, permit no one to pass either way.

The investing corps is accompanied by officers sent out by the chief of staff of the army, and by the

chiefs of artillery and engineers, to determine positions for the camps, to gain information of the
resources of the locality, and to indicate the proper
point at which to make the attack. They make a
sketch, on a scale of one two-thousandth of all the
ground within 600 yards of the work, upon which
they mark the salient, and at night they go up to the
glacis to examine the soil, and examine more nearly
the details of the fortification. The general officers
afterward renew these examinations in company
with the officers who have made them, and the general-in-chief then determines upon the point of
attack, after full consideration of all the information
at hand. The plan of the attack is then agreed upon,
and marked upon the drawing already made.

It is usual to attack the salient portions of a work,
and those where the works do not require to be taken
in succession. Every advantage should be taken of
covers and ridges of ground which give protection
from the fire of the work; hollows, which are entirely in view of the work, are to be avoided.

The infantry goes into camp near the point of
attack, beyond cannon range of the work; a portion
of the cavalry on the flanks, in order to repulse sorties, and the remainder keeping watch over the
ground in the vicinity.

It is well to have two artillery parks, which are also
beyond cannon range, and about 100 yards distant
from each other, one of them containing the heavy
material, and the other serving as a workshop and
place of distribution for the articles in daily use; the
artillery troops are placed in the vicinity of the large
park.

The camps and parks are often intrenched. From ten to fifteen days should be allowed for the arrangements between the investment and opening the trenches.

The infantry performs the trench duty, which is divided into two parts. 1st. Guarding the trenches, by battalion, and for tours of twenty-four hours. 2. Work in the trenches, by company, and for twelve hours at a time.

The guards of the trenches should be in number about three-quarters of the garrison. In constructing batteries, about ten or twelve men are allowed to each piece. In the trenches, one man is allowed for four or six feet of the length of the parallels.

It has been seen before, that officers of the *staff-corps* may be called upon to perform duty as staff-officers in the trenches, under the name of *majors, or aides-majors of the trenches*. The *major of the trenches* is intrusted with all the details relating to the assembly of the guards and workmen; he may likewise be called upon to distribute the guards along the different points of the attack, in conformity to the orders of the general of the trenches, and to supply working parties upon the requisition of the artillery and engineer officers. In order that he may be prepared for the performance of this duty, the chief of the staff should inform him in advance of the operations of the twenty-four hours of his tour.

The *major of the trenches* arranges the guards and workmen in the best manner, when they are proceeding to their duties, in order that each detachment may arrive at its own post without confusion.

The guards are placed in their usual battle order, and are divided into two lines near the trenches, in order to protect the work. The first line may be formed of the platoons of the flank companies of their battalions, and are placed about fifty yards to the front of the workmen, and lying down; in front of these, about the same distance, are sentinels, who stand or kneel, and keep a watchful eye over the ground around. The second line may be composed of battalions in column, posted in rear of the workmen. The mass of the troops are placed near the depots, which are to the rear of the trenches. This arrangement permits the troops in front to act in the most efficient manner in repelling sorties, while preserving a secure line of retreat upon their supports.

The companies of workmen are also as far as possible arranged in the trenches, according to the usual battle order of their regiment.

At dusk, the marks are established to show the position of the parallels, approaches and batteries; the work is executed at night.

The first parallel should not be more than 600 yards from the outworks of the place. The second parallel is usually 325 yards from the same points, the object being to have it at a somewhat greater distance from the work than from the first parallel. The third parallel is about sixty yards from the salients of the covered way.

In case a sortie is made, the guards of the trenches, supported by their reserves, make the best dispositions for repelling the enemy; if he penetrates to the trenches, the workmen retire; if not, they stand to their arms. After the completion of the third parallel, sorties are repulsed by a well-sustained fire. Always avoid pursuit of a sortie party.

When the third parallel is completed, an attack may be made by main force, by means of steps arranged against the parapet of the parallel, to enable the troops to pass rapidly out, after a heavy fire has been directed against the place, when they take possession of the covered way; or the attack may progress foot by foot by means of approaches in full and double sap, which lead to what is called the crowning of the covered way. Next comes the establishment of the breach and counter batteries, and then the descent into the ditch.

When the breach is wide enough for six men abreast, preparations for the assault may be made; but before making the assault, examinations should be made, to see, if it be practicable, whether the work is retrenched, or the fires of the flanks extinguished.

Assaults of demi-lunes are made at night. From four to eight select companies are taken, divided into three divisions, the two first being followed by a body of workmen; and having arrived at the breach, each division separates to the right and left to protect the workmen.

Assaults of the body of the place are made in the day.

Such is a summary of the dispositions adopted in regular sieges. If it becomes necessary to raise the siege, it should only be done after a heavy fire has been directed against the place.

ART. 89.—Defence of Places.

In order to defend a place, it is proper to begin by

carefully examining the surrounding ground, the communications it offers to the enemy, and their bends, the commanding points, the resources of the neighborhood; what should be the best arrangement of the artillery and musketry, the best position for the stores of powder and materials. A plan of the whole should be made.

A state of siege should be declared when the enemy comes within the limits of active operations for the place.

Active operations should be made so soon as an enemy is within three days' march. The garrison should then be divided into three parts, nearly equal: 1st. For the guards of the works, one half being under arms in the front of attack, as follows: forty men to each bastion and demi-lune; to the covered way one man to a yard along the front attacked, and one man to two yards on the adjacent fronts. 2d. For posts, reinforcements, sorties, this portion bivouacking in the ramparts and in the dry ditches. 3d. Resting, or under arms in the interior.

A hexagon requires about 3,200 infantry. The minimum armament of a front of attack is forty-eight pieces.

But little cavalry is necessary in a besieged place. During the early periods of the siege it assists in sorties, is employed in patrolling, and in completing the provisioning of the place.

During the investment, numerous parties scour the country around to prevent reconnoitring. Half of the second portion of the infantry bivouacs in the covered way, detaching advanced posts of eighty men, who form, at the foot of the glacis, a chain of marksmen, lying flat on the ground to hide themselves from the enemy's view. These detachments are under the command of an officer of rank; they retire when the siege works begin, in order to unmask entirely the fire of the artillery of the work.

If the trenches are opened too near the work, a sortie is made to hinder their execution. The sortie party will assemble in the places of arms of the covered way, being composed of two select companies, one battalion, and one squadron divided into two parts, one on each flank, with two supporting pieces of artillery. The artillery advances one-third of the distance, and when the party falls back, it takes position in the centre; the two companies then cover the rear. Generally sorties are only useful after the execution of the second parallel on account of the great distance previously.

Sorties in force are made at daybreak, preceded by a heavy and continued fire: three or four columns marching directly upon the siege works, while the flanks are also assailed, and efforts made by getting in rear to cut off the workmen. The sortie party should be followed by workmen, as the object of the operation is to destroy the works of the enemy: his guns should be spiked, and balls wedged into the bores, and the carriages blown up. At a later period of the siege, sorties in force may be made by passing the troops together over the crest of the covered way by means of ladders prepared for the purpose. They should retire into the collateral places of arms, covered by the fire of the guns of the place.

The garrison should use every means of annoying

the besiegers; by feints of sorties of small bodies of men, which force the troops in the trenches to prepare for defence, and they may thus be drawn under the fire of the place.

The best method of defending the covered way is by offensive returns, continually annoying the enemy by sorties in small bodies, by musketeers sheltered behind the traverse, and in intrenchments in the places of arms. A few skilful marksmen stationed on the ramparts may greatly harass the workmen: from the ramparts the infantry keep up a constant fire of musketry, while the besieger is making the trenches and working at the descent to the ditches. When the ditch is dry, sorties upon the sap in the ditch should be made: if full of water, efforts should be made to destroy the bridge or dike. Finally, when the assault of the breach is made, it should be obstructed in every possible way, both with material obstacles and with the fire of soldiers. When the besieger has effected a lodgement on the breach in the body of the place, a defence may still be made behind barricades in the interior of the city. A capitulation should be agreed to only when several assaults have been sustained on the body of the place, when efficient defence can no longer be made, and when provisions and munitions are exhausted.

ART. 90.—Detachments.

These are bodies of troops intended to act apart from the general line, and at greater or less distances, according to circumstances, from the mass of the army. They should be few, because they weaken the army. Their communication with it should be constantly kept up. A detachment should never exceed a fourth of the main body.

Detachments of some magnitude intrusted with secret and important duties, should generally be accompanied, if not commanded, by officers of the staff, because the duties of these more than of officers of troops bring them to a better knowledge of ground, enable them to have a better appreciation of the importance of their mission, and of any information collected, as they are more accustomed to understand the connection between the secondary operations and the great movements of the campaign, and they are often better able to surmount unexpected obstacles.

Dispose the troops so that during the march the different parts may be in sight of each other, except in a flat country, or when the detachment is large, when the advanced guard may be a half day's march before the main body: in a plain country divide up the artillery in the intervals of the infantry; in a broken country, place the cavalry after the infantry, and the artillery still to the rear; take one-sixth of the detachment to form the advanced guard: do not take more than one-third for the duties of advanced guard, rearguard, and flankers, unless the detachment is very feeble, when one-half may be taken in mixed detachments; regulate the march of the cavalry by that of the infantry.

ART. 91.—Convoys and their Escorts.

A train of 100 to 500 carriages should be divided into several parts, divisions of 100 carriages being separated by thirty or forty yards, and formed into sections of twenty-five or thirty carriages, with intervals of twelve to twenty yards. A six-horse team will occupy about seventeen yards, allowing four to a horse, four to the carriage, and one for the interval between consecutive vehicles. The length of a train may hence be deduced.

A convoy moves as much as possible in double file, with the width of a carriage between them. A train will get over about two and a half miles in an hour, in a level country, over good roads, and not much over one and a half miles in a broken country.

A convoy should have scouts out in front and flank, at least three miles, except in a mountainous country, where they need not be so far, in which case a few troopers only will move in advance of the advanced guard, behind the rear-guard, and on the flanks of the escort.

The escort is divided into three parts; one-third furnishing the advanced guard and rear-guard, one-third the main body, and one-third the reserve.

In a broken country, the cavalry will not be more than one-fourth of the escort; in a hilly country, from one-sixth to one-eighth. Never park in rear of a defile. Park only where you intend to pass the night, or when warned of the approach of the enemy, and in this last case, half of the escort does picket duty. It is better to bivouac than to canton in a village, and when there is no cause for apprehension, the park may be arranged with a front of several files; if, on the contrary, it is threatened, park in a circle or in square, the poles being inside.

The strength and composition of the escort of a convoy depend on the country the nature and value of the convoy, and the dangers it may incur. A larger escort is required for a convoy of powder, that the defence may not be near the train.

Cavalry is employed in escorts chiefly to reconnoitre; the proportion is larger as the country is more open.

Pioneers or working parties are attached to convoys to mend roads, remove obstacles, and erect defences. The convoys should always be provided with spare wheels, poles, axles, &c.

The commander of the escort should receive detailed written instructions. As far as the defence permits, the commander of the escort should refer to the officer in charge of the convoy, for the hours of departure, the halts, the parking, and order of the train, and the precautions against accident.

Officers who accompany the convoy, but do not belong to the escort, should exercise no authority in it, except by consent of the commander. If these officers are junior to the commander, he may assign them to duty, if the defence requires it.

A small party of infantry should be attached to each division of the convoy.

Generally, munitions of war are at the head of the convoy, subsistence next, and then other military stores, the sutler last. But always that portion of the convoy of most importance to the army should be in the safest place.

The commandant should send out reconnoitering parties, and never put the convoy in motion until their reports are received. He always forms an advance and rear-guard, and keeps the main body under his own immediate order, at the most important point, with small guards or posts at other points.

In an open country, the main body marches by the side of the road opposite the centre of the convoy; in other cases, near the head or rear of the column, as the one or other is more exposed.

The advanced guard precedes the convoy far enough to remove all obstacles to its advance. It examines the woods, defiles, and villages, and by mounted men gives information to the commander, and receives his orders. It reconnoiters places for halts and parks.

If the head of the column is threatened, the advanced guard seizes the defiles and places which the enemy might occupy, and holds them until the main body advances to the front, and relieves it; the main body holds the positions until the head of the column arrives, and then leaves detachments which are relieved by the parties marching with the divisions: the posts are not abandoned until the whole convoy has passed, and the position is no longer important.

When the rear is threatened, like measures are taken; the rear-guard defends the ground, and retards the enemy by breaking the bridges and blocking the road.

If the flanks are threatened and the ground is broken, and many defiles are to be passed, the defence of the convoy becomes more difficult; the advanced and rear-guards must be reduced, the flanks strengthened, and positions which will cover the march of the convoy must be occupied by the main body of the troops before the head of the convoy reaches them, and until it has passed.

If the convoy is large, and has to pass places
that the force and position of the enemy make dangerous, the loss of the whole must not be risked; it
must pass by divisions which reunite after passing.
In this case, the greater part of the troops guard the
first division; they seize the important points, and
cover them with light troops, or, if necessary, with
small posts, and hold them until all the divisions
have passed.

If there is artillery in the convoy, the commander of
the escort uses it for the defence.

To move faster and make the defence easier, the
carriages move in double file whenever possible. If a
wagon breaks, it is at once removed to the side of the
road, and when repaired, takes the rear: when it cannot be repaired, its load and horses are distributed to
some of the other wagons kept in the rear for that
purpose.

Convoys by water are escorted on the same
principles. Each boat has a small guard; one portion
of the escort precedes or follows the convoy in
boats.

The cavalry march opposite the convoy; the
advance and rear-guard move by land, and all are
connected by flankers with the convoy. Where a river
runs through a narrow valley, the body of the infantry
moves by land, to prevent the enemy from occupying
the heights, and disturbing the convoy.

Convoys halt every hour, to let the horses take
breath and the wagons close up. Long halts are made
but seldom, and only in places that have been examined, and are capable of good defence.

At night the park is arranged for defence, and in

preference, at a distance from inhabited places, if in an enemy's country.

The wagons are usually parked in ranks, axle to axle, poles in the same direction, and with sufficient space between the ranks for the horses. If an attack is feared, pack in square, with the hind wheels outside and the horses inside.

On the appearance of the enemy during the march, the commander closes up the wagons, and continues his march in order; he avoids fighting; but if the enemy seizes a position that commands his road, he attacks vigorously with the mass of his force, but is not to continue the pursuit far from the convoy. The convoy halts, and resumes the march when the position is carried.

When the enemy is too strong to be attacked, the convoy is parked in square, if there is room; if not, closed up in double file; at the front and rear the road is blocked by wagons across it. The drivers are dismounted at the heads of the horses, but they are not permitted to escape. The light troops keep the enemy at a distance as long as possible, and are supported when necessary, but prudently, as the troops must be kept in hand to resist the main attack.

If a wagon takes fire in the park, remove it if possible; if not, remove first the ammunition wagons, then those to leeward of the fire.

When a whole convoy cannot be saved, the most valuable part may be sometimes, by abandoning the remainder. If all efforts fail, and there is no hope of succor, the convoy must be set on fire, and the horses killed that cannot be saved; the escort may then cut its way through.

If the convoy is of prisoners of war, every effort should be made to reach a village or strong building where they may be secured. If forced to fight in the field, the prisoners must be secured, and made to lie down, until the action is over.

The most favorable times for attacking a convoy are at its halts, or when preparing to park, or when passing through a wood or defile, a winding part of the road, a bridge, or ascending a hill.

The infantry should be equal to the escort; the cavalry double the enemy's. In a plain, a detachment charged with the attack of a convoy, if the latter is numerous, is commonly divided into three parts, one attacking the centre, one the head, and one the tail, a reserve being kept at hand. If the convoy is small, one portion of the attacking party is directed against the mass of the escort; a second is to harass the wagons, endeavoring to cut the traces; the third is the reserve.

If the convoy is parked, try to chase off the escort by demonstrations of cavalry, while the infantry attack the troops remaining near the convoy.

ART. 92.—Detached Posts.

These are so chosen that an enemy can only reach them after passing formidable obstacles; the troops holding them should be in number proportioned to their size and importance. The garrison is usually divided into three parts, one-third being keep under arms, one-third on picket duty, and one-third in reserve. Small posts of five or six footmen and several troopers, guard the approaches; a platoon or two of cavalry patrol to some distance; artillery is only useful in a broken country where the enemy has, for example, but a single line of approach to the post.

Before occupying a post, the detachment to which it is assigned forms in battle order at some distance, and has a visit made to the place; a guard is then established; the position is carefully examined to learn its resources and means of defence; if possible, shelters for the troops are constructed.

Posts, whether intrenched or not, are carried by means of false and true attacks combined; each is preceded forty or fifty paces by skirmishers, and each party is divided into three sections. If the post has intrenchments, the first section is followed by workmen, who are to destroy the works; the second, slinging their muskets on their backs, carry ladders and fascines; the third is the reserve.

ART. 93.—Villages.

A village occupied by a detachment, is defended, like an isolated post, by advanced parties covering the approaches, by intrenchments occupied by troops, by houses arranged for defence.

The weak points are strengthened by bodies of troops placed at the junction of streets; the artillery commands the main avenues; a reserve is concentrated at the middle of the village, on the most favorable point, in readiness to move in any direction to meet the enemy. Sometimes this reserve, when the locality does not give space enough for it, is placed behind the principal communication, and in column, or even at the outskirts of the town, and deployed. Sorties are only made in case of decided superiority on your part, or of faults committed by the enemy;

they should be conducted with vigor, but with circumspection.

When the village is a part of the general order of battle, the defensive arrangements should be rather exterior than interior. The infantry is no longer massed in the interior, but rather in the skirts of the town, occupying such houses and enclosures as will threaten the flanks of the column of attack. Skirmishers, with strong supports and reserves, guard the town, and artillery on the flanks, also in the outskirts, crosses its fire on the principal avenues, while the cavalry takes position in rear. This arrangement is suited to the offensive defence, and has the advantage of not accumulating the combatants in the narrow streets, which soon become blocked up.

The attack of a village is executed upon the same principles as any other position or post.

True and false attacks are made. The head of each is formed of skirmishers, for which one-sixth of the disposable troops are employed. Then come the supports at about 100 paces, deployed in column, according to the character of the ground. There will be one reserve or several, depending also on the ground, and the distance apart of the several attacks. About one-third of the troops form the reserve. As soon as the outskirts are taken, columns are thrown around to cut off the retreat, and attack the reserves of the enemy. When, at last, the village is carried, the mass of the troops is rallied in order to oppose offensive returns, while the pursuit is made by skirmishers.

Fire is often used to hasten the surrender of a town, and drive out its occupants.

ART. 94.—Defence and Attack of Woods.

In the defence of woods, as in the attack, the troops are divided, as in the case of a village, into three parts: 1st, a line of skirmishers; 2d, supports to the mass of the troops; 3d, reserve.

In the defence, skirmishers spread along the skirts, are sustained in the rear by posts occupying the junctions of roads, the roads and the open spaces, while the main body is established in a central intrenched position if the time and means allow. The salients of the woods are protected by abatis.

In the attack, the infantry surrounds with skirmishers the salients of the woods and the crossings of the main roads, the skirmishers being followed up and supported by numerous small columns of attack. The salients once taken, they are occupied in force, and the skirmishers are gradually pushed forward, and columns of attack following up the movement, and the main body of the enemy is finally assailed, and driven out of position.

In all cases the small columns follow the skirmishers with great circumspection, guarding carefully against flank movements the enemy make against them, and taking advantage of every defensive position offered by the ground.

ART. 95.—Foraging Parties.

Foragers must carry their arms, marching in good order, and escorted by a detachment that sends to front, flank and rear, sufficient portions to cover the operation.

On arriving at the locality where the foraging is to be done, these detached portions cover the operation with all the precautions indicated for grand guards, small posts and sentries. The main body of the escort takes the best dispositions to protect the affair, and rally the small posts and foragers, either in case of danger or of return. Sometimes, when going far from the camp or bivouac, reserves are left at intermediate points, and are picked up when retiring. Whilst the operation is proceeding, the men having done their forage duty, come together at a given place, and when it is completed, and all the men are assembled, they return to the principal corps in the same order as they came, unless the circumstances require some modification. Should the foraging party be attacked, the sentries signal the enemy, and begin skirmishing, the posts lending their support, and the chief of the escort takes the necessary measures to repel the attack. In the mean time, the foragers discontinuing their work, retire with what they have already taken, to the site indicated for rallying. If the enemy is discouraged and the danger ceases, they begin afresh; otherwise the retreat is effected in the best possible order. Should very superior forces present themselves, the foraging expedition must be entirely abandoned; the foragers throw away the provisions already gathered, and are employed for the defence while retreating. These are dangerous operations, in which resources are squandered, rapine originates, and discipline is likely to suffer; they should therefore only be resorted to when it is impossible to have regular distributions. With a commissariat properly organized, cavalry forages should only be had recourse to, and only when it is impossible to find food for the horses otherwise.

ART. 96.—Levying Contributions.

When war contributions are to be levied, it should be done under the protection of an imposing escort of infantry, cavalry, and horse artillery.

The operation is begun at the more distant points. Secrecy is rigidly preserved up to the moment of leaving and during the whole march; avoid passing through inhabited places, and arrive in the night at the intended destination; carefully examine the locality; place posts and sentinels at the avenues of approach and departure, and take hostages.

ART. 97.—Partisans.

Sometimes a body of partisans is attached to an army. They assist in the operations by deceiving the enemy, rendering him anxious for his communications, intercepting his couriers, threatening or destroying his magazines, carrying off his detached parties and convoys. They march at night more than by day: during the day they rest in retired places, being careful to keep out small detachments and scouts: they keep good guides and make great use of spies: they avoid as much as possible cities and towns, and when they enter them, they secure hostages, if necessary: finally, they give the country no rest, beating about rapidly from point to point.

ART. 98.—Field Works.

In the construction of field works, the following principles should, as far as practicable, be observed. 1st, the works to be flanked should never be beyond effective musket range from the works flanking them. 2d, the angles of defence should be about right angles, certainly not less. 3d, the salient angles of works should be as obtuse as circumstances will permit, sixty degrees being the minimum. 4th, although ditches cannot be always fully flanked, they should be as effectually as may be. 5th, in constructing field works, reference should be had not only to the direct and immediate obstacles the work itself presents to the enemy, and the positive effects of fire on the approaches to it; but likewise the relative value of the work must be considered as to the support it can give to, or receive from other works. 6th, the outline of a field work should be proportioned to the number of men intended to defend it. 7th, the ground over which an enemy must pass to the attack should, if possible, be seen both in front and flank.

Redan.—This is a work consisting of two faces, each thirty to sixty yards long; the gorge or entrance in the rear being open. It is used to cover a point in its rear, such as a bridge, defile or ford. Having no flank defences, its salient is unprotected, and to obtain a fire in the direction of its capital, a short face, called a pan coupé, is sometimes made in its salient angle. Flanks perpendicular to the faces are sometimes added.

Lunette.—This consists of two faces from forty to sixty yards long, and of two flanks from fifteen to thirty yards. It is used for the same purposes as the preceding. It has the same defects, but possesses the advantage of sweeping with the fire of its flanks ground which might be badly defended by its faces.

Tenaille.—This is an inverted redan.

Indented Line.—This is a succession of tenailles, having long faces and short alternately, the long from fifty to eighty yards, and the short from fifteen to twenty-five yards. It serves to convert the fire of a right line into a flank and cross fire.

Swallow-tail or Priest-cap.—A tenaille at the extremities of which are added two long faces extending to the gorge. The faces of the tenaille may be thirty yards, and the long faces from sixty to one hundred.

Double Swallow-tail.—A double tenaille with long faces as in the simple.

Redoubt.—Any enclosed work of a polygonal form without re-entering angles, is a redoubt. This work is used to fortify a position which can be attacked on all sides, the works which have already been described, being unsuitable for this purpose, as their gorges are open, and therefore require to be supported by troops, or works in their rear, except when they are so situated that an attack cannot be made at the gorge. The square is the most common form of the redoubt, on account of the ease with which it is constructed, and the advantage it possesses when combined with several others, of protecting the spaces between them by a cross fire. All redoubts have the same effects. The ditches are unprotected, and there is a sector without fire in front of each salient. The angles may be cut off by pan-coupés or rounded. The size of square redoubts may vary between fifteen and forty-five yards a side. The minimum is for one rank of defenders, twenty-five yards for two ranks, and thirty yards for three ranks. The redoubt of fifteen yards a side will be suitable for a detachment of fifty men. That of forty yards will answer for 500 men and two pieces of artillery. The entrance to the redoubt may be six and a half to ten feet wide, and covered by a traverse on the inside.

Star Fort.—This is an enclosed work with salient and re-entering angles, the object being to remedy the defects of the redoubt, which is effected but partially. The staff fort, laid out on the same polygon as a redoubt, has less interior capacity and longer interior crest, thus requiring more men for its defence, and giving them less space. The faces may vary from thirty to sixty yards.

Bastion Fort.—This satisfies more fully the conditions of a good defence than any other work, but owing to the time and labor required for its construction, it should be applied only to sites of great importance, which demand the presence of troops during a campaign. The side of the polygon on which it is laid out may range between 250 and 125 yards.

FIG. 14.

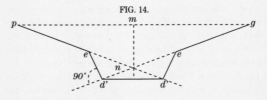

$a=pq$. In the square $mn=\frac{a}{8}$, $e'd'$ and ed are perpendicular to pd and gd'; $ep=eg=\frac{2}{7}a$ or $\frac{1}{3}a$. In the pentagon $mn=\frac{a}{7}$, in the hexagon $mn=\frac{a}{6}$, and the same for higher polygons.

Tete-de-pont.—To arrange a tete-de-pont the important things to be attended to are that all the ground over which the enemy may approach the bridge shall be thoroughly swept by fire, and the capacity of the work should be such that it will cover the bridge or bridges, and contain troops enough for a strong defence. A redan, lunette or priest-cap may be used. The long faces may be flanked by musketry or artillery from the opposite bank. The *simple crown tete-de-pont* is formed of a central bastion and two half bastions connected by curtains. The *complex crown* consists of a polygon of three or more sides on each of which a bastion front is constructed.

FORTIFIED LINES.

When a considerable extent of ground is to be fortified, use is made of lines composed of the simple works already described.

FIG. 15.

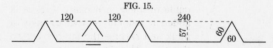

Lines of Redans connected by Straight Curtains. (Fig. 15.)—Employed when the line is developed in a plain. The distance between the salients is calculated for the range of small arms; it is not taken less than 160 yards; straight curtains connect the redans, the length of faces is sixty yards. The salients and ditches of the redans are not defended, the ground in front of them being without fire.

Lines of Redans with Broken Curtains.—These are employed when they may be protected from enfilade fire. The curtain is broken forward so as to

FIG. 16.

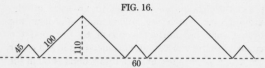

45   100   110   60

FIG. 17. 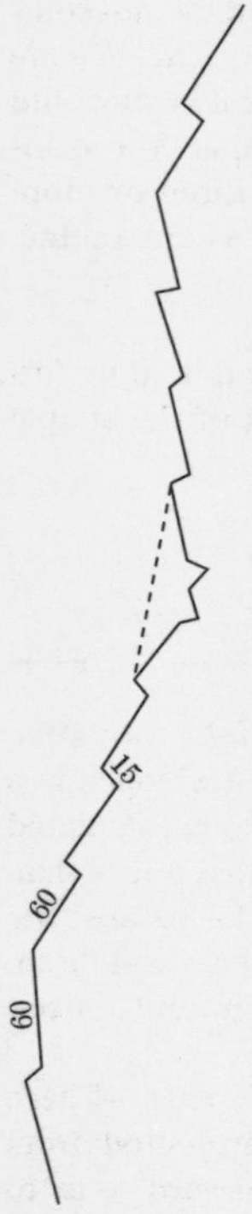   form small redans with faces perpendicular to those of the large.

Cremaillere Line. (Fig. 17.)—The flanks should be turned toward the point to be defended.

The salient toward which the flanks are turned, is thus well defended. The re-entering is arranged so as to have a cross-fire in front of it. The flanks are from fifteen to thirty yards, the faces from sixty to one hundred. An abatis, thrown up in this form, with a slight parapet behind it, will make a formidable obstacle, especially if there is added a redoubt or two to take in flank and reverse the approaches to the line. This line may readily be adapted to the irregularities of ground, as, for example, in following the winding of a river bank or the slope of a side hill. The long branches in this case should be kept as nearly horizontal as possible. Two cremailleres traced upon the opposite slopes and meeting at the bottom of the valley, make an excellent defence for a defile. More complex and irregular lines are used when the

15

60

60

character of the ground requires it, the problem always being with the least expenditure of labor and time to get the best practicable direct and cross fire over the approaches to the position.

LINES WITH INTERVALS.

These are arranged to suit the ground on which they are to be placed, being composed of detached works flanking each other. In general, lines with intervals should be preferred to continued lines, being more suitable for active defence.

They may be formed of lunettes or redoubts arranged in quincunx order. There might be, for example, a few hundred paces to the front of the intervals of the troops, a line of lunettes or redoubts with their salients turned to the enemy, sufficiently capacious to contain from 300 to 400 men, with several pieces of artillery: behind the intervals of these are redan batteries to flank them; between the batteries and behind the redoubts epaulements serve as covers to squadrons of cavalry; the remainder of the troops being to the rear, ready to act according to circumstance.

To cover an army we may make use of a system of couples of works alternately salient and re-entering, the salient couples being at the natural points of attack. It is a succession of bastions connected by curtains. (Fig. 18.)

Passages of six yards are left for the light cavalry. Epaulements mask the openings left for sorties in force. Square redoubts should be placed in proper position to cover the flanks of the position when they do not rest on strong natural obstacles.

FIG. 18.

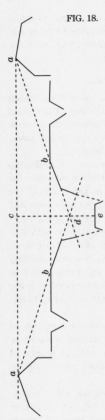

aa=720 yds. cd=120 yds.
bb=240 " de=65 "
ad=400 yds.

Certain portions of the works may be at times advantageously occupied by obstacles, such as woods, farm-houses, &c. The thickness of parapets of all the flanks and of the faces of the re-entrant works is four and a half feet, and the height the same; the parapets increase in height and thickness from the shoulders of the advanced bastions to their salients, at which points they are six and a half to eight feet high, and twelve to fifteen feet thick. The ditch and glacis will have a constant breadth from the shoulders to the salients.

A step, intended to receive voltigeurs, is made in the counterscarp four feet below the natural ground; moreover, the broken curtains which connect the bastions are provided with steps, and barbettes are arranged to facilitate the fire of the pieces.

In the system the troops may be disposed as follows: the battalions of the first line are distributed along the works, or in double column behind the epaulements for sorties in force.

The portion intended to line the works is distributed by company, two to each face, and one to each flank. The grenadiers act as a reserve, the voltigeurs being arranged as skirmishers, or placed upon the banquette of the counterscarp. The cavalry, except the reserve, is in columns of squadrons, a regiment in each, drawn up to the rear of the epaulements for sorties, a portion behind the battalions of the first line, and a portion behind the battalions of the second line.

Upon the perpendicular to each inclined front, between the first and second lines, is a squadron of light cavalry in column by platoons. The second line is held in double column, the centre of each column being immediately in rear of the salient of the work in front of it.

The reserve is 500 paces in rear of the second line, formed in three masses of all arms, one being for the support of the centre, and one for each wing. Thus drawn up, the army is ready to receive an attack, protected by the artillery, which, except that of the reserve, is in battery principally upon the flanks and salient of the retired works.

GENERAL RULES.

Intrenchments and their different parts should defend each other by mutual flank fires, and the flanking should be a rectangular one.

The works should be arranged so as to facilitate sorties and offensive returns; the sortie passages should be at least ten feet wide, closed by barrier gates or chevaux-de-frise, and covered by a redan in front of the ditch, or by an interior traverse: a mound of earth may be left in the ditch for a bridge, or one may be built of wood, and destroyed after passage in case of retreat. The interior space or the capacity of a work and its development are determined from the following data: each foot soldier will occupy one yard, linear measure, along the interior crest, and each cannon from five to six yards. The space requisite to lodge each man is one and a half square yards; and about sixty square yards should be allowed for each gun; for a powder magazine for three or four cannon, fifteen to twenty square yards. When traverses are used, space must be allowed for them, which will depend upon the circumstances of the case.

For a good defence, two ranks of musketeers should be on the banquette, and the reserve may be one-half the entire force, and should never be less than one-fifth.

Positions should be sought where defilement will be unnecessary or very simple. The principal faces should be directed toward hollows, marshes, inundations, inaccessible points, or heights beyond cannon range. In a hilly country, the form of the crests is followed by the works, so that the slopes may be completely swept by their fire. If the slope is steep and the post of no great importance, or time presses, the ditch in front may be omitted.

PROFILES OF WORKS. (FIG. 19.)

The interior crest should not be less than six and a half feet above the ground, when the work is to cover foot soldiers, nor less than eight feet when mounted men; the relief should not exceed twelve feet. The command over the glacis, or over works in front of it, should be at least five feet; the interior slope is three perpendicular upon one base, and its height above the banquette four and a quarter feet; the banquette for two ranks should be four feet in width, for one rank but two feet, and if there are three ranks, four feet, the third rank standing on the banquette slope, which should not be steep, about one perpendicular to two base. The inclination of the top of the parapet is seldom greater than one-fourth, and is usually one-sixth; it is usually directed to the edge of the counterscarp, and should never pass more than three feet above it. The exterior slope is the natural slope of the earth, three on two in stiff earth, two on three in loose earth, and one on one in ordinary soil. The ditch should furnish the earth for the parapet. Its minimum width to be efficient as an obstacle is twelve feet, and its depth should not

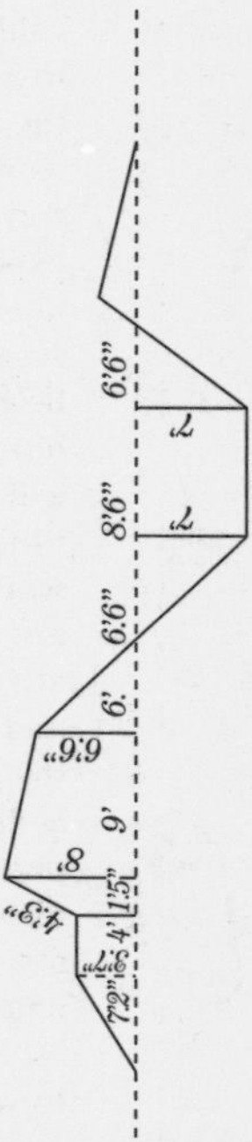

FIG. 19.

be less than six feet, nor more than twelve. The slope of the scarp is usually three on two, and of the counterscarp, two on one in ordinary soil. The glacis is formed of the excess of earth, if there be any. In order that a covered way may receive defenders, the relief of the work should be at least twelve feet, and that of the covered way at least six and a half feet.

FIG. 20.

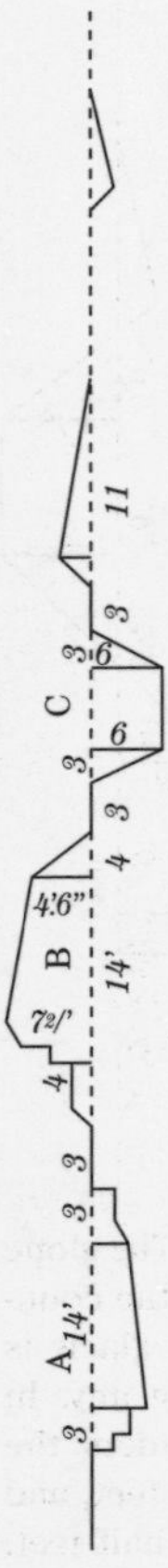

The thickness of parapet varies with the calibre of the enemy's guns, the rule being to make the thickness one and a half times the penetration of the missiles. For field works the thickness of parapet usually varies between nine and fifteen feet, when exposed to artillery. If exposed only to musketry, it may be from four and a half to six feet. The berm is a defect, and should be omitted, if the soil permits: if any is introduced, make it not less than one and a half feet wide. Figures 19 and 20 give profiles of field works. To execute the work shown in figure 20, fifty-three men are necessary, disposed as follows: there are three working spaces, A, B, and C; A and C for the excavation on each side of the parapet, and B for the embankment. A is divided into two parts of nine men each, one-half acting as a relay for the other. B is also is two parts, first part of twelve men, six to smooth the earth furnished by C, and six to ram; second part of eight men, four to smooth the earth from A, and four to ram. C is also in two parts, first of four men to embank and smooth the glacis; second part of eleven men to dig and throw the earth on the parapet. About fifteen yards in length of interior crest may be thus executed in eight hours. The men may be from four and a half to six feet apart along the direction of the interior crest, not to be in each others' way.

TRACING AND THROWING UP A WORK.

The operations required in throwing up a work may
be divided into three parts, 1st, tracing upon the
ground, construction of the profiles, commencing the
excavation; 2d, excavation of ditch and embankment
of parapet, with revetment of slopes, finished; 3d, the
accessories, magazines, &c.

The work is commenced by marking on the ground
the interior crest, the foot of the interior slope, and
the banquette, which is done by a little furrow made
with a pick moved along cords stretched in the direction of the lines just mentioned; this being done, and
the ground being supposed uneven, which makes the
relief different at the different angles, on account of
the necessity of defiling, this operation must be next
attended to in order to be able to set up the profiles.
The object of defilement is to protect the interior of
the work from fire coming from elevated points within range of the enemy's fire-arms. It is begun by determining a plane which is assumed as an artificial plane
of site, upon which the work is constructed as upon
the ground. This plane is taken tangent to the commanding points, and passing through a certain line
within the limits of the work. This line must be so
taken that the plane through it and tangent to the
ground will pass at least three feet above every point
of the ground within the limits of the work.
Determine the position of this line by the heads of
two stakes, then through it pass a number of planes
tangent to the high ground within cannon range;
mark the intersection of each of them with a stake
planted at the salient of the work, and that one
whose intersection is the highest gives the artificial

plane of site. A plane parallel to this, and five feet
above it, is the plane of defilement, and it is evident
that if the interior crest is kept in that plane, the
whole of the interior of the work will be unseen from
the enemy's positions.

If the work is commanded by lateral heights, two
artificial planes of sight are necessary, each tangent
to the ground on its own side, and having a line of
intersection projected in the capital of the work,
three feet above the ground at the gorge, and one and
a half higher at the salient. Planes parallel to these
and five feet higher will be the planes of the interior
crest of the halves of the work; but it remains yet to
construct a traverse along the capital to protect the
work from reverse fire. To get the height of this traverse, suppose a vertical plane passed through the
capital of the work. Suppose the foot of the interior
slope of each face adjacent to the salient raised one
and a half feet; through each of these pass a plane
tangent to the high ground on the other side; take
two planes parallel to these and five feet higher;
mark their intersections with the vertical plane
through the capital, and that which is the highest
will be the ridge line of the traverse. The work will
then be protected by its parapet from front fire, and
by the traverse from reverse fire. Both should
be shot proof.

For closed works, let *abcd* be a redoubt to be
defiled from *P*; to find the proper height for crest *abc*,
take a line *bc* such that it shall nowhere be less than
three feet above the ground, and through it pass a
plane tangent to *P*; a plane parallel to this and
five feet above it will fix *abc*: *bdc* may be kept

FIG. 21.

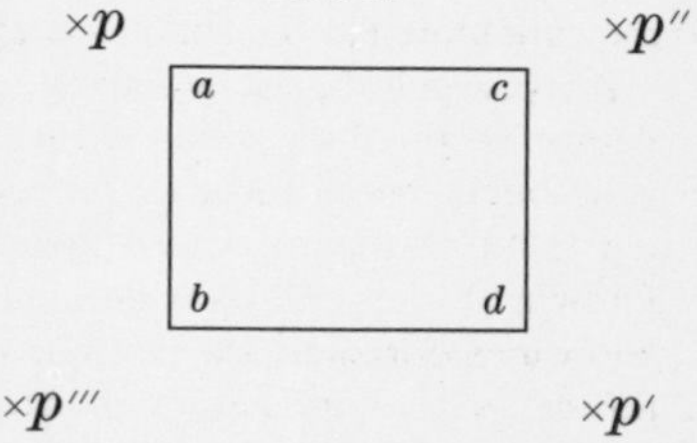

×p ×p''

×p''' ×p'

in the same plane, if it gives sufficient height in this part of the work to the parapet; and if not, raise up d to a sufficient height, and as this will expose it to P, a traverse must be put along bc: to determine its heights, find a point at d, one and a half feet higher than the banquette, and through it and P draw a line; take a line five feet higher, and the point where it pierces the vertical plane through bc will be the required height of the traverse. To protect abc from P' a traverse along bc will be requisite, provided sufficient height is given it. If there are still other dangerous points, P'' and P''', it may be necessary to erect another traverse along ad.

To avoid too high relief, when the height of the artificial plane of site exceeds eight feet at the salient, successive parallel traverses may be placed. On account of the inequality of the relief of a work, in consequence of the irregularity of the ground and the conditions of defilement, the profiles at the different angles, taken perpendicular to the interior crest, are different. These profiles are constructed with the assistance of a few men, who are provided with picks, stakes, poles, laths, nails, saws, and hammers. The perpendicular profiles being traced, the oblique ones at the angles are readily deduced by sighting along the perpendicular ones; when the corresponding lines of two adjacent faces are not in the same plane they are united in the simplest way.

The parapets being thus fixed, the next step is to determine the dimensions of the ditch: for that purpose calculate the surface S, of each profile by dividing it into surfaces whose measure is simple and known. From this surface subtract the usual allowance for increase of bulk of earth, by being thrown out of its natural bed (one-sixth for stiff earth, one-tenth for loose, and one-eighth for ordinary earth); assume a depth h for the ditch, and divide S by h, we thus obtain a mean width l: add and subtract the half sum of the bases of the scarp and counterscarp slopes, in order to have the width at the top and bottom. Then trace with the pick the lines of the scarp and counterscarp and the feet of the slopes; observe then if the superior slope prolonged passes more than three feet above the counterscarp. If it is desired to have a covered way, place it about half the depth of the ditch, removing the earth for a space equal to half the desired width, and throwing it to the rear to complete the width. The ditch is rounded off at the angles, the curve being traced with the foot of scarp at the salient as a centre: but if the ditches which meet are of unequal widths, prolong the counterscarps to meet and bisect their angle, and from the point of intersection of the scarps let fall perpendiculars on the counterscarps; one of these perpendiculars cuts the bisecting line of the angle of the counterscarps in a point which is taken for the centre of the arc of the curved portion of the counterscarp.

If a barbette is placed in the salient, a pan coupé

of eleven feet is laid off, and from the middle of this a length of twenty-four feet along the capital to the rear; at the extremity of this distance lay off five feet on each side, on a perpendicular to it, and from the points thus formed let fall perpendiculars on the faces; we have the limits of the top surface of the barbette for the piece. A ramp ten feet wide is laid out along the capital. If there is more than one piece we allow for each a length of eighteen feet along the interior crest. The slope of the barbette on each side of the ramp is the natural slope of the earth. The distance of the barbette below the interior crest varies with the calibre of the piece, from about two and three-quarters feet to four. Between the platforms of the pieces, little ditches are dug sufficiently deep to put the men under cover. If a barbette is placed along a face, it should have a width of twenty feet and a length of twenty-four, and for each additional piece a distance of eighteen feet is allowed along the interior crest.

Generally the workmen are placed in four ranks, two on the bottom of the ditch between the lines, corresponding to the feet of the scarp and counterscarp slopes, a third on a berm which is about halfway down the ditch and about four feet in width, and finally a fourth, along the interior crest. The first rank in the bottom of the ditch has picks, the other three having shovels. These workmen, in each rank, are about four and a half or six feet apart; each space is marked off by lines on the ground; and to get them in position, the line of the scarp is divided into lengths of four and a half feet, and that of the counterscarp into the same number of equal parts.

In the first stages of the work the ditch is excavated only to half its final depth, and to the mean width: the earth of the parapet is levelled off to a height of three feet, and rammed in layers of one foot; at the second stage the excavation and embankment are completed, according to the profiles determined upon. The last business is to finish the slopes carefully.

We may estimate the number of days necessary to the execution of work by recollecting that a working part of four men can remove two cubic yards a day in stiff earth, and four or five in ordinary loose earth.

Multiply the area of each profile by the distance 1.50: we then have the excavation of each working

party, and taking a mean excavation D, $\dfrac{D}{2}$ is the

number of days, supposing that the working party consists of four men, who remove two cubic yards a day, and that there are as many working parties as there are lengths of 1.50 yards, or four and a half feet in the development of the work. If it is desired to have the depth of daily excavation, divide two cubic yards by the area of the space occupied by a working party.

The excess of the excavation forms the glacis; this glacis may be established by trial, or the excess of the excavation over the embankment may be calculated; for that purpose, if there is no barbette, it will be sufficiently accurate to take on each face the difference between the development of the parapet and of the corresponding ditch, and to multiply this by a mean profile: the sum of the differences is the total excess: let E be this excess, and let h be the height of the glacis; finally, let d be the development of the work, then $x + \dfrac{hd}{2} = E$, x being the breadth of the glacis. But if there is a barbette, its volume diminishes by just so much the glacis: calculate this volume with that of the corresponding portion of the parapet, and at the same time that of the ditch in front; the difference is to be subtracted from the differences already determined for the remaining portions of the work. To make this calculation the barbette may be divided up into suitable solids.

The interior slope is revetted in works which are rapidly built; for this purpose use sods arranged as headers and stretchers, the latter being twelve inches square and four inches thick, while the headers are twelve inches wide, eighteen inches long and four inches thick. Thirty sods (one-third headers) form one square yard, and a working party of three men will provide 100 sods in an hour—the first man making the cuts, the second taking up the sods, and the third giving them proper thickness; an expert will in a day revet forty square yards with the aid of two assistants to hand him the sods.

To revet with fascines, use those nine or ten feet long, or more, and nine inches in diameter. A row of fascines is first placed about half its thickness below the tread of the banquette, each fascine being held in place by two or three pegs driven into the ground, the knots of the withes being turned in next the parapet: a second row is placed on the first sufficiently to the rear to give the proper slope, and it is also held in place by pegs, but at the third row the fascines are secured by long anchoring withes, fastened to anchoring stakes driven in the mass of the parapet. Three men will make twenty-five square yards of the revetment in ten hours. The earth is rammed behind the fascines as they are placed. In the sod and fascine revetment the different courses should break joints.

The hurdle revetment may be also used. Take hurdles six feet long, each being fastened at its extremities and middle by two anchoring withes, when the revetment is made as the parapet rises; but if the revetment is made after the parapet is formed, the hurdles are held fast in place by pegs with forked ends: if the wattling is made in its place the stakes are first driven into the banquette, and held in position by anchoring pickets: the twigs are then woven around the stakes. The sand-bag revetment is excellent for temporary purposes. When empty the bag is two and two-thirds feet long and one and one-sixth wide.

For the reception of stores, excavations are made in traverses, or under the parapet, which are lined with fascines or gabions. These may be four feet deep, six feet long, and from three to six feet wide. Blindages may be made for the same purpose, of trunks of trees, hastily squared on one side each, placed leaning side by side against the side of a traverse, or some similar mass, and covered over the sand-bags, or sods, or earth.

To field works are added accessories, whose object is to delay the approach of the enemy, to keep him in an exposed position under the fire of the works, and to render the assault difficult and dangerous. *Palisading* is placed in the ditch at the foot of the counterscarp: this consists of triangular stakes planted in an upright position, and having their upper ends pointed; they are about six or eight inches on a side, and ten feet long. They are sunk two or three feet in the ground, and placed about three inches apart. From eight to ten palisades are allowed to two lineal yards. A working party of three men will plant twenty yards in an hour. To overturn them, powder is used. Fifty pounds of powder in a bag, securely fastened to a palisading, will blow it down.

These stakes are sometimes placed at the top of the scarp, in a position nearly horizontal, the points outward, and inclining downward. This makes a *fraise*.

The gorges of open works are sometimes closed by a *stockade*, which is made of trunks of trees eight inches in diameter, having loopholes made in them a yard apart and two yards above the ground; an interior banquette being arranged for the men to stand on in firing.

Abatis, formed of trunks and thick branches of trees fastened together, and fixed in the ground by crotchet pickets, may be placed in front of the counterscarp, a shallow excavation being made for it.

Trous-de-loup, or inverted truncated cones, may be dug in quincunx order, laid out by the use of an equilateral triangle of cord fifteen feet on a side; the upper diameter is six feet and the lower eighteen inches. The depth should be six feet, and a sharp stake should be in the centre.

Fougasses may be also used in defending field works. To make a fougasse, an inclined funnel-shaped excavation is made, to the depth of five or six feet. At the bottom of the funnel a box is placed, containing fifty-five pounds of powder with which a powder-hose communicates. A strong shield of wood, formed of batten well nailed together, is placed in front of the box, and three or four cubic yards of pebbles, or an equal weight of brick-bats or other materials are filled in against the shield. Earth is then well rammed around the shield, on top and behind, to prevent the explosion from taking place in the wrong direction. A fougasse of this size, when sprung, will scatter the pebbles over a surface sixty yards in length and seventy in breadth.

ART. 99.—Field Ovens, Kneading-Troughs, Cooking, &c.

Earthen Ovens.—To construct with rapidity an earthen oven, dig a slope with a step (Fig. 22), and on

FIG. 22.

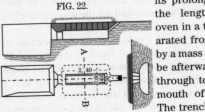

its prolongation, dig the length of the oven in a trench separated from the step by a mass of earth, to be afterward pierced through to make the mouth of the oven. The trench when finished, should be two feet eight inches in depth, one foot four inches in breadth, and ten feet long. Then dig on the sides portions of an oval arch, so as to have the arch with a span of three feet three inches,

which is also the breadth of the hearth. Then pierce
the mouth and cover the trench with from three to
five sods as arch stones, leaving a chimney space to
the bottom. Ovens for from 100 to 250 rations may be
thus made.

In a stiff soil, an oven may also be made by forming
a slope six feet in height; open in this slope a very
low and narrow branch, which make six feet long; at
four feet from the mouth, form two small branches
perpendicular to the first, excavating the earth
between the branches, giving an elliptical form to the
hearth, which slopes toward the mouth, and finishing
the upper part in shape of an arch; a chimney may be
added, but it is often dispensed with. The oven is
heated for ten hours to dry, and then the bread may
be baked; the subsequent heatings last only two or
three hours.

Wooden Ovens. (Fig. 23.)—To construct a wooden
oven, make an excavation ten

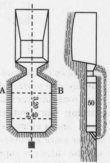

FIG. 23.

and a half feet in length, eight
feet in breadth, and one foot
eight inches in depth, giving a
slight slope to the hearth
toward the front.—The trench
is covered with pieces of
wood, oak or fir, from six to
ten inches square, placed
close together, and the wood
is covered with earth carefully rammed, the chimney-place
being sodded. The fire-place
is dried by heating for seven or eight hours, but subsequent heatings require only two hours. Such ovens

will stand quite well five or six bakings. They require only two hours to make them, when the wood is prepared. If the wood should take fire, it may be extinguished by closing the mouth and chimney; if entirely burnt out, the wood may be replaced in half an hour.

Oven of Gabions. (Fig. 24.)—Take two gabions of semicircular cross-section, made each with twenty

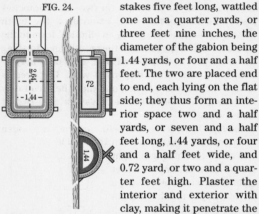

FIG. 24.

stakes five feet long, wattled one and a quarter yards, or three feet nine inches, the diameter of the gabion being 1.44 yards, or four and a half feet. The two are placed end to end, each lying on the flat side; they thus form an interior space two and a half yards, or seven and a half feet long, 1.44 yards, or four and a half feet wide, and 0.72 yard, or two and a quarter feet high. Plaster the interior and exterior with clay, making it penetrate the interstices of the gabions. If clay cannot be procured, use any rich earth, adding hay or straw if necessary. The front and back are closed with sods, or with a wattling plastered as the remainder. A mouth is made, and a chimney opening at the other end. The wicker-work is covered with earth to retain the heat, and the sides are supported at the same time. Withes are attached to the top of the basket-work, passed through the earth, and fastened to the ridge-pole of a wooded horse straddled across the structure. Eight of these may be made in twenty-four hours.

Kneading-Troughs. (Fig. 25.)—An expeditious method of making a kneading-trough in the field is to dig two trenches of unequal size, parallel to each other, of which the smaller should be lined with boards.

FIG. 25.

KNEADING TROUGH

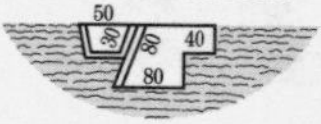

The bakers stand in the larger trench, and knead in the other. Dough is kneaded with six parts of flour, four of water, and half a part of salt to the 100 parts.

To make sure of the rising of the bread, dig a trench half a yard deep, and of convenient length and breadth; warm it with wood in small sticks, then place the bread on brushwood, covering the trench with branches, planks and hay.

Cooking other food than bread is performed by means of stoves of earth arranged to receive the camp pots, which contain enough for eight men.

For that purpose (Fig. 26), an elliptical excavation is made, of which the long axis is 0.28 yard or eleven inches, and the short axis 0.25 yard, or ten inches, the depth being 0.40 yard, or one foot four inches. At 0.20 yard, or eight inches from the bottom, and from that point to the top, this excavation is increased in diameter in every direction 0.02 yard, or one inch, so as to make it 0.32 yard, or thirteen inches by 0.27 yard, or ten inches in its upper part, thus making an offset upon which a camp-kettle can be placed. At the level of the offset, and all around it, a small cylindrical space is cut, two inches wide and two inches high. A hole to stand in is dug 0.60 yard, or two feet deep, and separated from the first

FIG. 26.

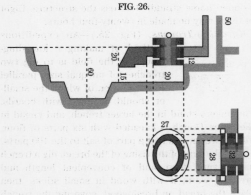

excavation by a mass of earth about one foot thick,
through which an opening six inches square is
pierced, at the level of the fire-floor. Steps are
arranged for descent into the standing hole, and opposite to this a horizontal opening is made at the level of
the offset, and from its extremity a chimney erected,
which may be made as high as necessary with sods.

CAMP COOKING.

Bones should never be thrown away, but broken up
and boiled repeatedly. Meat or bones should always
be put into the cold water for making soup, and
boiled with it, not put into boiling water.

Meat, previously wrapped in paper or cloth, may be
baked in a clay case, in any sort of pit or oven, well
covered over, and with good economy.

Upon giving men time and opportunity to cook, and
enforcing attention to comfort, depends much of
their cheerfulness and efficiency.

Cooking Fires.—In cooking for a large party with a small supply of fuel, either dig a narrow trench, above which all the pots and kettles may stand in a row, and in which the fire is made; the mouth being open to the wind, and a small chimney built at the other end, or else use the arrangement shown above.

Kabobs.—For a hurried dinner, boil the rib-bones, or skewer your iron ramrod through a dozen small lumps of meat, and roast them. In all cases, if your meat is of a tough sort, hammer it from time to time, when half done, to break up its fibre, and then continue the cooking.

Salt Meat, to prepare hurriedly.—Warm it slightly on both sides; this makes the salt draw to the outside; then rinse it well in a pannikin of water. This is found to extract a great deal of salt, and to leave the meat in a fit state for cooking.

RECEIPTS BY M. SOYER.

Stewed Salt Beef and Pork.—Put into a saucepan about two pounds of well-soaked beef, cut in eight pieces, half a pound of salt pork, divided in two, and also soaked; half a pound of rice, or six tablespoonfuls; one quarter of a pound of onions, or four middle-sized ones, peeled and sliced: two ounces of brown sugar, or one large table-spoonful; one quarter of an ounce of pepper, and five pints of water, simmer gently for three hours, remove the fat from the top, and serve. This dish is enough for six people, and if the receipt be closely followed, you cannot fail to have an excellent food.

Mutton Soup.—Put the rations of six into a pan,

six pounds of mutton, cut in four or six pieces; three quarters of a pound of mixed vegetables, or three ounces of preserved; three and a half teaspoonfuls of salt; one teaspoonful of sugar, and half a teaspoonful of pepper, if handy; six ounces of barley or rice, or five table-spoonfuls of either; eight pints of water; let it simmer gently for three hours and a half, remove the fat and serve. Bread or biscuit may be added in small quantities.

Plain Pea-Soup.—Put into a pan two pounds of pork well soaked, and cut into eight pieces; pour six quarts of water over; one pound of split peas; one teaspoonful of sugar; half a teaspoonful of pepper; four ounces of fresh vegetables, or two ounces of preserved, if handy; let it boil gently for two hours, or until the peas are tender. When the pork is rather fat, as is usually the case, wash it only; one quarter of a pound of broken biscuit may be used for the soup. Salt beef, when rather fat, and soaked, may be used for pea-soup.

French Beef Soup.—Put into the kettle six pounds of beef, cut into two or three pieces, bones included; one pound of mixed green vegetables, or half a pound of preserved; four teaspoonfuls of salt; one teaspoonful of pepper, one of sugar, three cloves, and eight pints of water. Let it boil gently three hours; remove some of the fat, and serve. The addition of one and half pounds of bread, cut into slices, or one pound of broken biscuits, well-soaked, will make a very nutritious soup. Skimming is not required.

How to Stew Fresh Beef, Pork, Mutton, and Veal.— Cut or chop two pounds of fresh beef into ten or twelve pieces; put these into a saucepan, with one and a half teaspoonfuls of salt; one and a half tea-spoonfuls of sugar; half a teaspoonful of pepper, two middle-sized onions sliced, and half a pint of water. Set on the fire for ten minutes, until forming a thick gravy. Add a good table-spoonful of flour, stir on the fire a few minutes; add a quart and a half of water; let the whole simmer until the meat is tender. Beef will take from two and a half to three hours; mutton and pork about two hours; veal, one hour and a quarter to one hour and a half; onions, sugar, and pepper, if not to be had, must be omitted; it will even then make a good dish; half a pound of sliced potatoes, or two ounces of preserved potatoes; ration vegetables may be added, also a small dumpling.

Plain Boiled Salt Beef.—For six rations, put in saucepan six pounds of well-soaked beef, cut in two, with three quarts of cold water, simmer gently three hours, and serve. About one pound of either carrots, turnips, parsnips, greens or cabbage, or dumplings, may be boiled with it.

Plum Pudding.—Put into a basin one pound of flour, three-quarters of a pound of raisins (stoned, if there is time), three-quarters of a pound of the fat of salt pork (well-washed, cut into small dice, or chopped), two tablespoonfuls of sugar or molasses; add half a pint of water, mix all together; put into a cloth tied tightly; boil for four hours, and serve. If time will not permit, boil only two hours, though four are preferable. How to spoil the above—add any thing to it.

ART. 100.—Sundry Hints.

Precautions against Thirst.—Drink well in the morning before starting, and nothing till the halt; keep the mouth shut; chew a straw or leaf, or keep the mouth covered with a cloth; all these prevent suffering from extreme thirst. Tying a handkerchief, well wetted in salt water, around the neck allays thirst for a considerable time.

To Purify Water that is Muddy, Putrid or Salt.—With muddy water, the remedy is to filter; with putrid, to boil, to mix with charcoal, or expose to the sun and air; or what is best, to use all three methods at the same time. With salt water, nothing avails but distillation.

To Filter Muddy Water.—When at the watering place there is nothing but wet sand, take a good handful of grass, and tie it roughly together in the form of a cone, six or eight inches long; then dipping the broad end into the puddle and turning it up, a streamlet of partly-filtered water will trickle down through the small end. For a copious supply, the most perfect plan, if you have means, is to bore a cask full of auger holes, and put another small one, that has had the bottom knocked out, inside it, then fill up the space between the two with grass, moss, &c. Now sinking the whole in the midst of the pond, the water will filter through the auger holes and moss, and rise up clear of, at least, weeds and sand, in the inner cask, whence it can be ladled. With a single cask, the lower parts of the sides may be bored, and alternate layers of sand and grass thrown in, till they reach above the holes; through these layers the water will strain. Or any coarse

bag, that is keep open with hoops, made on the spot,
may be moored in the muddy pool, by having a heavy
stone put inside it, and will act on the same principle,
but less efficiently, than the casks. Sand, charcoal,
sponge, and wool are the substances most commonly used in filters; peat charcoal is excellent. A small
piece of alum is very efficacious in purifying water
from organic matter, which is precipitated by the
alum, and a deposit left at the bottom of the vessel.

Putrid Water should always be boiled with charcoal or charred sticks before drinking, as low fevers
and dysenteries too often are the consequences of its
being used indiscreetly, but the charcoal entirely dis-
infects it; bitter herbs, if steeped in it, or even rubbed
well about the cup, are said to render it less unwhole-
some. The Indians plunge a hot iron into putrid and
muddy water.

When carrying water in buckets, put a wreath of
grass, or something floating on the top of the water,
to prevent splashing; and also make a hoop, inside
which the porter walks, while his laden hands rest on
the rim, the office of the hoop being to keep the
buckets from knocking against his legs.

Touch-Paper.—If the ashes of a cigar be well
rubbed into a bit of paper, they convert it into touch-
paper. Gunpowder also, if rubbed into paper, has the
same effect; and injured gunpowder will do as well
for this purpose as good. To prepare a store of
touch-paper, a strong solution of saltpetre in water
should be obtained, and the paper or rags, or fungus
dipped into it, and held to dry. This solution may be
made by pouring a little water on a charge of gunpowder or on cigar ashes, which will dissolve the

saltpetre out of them. Boiling water makes a solution forty-fold stronger than ice-cold water, and about eight times stronger than water at 60 degrees Fahr.; and unsized paper, like blotting-paper, is the best suited for this purpose.

To Kindle a Spark into a Flame, the spark should be received into a kind of loose nest of the most inflammable substances at hand, which ought to be prepared before the tinder is lighted. When by careful blowing or fanning the flame is once started, it should be fed with little bits of sticks or bark, split with a knife or rubbed between the fingers into fibres, until it has gained enough strength to grapple with thicker ones. There is a proverb—"Small sticks kindle a flame, but large ones put it out."

Fuel.—There is something of a knack in finding firewood. It should be looked for under bushes; the stump of a tree, that is rotted nearly to the ground, has often a magnificent root, fit to blaze throughout the night. Dry manure of cattle is an excellent fuel. Dry fuel gives out far more heat than damp. Bones of animals furnish also an excellent substitute for firewood.

Mattresses, Blankets, and their Substitutes.—A good substitute for a mattress is to strew the ground with dry grass and other things plucked up from the ground. Leaves, fern, feathers, heather, rushes, reeds, hay, straw, fodder, wood shavings, &c., may be used to advantage. Empty bags, skins, saddle-cloths, spare clothes, &c., may be used. It gives great comfort to have scraped a little hollow in the ground, just where the hip-bone would otherwise press.

Work hard at making the sleeping place dry and

comfortable; it is wretched beyond expression for a man to lie shivering, and to think with self-reproach, how different would be his situation if he had simply had energy and forethought enough to cut and draw twice the quantity of firewood, and to labor an extra half hour in making a snugger berth.

Pillows.—Without some sort of pillow it is difficult to sleep. A mound of earth scraped together soon wears down. A bag filled with earth or grass keeps its shape. A stone or billet of wood is better than nothing. Saddles are much used.

Huts, Tents, Booths, &c.—Where there are trees, a booth may be erected with a little care. Drive sticks, four feet long or more, into the ground, and bending their tops together lash them fast with string or withes, or strips of bark. Then by heaping leaves and broad pieces of bark over all, and banking up the earth on either side pretty high, an excellent kennel is made. If daubed over with mud or clay it becomes more air proof.

Pitching a Tent is quite an art, so as to let in or exclude the air at will, to take advantage of sun, shade, &c. Before a storm, dig a ditch as deep as you can, around the outside of the tent, to turn aside the water, and to drain the ground on which it stands— even a furrow scratched with a tent peg is better than nothing.

Be careful that the tent is not too much strained, else the shrinking of the materials in the rain will tear up the pegs. The ground is often such that the pegs will not hold: if it be sandy, scrape the surface sand away before driving them in, and put flat stones under the poles to prevent them from working down and thus leaving the tent slack and unsteady. If the sand is very deep, it is an excellent plan to bury sticks or bushes two or three feet deep, and to tie the tent corners to the middle of them instead of to pegs. Bags of sand may be also buried.

Heavy saddles or other things may be used for fastening tents to, when pegs cannot be driven, or will not hold. A tent should never be pitched in a slovenly way, as it is far more roomy, secure, and graceful when stretched.

To dry clothes at a smouldering fire, it is very convenient to make a dome-shaped frame-work of twigs, by bending each twig into a half circle, and planting both ends of it in the ground, one on each side of the fire. Then laying the wet clothes on this frame-work, they receive the full benefit of the heat, and the steam passes readily upward.

Shooting From a Horse.—Use the spur, but never the whip; else when you raise your gun to fire, he will feel a dread that it may be the whip, and is sure to be a little unsteady.

To Cut Chaff.—Tie a sickle against a tree with its blade projecting; then standing in front of the blade, hold a handful of straw across it with both hands, one on either side of the blade; pull it toward you, and the straw will be cut through; drop the cut end, seize the straw afresh, and repeat the process.

Saddles.—Sore backs are the plague of beasts of burden, for if the skin be once broken, it will never heal thoroughly during the journey. The first appearance of a sore back is a small, hardish swelling: this must be at once attended to by folding the saddle cloth in some appropriate way, or even by pick-

ing out the saddle stuffing, so as to ease all pressure
from it, otherwise it will grow larger and larger, and
a single day will convert what might have been easily cured into a serious and irremediable gall.

ART. 101.—Medical and Surgical Hints.

Camps.—The position of camps is very important.
The neighborhood of marshes, grounds liable to be
flooded, or surrounded with stagnant water, low
places covered with brushwood, are all injurious to
health. The noxious effluvia from these are increased
in proportion to the heat and season of the year. The
danger of such situations is in some degree dependent on the temporary or permanent nature of the
camp; ground may be occupied for one night which
would be very bad for a permanent station. If compelled to encamp on wet or marshy ground, cut
drains across the land and around the tents. A water-
proof sheet to sleep on is very useful; dry straw or
heath, if at hand, answers temporarily. The situation
is sometimes under no control; if it is, a dry elevated
position, remote from marshes, swamps, stagnant
water, or underwood, should be selected. It is best
on a gentle declivity, with a dry soil, and near a
running stream. To ascertain the nature of the soil,
dig to some depth to see if moisture is retained.
A camp should not be formed on ground recently
occupied, nor on a battle-field. Tents should be
well ventilated, especially if straw is used. The general cleanliness of camp is very important, more
especially if stationary. It is advisable occasionally
to change the ground, if possible. The opinion of
natives often affords assistance in ascertaining the

prevailing diseases, and the general mode of living of the inhabitants may be a useful guide.

Bivouac.—If possible, on dry ground, near wood and water. In these cases, hoods to the overcoats or water-proofs are very beneficial. Fires should be lighted, and if an extended front is objectionable, they can be made in circular clusters, the men lying between. The men should sleep by squads close together, and in wet weather or cold, a half ration of rum is serviceable before sleeping. A water-proof sheet, with eyelet holes at the corners, may be readily stretched over sticks, and affords a good protection against heavy dews. In very cold weather, sentries should be relieved hourly or half-hourly, and when relieved should pace about briskly to remove all numbness before lying down. If obliged to sleep on snow, it should be piled upon each side. It is useful to smear the face and ears with oil before going on duty in very cold weather.

Diet.—The importance of wholesome food to the preservation of health, and its efficacy in resisting the inroads of disease are evident. The food of the soldier may be coarse, but it should be wholesome, nutritious, and abundant. It is desirable, as far as possible, to issue rations daily; when more is issued at once, the soldier is apt to eat most of it in one day or waste it. Salted provisions should be well steeped in water before being cooked. There are obvious advantages in cooking in messes; the men prefer to roast or boil their own ration, but this does not make the most of it. It should be boiled with vegetables to make soup, which is always best made in messes. In addition to cabbage, turnips or carrots, there are various wild vegetables, such as cresses, sorrel, and others, which are excellent additions to soup. The use of compressed vegetables obviates all inconvenience from want of fresh, but they require more cooking. The best rule in cooking meat is to boil slowly, and to roast quickly. It is very necessary for troops to have a morning meal of tea or coffee before undergoing great exertion; it is the best safeguard against malaria, damp or cold: a full meal is not necessary.

Clothing.—This should be adapted to the climate, as far as possible, whether to protect the body from heat or cold. There should be nothing to impede the free action of the limbs or chest. In hot climates the head must be protected from the sun. Flannel shirts are very serviceable. Personal cleanliness is very important; bathing is highly beneficial when practicable at proper seasons.

Surgical Hints.—These are only for guidance when a medical officer is not at hand. The most useful thing is to be able to stop bleeding when profuse, as in many cases life may be preserved by the immediate adoption of simple means.

Bleeding from wounds is of two kinds: 1st, from *veins*, when the blood is dark in color, and flows slowly; 2d, from *arteries*, when the color is bright, florid red, and it issues in jets, or forcibly and rapidly.

Means for Suppressing Bleeding.—In the first class of cases, which are commonly caused by the wound of some superficial vein, pressure by the fingers, or a bandage of any kind passed around the limb *below* the wound (that is, further from the centre of circulation), and *moderately* tightened, is sufficient. This kind of bleeding is seldom profuse, except when combined with the wound of some artery which requires more vigorous temporary measures.

In the second class of cases, an artery in a limb is wounded, and there is a profuse and rapid flow of bright blood. The limb should be firmly grasped by one or both hands, placed *above* the wound, that is, nearer the centre of circulation. By making a firm pressure, the bleeding can be restrained until a tourniquet is applied. When this instrument is not at hand, a handkerchief folded up, sash, brace, or any similar article is to be passed around the limb, the ends tied, and by means of a stick twisted tightly enough to stop the bleeding.

Bleeding from wounds caused by shot is rarely profuse, and even when a limb is severely wounded, or carried away by a round shot, it does not always occur to a great extent: in such cases, however, it is desirable to put the bandage on as described, leaving it to be tightened should it be necessary. Stimulants should be given very sparingly.

Temporary Removal of Wounded Persons.—If a limb is broken or so injured as to be useless, the object is to prevent the pain and mischief caused by moving the limb without support.

If the arm is injured to this degree, let the elbow be bent at a right angle, and gently supported in a common sling, suspended around the neck. The wounded person will generally be able to walk with greater comfort for a small distance than by being carried. If the leg or thigh is rendered useless, let the person remain on the ground, and by tying the sound limb to the injured one considerable support is obtained: a scabbard may be used for the same purpose. If a stretcher is not to be had, a blanket drawn under the body and carried by the ends, affords a substitute.

ART. 102.—Promotion in the French Army. (Law of April 14, 1832.)

1. No one can be a corporal until he has served at least six months as a private in one of the corps of the army.

2. No one can be a sergeant until he has served at least six months as a corporal.

3. No one can be a sub-lieutenant unless he be eighteen years of age, or have served at least two years as a non-commissioned officer in one of the corps of the army, or have passed two years at a military school and undergone a satisfactory examination at leaving.

4. No one can be a lieutenant unless he has served at least two years as sub-lieutenant.

6. No one can be a captain without serving two years as lieutenant.

7. No one can be chief of battalion, chief of squadron, or major, without serving at least four years as captain.

8. No one can be lieutenant-colonel without serving at least five years as chief of battalion, chief of squadron, or major.

9. No one can be colonel without serving at least two years as lieutenant-colonel.

10. No one can be promoted to a grade higher than that of colonel without serving at least three years in the grade immediately below.

18. The time of service required for passing from one grade to another may be reduced one half in war.

19. The conditions imposed for passing from one grade to another can be set aside only: 1st, for distinguished conduct duly set forth and published in the orders of the day to the army, or, 2d, when vacancies in corps in presence of the enemy cannot be otherwise filled.

20. In time of war, and in corps in presence of the enemy, half the promotions to grades of lieutenant and captain are by seniority, and all promotions to grades of chief of battalion or squadron are by selection.

21. In no case shall any one be appointed to a grade without command, nor be granted an honorary grade, nor shall any rank be given superior to that of actual command.

LAW OF MARCH 16, 1838.

11. Infantry solders can be admitted into elite companies only after serving six months.

In all arms where there are soldiers of a first class, the same length of service is required to pass from second to first class.

In the infantry, the soldiers of the elite companies, and in the cavalry, the soldiers of the first class are nominated for selection by the chiefs of corps.

In the other arms, and in all the special corps, passage from the second to the first class is by seniority, except in cases coming under Art. 93.

93. In troops in the field, the time of service required to pass into the elite companies, or to the first class may be reduced one-half. Soldiers distin-

guished by some act of daring or personal sacrifice, announced in orders before the regiment, may have these conditions set aside.

94. In corps where battalions, squadrons, or detachments only are in the field, all the vacancies in the grades of non-commissioned officers belong exclusively to the troops in the field.

95. All the sergeants of the portion of a corps in the field are candidates, together with the sergeants on the list for promotion, but not in the field; for the vacancies of sub-lieutenants open to sergeants, no matter where the vacancies occur. In the portion of the corps not in the field, the same order of turns is followed as before the separation. In the portion in the field, the first vacancy is given to one of the sergeants in that portion: the second and third are given in conformity with the special arrangements of each year. When the whole corps is in the field, the same order of appointment is followed as before entering upon the campaign.

Where a sergeant deserves promotion for distinguished conduct and there is no suitable vacancy in his regiment, he is nominated for a vacancy in another regiment of the same arm.

96. Promotions to the grades of lieutenant and captain are made as follows: Half of the vacancies in battalions, squadrons, or detachments which form part of an active army, and two-thirds in the part not in the field, are filled by seniority. All the officers of the active portion of the corps are candidates, together with those officers of the non-active portion who are on the list for such promotion, for places to be filled by selection, wherever these may occur.

Whenever on account of distinguished service mentioned in orders, a sub-lieutenant or lieutenant deserves promotion, and there is no suitable vacancy in his regiment, he is nominated to a vacancy (to be filled by selection), in some other regiment of the arm.

For the execution of these arrangements, the order of returns (1st turn being that of seniority; 2d, of selection; 3d, of seniority, and so again, beginning with a seniority place), is followed before the division of corps, and is continued in that portion of it which does not enter the field. In battalions, squadrons or detachments in the field, a new arrangement is made after the separation, that is to say: the first vacancy is filled by seniority, if the last promotion was by selection, and the reverse. This arrangement also prevails in corps, all of whose parts are in the field.

97. Promotion to the grade of chief of battalion or squadron in troops in the field, taking place only by selection, all the captains of the corps or parts of corps in the field are candidates (along with the other captains of that arm who are on the list for promotion by selection) for such vacancies, without prejudice, however, to the seniority rights of those captains not in the field.

103. Propositions for appointment of non-commissioned officers are to be made to the colonel of the regiment by captains, accompanied by remarks of the chief of battalion or squadron and the lieutenant-colonel. The colonel appoints from the list those who are to fill vacancies. He may also, besides this list, select from those distinguished by brilliant services. For promotion to the grade of sub-lieutenant, lieutenant, and captain, the chief of the corps or regi-

ment recommends, after taking the advice of the chiefs of battalions or squadrons, and also of the lieutenant-colonel, if present. For promotion to the grade of chief of battalion or squadron, the general of brigade recommends, after taking the advice of the colonels or chiefs of corps in his brigade. For promotion to the grade of lieutenant-colonel, the general of division recommends, after consulting the colonels or chiefs of corps, and the generals of his brigades. For promotion to the grade of colonel or general of brigade, the general in chief recommends, after consulting with generals of brigade and division for promotion of a colonel, and with generals of division for promotion of a general of brigade. These recommendations for the different grades are transmitted through the proper channels, to the commander-in-chief of the army, to the minister of war. The chiefs of corps and general, to whom this right of nomination is given, designate for each vacancy three candidates taken from among the officers and non-commissioned officers under their orders, who have been presented for promotion in the prescribed form. The number of candidates for the grades of lieutenant-colonel, colonel and general of brigade, may be reduced.

109. Officers captured by the enemy do not have their places filled unless the exigencies of the service positively require it, and only upon the order of the minister of war.

Officers, prisoners of war, will retain their right of seniority for promotion; but they can only be promoted to the grade immediately superior to that they had when captured.

110. All officers, from the grade of sub-lieutenant to colonel inclusive, who, upon returning from captivity, find the place filled, which they had before their capture, as well as that to which they might through seniority have ascended, are placed upon a retired list until vacancies occur.

111. If an officer, who has deserved promotion for gallant conduct, is captured before receiving it, he may still receive it upon the recommendation of the commander-in-chief.

ART. 103.—In the Regular army of the United States, the following are the Laws Relating to the Promotion of Officers and Non-Commissioned Officers.

(March 30, 1814.) "Promotions may be made through the whole army in its several lines of light artillery, dragoons, artillery, infantry, and riflemen, respectively."

(July 6, 1812.) "Promotions by brevet may be conferred for gallant action or meritorious conduct."

(March 3, 1851.) "All promotions in the staff departments or corps shall be made as in other corps of the army."

(March 3, 1853.) "Any lieutenant of engineers, topographical engineers or ordinance, having served fourteen years continuously as lieutenant, shall be promoted to the rank of captain: provided the whole number of officers in either of said corps be not increased beyond the number fixed by law, and that no officer be promoted before those ranking him in the corps."

(August 4, 1854.) "Authorizes the President to confer brevet of second lieutenant on meritorious non-commissioned officers, after examination before a board of officers, and to attach them to regiments."

(August 3, 1861.) "Whenever any army captain of the quarter-master's department shall have served fourteen years' continuous service, he shall be promoted to the rank of major. When officers are retired, the vacancies are filled by regular promotion of juniors of the arm or corps."

The regulations on the subject are the following: All vacancies in established regiments and corps, to the rank of colonel, shall be filled by promotion according to seniority, except in case of disability or other incompetency.

Promotions to the rank of captain shall be made regimentally; to major and lieutenant-colonel and colonel, according to the arm, as infantry, artillery, cavalry, &c.; and in the staff department, and in the engineers, topographical engineers, and ordnance, according to corps.

Appointments to the rank of brigadier and major-general will be made by selection from the army.

The graduates of the military academy are appointed to vacancies of the lowest grade, or attached by brevet to regiments or corps, not to exceed one brevet to each company; and meritorious non-commissioned officers, examined by an army board, and found qualified for the duties of commissioned officers, will, in like manner, be attached to regiments as brevet second-lieutenants.

Whenever the public service may require the appointment of any citizen to the army, a board of officers will be instituted, before which the applicant will appear for an examination into his physical ability, moral character, attainments, and general fitness for the service. If the board report in favor of the applicant, he will be deemed eligible for a commission in the army. As far as practicable, all appointments and details on the staff will be equalized in the several regiments.

General officers appoint their own aides-de-camp.

An office shall not fill any staff appointment or other situation, the duties of which will detach him from his company, regiment, or corps, until he has served at least three years with his regiment or corps; nor shall any officer (aides-de-camp excepted) so remain detached longer than four years.

ART. 104.—Exchange of Transfer of Officers and Soldiers.

The transfer of officers is settled by custom and regulation, there being no law on the subject. It is made by the War Department on the mutual application of the parties desiring the exchange. The following are the regulations: An office shall not be transferred from one regiment or corps to another, with prejudice to the rank of any officer of the regiment or corps to which he is transferred.

No non-commissioned office or soldier will be transferred from one regiment to another without the authority of the commanding general. A colonel may, upon the application of the captains, transfer a non-commissioned officer or soldier from one company to another of his regiment, with consent of the department commander, in case of change of post.

When soldiers are authorized to be transferred, the transfer will take place on the first of the month, with a view to the more convenient settlement of their accounts.

ART. 105.—Leaves of Absence.

The law provides that every colonel or other officer commanding a regiment, troop, or company, and actually quartered with it, may give furloughs to non-commissioned officers or soldiers, in such numbers and for so long a time as he shall judge to be most consistent with the good of the service; and a captain and other inferior officer, commanding a troop or company, or in any garrison, fort, or barrack of the United States (his field officer being absent), may give furloughs to non-commissioned officers or soldiers for a time not exceeding twenty days in six months, but not more than two persons to be absent at the same time, unless some extraordinary occasion should require it.

The law does not provide for leaves of absence to officers, and the following are the regulations on the subject:

In no case will leaves of absence be granted so that a company be left without one of its commissioned officers, or that a garrisoned post be left without two commissioned officers and competent medical attendance; nor shall leave of absence be granted to an officer during the season of active operations, except on urgent necessity.

When not otherwise specified, leaves of absence will be considered as commencing on the day the officer is released from duty at his post.

In time of peace, commanding officers may grant leaves of absence as follows: The commander of a post not to exceed seven days at one time, or in the same month; the commander of a geographical department not to exceed sixty days; the general commanding the army not to exceed four months. Applications for leaves of absence for more than four months, or to officers of engineers, ordnance, or of the general staff, or serving on it (aides-de-camp excepted), for more than thirty days, must be referred to the adjutant-general, for the decision of the secretary of war. In giving a permission to apply for the extension of a leave of absence, the term of the extension should be stated.

The immediate commander of the officer applying for leave of absence, and all intermediate commanders, will indorse their opinions on the application before forwarding it.

The commander of a post may take leave of absence not to exceed seven days at one time, or in the same month, reporting the fact to his next superior.

Three months' leave of absence will be allowed to graduates from the time of quitting, as cadet, the Military Academy.

No leave of absence exceeding seven days, except on extraordinary occasions, when the circumstances must be particularly stated (and except as provided in the preceding paragraph), shall be granted to any officer until he has joined his regiment or corps, and served therein at least two years.

Officers will not leave the United States, to go beyond sea, without permission from the war department.

An application for leave of absence on account of sickness, must be accompanied by a certificate of the senior medical officer present, in the following form:—

—— —— of the —— regiment of —— having applied for a certificate on which to base an application for leave of absence, I do hereby certify that I have carefully examined this officer, and find that (here the nature of the disease, wound, or disability is to be fully stated, and the period during which the officer has suffered under its effects,) and that in consequence thereof he is, in my opinion, unfit for duty. I further declare my belief that he will not be able to resume his duties in a less period than (here state candidly and explicitly the opinion as to the period which will probably elapse before the officer will be able to resume his duties, and when there is no reason to expect a recovery, or when the prospect of recovery is distant and uncertain, or when a change of climate is recommended, it must be so stated.)

Dated at —— this —— day of —— 18 —

Signature of the medical officer.

When an officer is prevented by sickness from joining his station, he will transmit certificates in the above form monthly, to the commanding officer of his post and regiment, or corps, and to the adjutant-general: and when he cannot procure the certificate of a medical officer of the army, he will substitute his own certificate, on honor, to his condition, and a full statement of his case. If the officer's certificate is not satisfactory, and whenever an officer has been absent on account of sickness for one year, he shall be examined by a medical board, and the case specially reported to the President.

In all reports of absence, or applications for leave

of absence on account of sickness, the officer shall state how long he has been absent already on that account, and by whose permission.

Furloughs to enlisted men will be granted only by the commanding officer of the post, or the commanding officer of the regiment actually quartered with it. Furloughs may be prohibited at the discretion of the officer in command.

Soldiers on furlough shall not take with them their arms or accoutrements.

FORM OF FURLOUGH.

To all whom it may concern:

The bearer hereof, —— —— a sergeant (corporal or private,) of captain —— —— company — regiment of — aged — years, — feet — inches high, —— complexion, —— eyes, —— hair, and by profession a ——, born in —— of —— and enlisted at —— in the —— of ——, on the —— day of ——, eighteen hundred and ——, to serve for the period of ——, is hereby permitted to go to ——, in the county of ——, state of ——, he having received a furlough from the — day of —— to the — day of ——, at which period he will rejoin his company or regiment at ——, or wherever it then may be, or be considered a deserter.

Subsistence has been furnished to said —— —— to the — day of ——, and pay to the — day of ——, both inclusive.

Given under my hand at ——, this — day of ——, 18 —.

Signature of officer granting.

ART. 106.—Courts Martial and Courts of Inquiry.

Any general officer commanding an army, or colonel commanding a separate department, may appoint general courts-martial whenever necessary. (65th Art. of War.) General courts-martial may consist of any number of commissioned officers, from five to thirteen, but not of less than thirteen, where that number can be convened without manifest injury to the service. (Art. 64.) No sentence of a court-martial shall be carried into execution until after the whole proceedings shall have been laid before the officer ordering the same, or the officer commanding the troops for the time being; neither shall any sentence of a general court-martial, in time of peace, extending to the loss of life, or the dismission of a commissioned office, or which shall, either in time of peace or war respect a general officer, be carried into execution until the whole proceedings shall have been transmitted to the secretary of war, to be laid before the President of the United States, for his confirmation or disapproval, and orders in the case. All other sentences may be confirmed and executed by the officer ordering the court to assemble, or the commanding officer for the time being. (Art. 65.) Whenever a general officer commanding an army, or a colonel commanding a separate department, shall be the accuser or prosecutor of any officer of the army under his command, the general court-martial for the trial of such officer shall be appointed by the President of the United States, and the proceedings and sentence of the said court shall be sent directly to the secretary of war, to be laid by him before the President for his confirmation or disapproval, or orders in the case.

(Act May 29, 1830.) Every officer commanding a regiment or corps may appoint, for his own regiment or corps, courts-martial, to consist of three commissioned officers, for the trial and punishment of offences not capital, and decide upon their sentences. For the same purpose, all officers commanding any of the garrisons, forts, barracks, or other places where troops consist of different corps, may assemble courts martial, to consist of three commissioned officers, and decide upon their sentences. (Art. 66.)

No garrison or regimental court-martial shall have the power to try capital cases or commissioned officers; neither shall they inflict a fine exceeding one month's pay, nor imprison, nor put to hard labor any non-commissioned officer or soldier, for a longer time than one month. (Art. 67.) The judge-advocate, or some person deputed by him, or by the general, or officer commanding the army, detachment or garrison, shall prosecute in the name of the United States, but shall so far consider himself as counsel for the prisoner, after the said prisoner shall have made his plea, as to object to any leading question to any witness, or any question to the prisoner, the answer to which might tend to criminate himself; and administer to each member of the court, before they proceed upon any trial, the oath prescribed in the articles of war for general, regimental, and garrison courts-martial. The president of the court then administers an oath to the judge-advocate. (Art. 69.) If a prisoner when arraigned stands mute, the trial goes on as if he pleaded not guilty. (Art. 70.) If a member be challenged by a prisoner, the court judges of the relevancy of the challenge. Only one member can be challenged at a time. (At. 71.) All members are to behave with decency and calmness, and in giving their votes to begin with the youngest. (Art. 72.) All persons who give evidence are examined on oath or affirmation. (Art. 73.) On trials of cases not capital before courts-martial, the deposition of witnesses, not in the line or staff of the army, may be taken before some justice of the peace and read in evidence; provided the prosecutor and person accused are present at the taking of the same, or are duly notified thereof. (Art. 74.) No officer shall be tried but by a general court-martial, nor by officers of inferior rank, if it can be avoided. Nor shall trials be carried on except between eight in the morning and three in the afternoon, excepting in cases requiring immediate example in the opinion of the officer ordering the court. (Art. 75.) No person to use menacing words, signs or gestures before a court-martial, or cause any disorder or riot, or disturb their proceedings, on the penalty of being punished at the discretion of the said court-martial. (Art. 76.)

(Act of July 29, 1861.) Every officer, non-commissioned officer or private of the militia in the service of the United States, who shall fail to obey a legal order of the President, shall forfeit a sum not exceeding one year's pay, and not less than one month's pay, to be determined and adjudged by a court-martial; and such officer shall be liable to be cashiered by sentence of court-martial, and be incapacitated from holding a commission in the militia for a term not exceeding twelve months, at the discretion of the court; and such non-commissioned officer and private shall be liable to imprisonment by a like sentence, on failure of payment of the fines adjudged against them for one calendar month, for every twenty-five dollars of such fine.

Courts-martial for the trial of militia shall be composed of militia officers alone.

(Act of August 5, 1861.) Flogging, as a punishment in the army, is hereby abolished.

FORM OF A GENERAL ORDER APPOINTING A GENERAL
COURT-MARTIAL.

Head-quarters of the Army }
March —, 18—. }

General Orders, }
No. —. }

A general court-martial, to consist of thirteen members, will convene at Fort Monroe, in the state of Virginia, on Monday, the second of April, 18—, at eleven o'clock, A. M., or as soon thereafter as practicable, for the trial of Captain A. B., of the first regiment of artillery, and such other prisoners as may be brought before it. The following officers are detailed as members of the court:

1. Colonel A. B.,	.	First regiment of ——.
2. Colonel C. D.,	.	Third regiment of ——.
3. Lieut.-Col. E. F.,	.	First regiment of ——.
4. Lieut.-Col. F. G.,	.	Second regiment of ——.
5. Major W. T.,	. .	Third regiment of ——.
6. Major N. M.,	. .	First regiment of ——.
7. Captain A. N.,	.	Third regiment of ——.
8. Captain B. N.,	.	First regiment of ——.
9. Captain C. N.,	.	Second regiment of ——.
10. Captain D. M.,	.	Third regiment of ——.
11. Captain E. L.,	.	First regiment of ——.
12. Captain F. II.,	.	First regiment of ——.
13. Captain G. W.,	.	First regiment of ——.

And the following officers are detailed as supernumeraries:

Captain N. P., . .   Second regiment of ——.

Captain D. B., . .   First regiment of ——.

Captain N. O., . .   First regiment of——.

Captain S. R., of the fourth regiment of ——, is hereby appointed judge-advocate.

By command of

Lieut.-Gen. ——,

——, Adjt.-Gen.

ANOTHER FORM OF ORDER.

General Orders,   Head-quarters,
No. —.   —— ——.

A general court-martial is hereby appointed to meet at ——, on the ——day of ——, or as soon thereafter as practicable, for the trial of ——, and such other prisoners as may be brought before it.

Detail for the court.

1. ——.	6. ——.	10. ——.
2. ——.	7. ——.	11. ——.
3. ——.	8. ——.	12. ——.
4. ——.	9. ——.	13. ——.
5. ——.		

——, Judge-advocate.

No other officers than those named can be assembled without manifest injury to the service.

By order of ——,

——, Asst. Adjt.-Gen'l.

MODE OF RECORDING THE PROCEEDINGS OF A GENERAL (OR OTHER) COURT-MARTIAL.

Proceedings of a general court-martial, held at Fort Monroe, in the state of Virginia, by virtue of the following orders, viz.: (here insert a copy of the order convening the court.)

The court met pursuant to the above orders.
Present:

1. Colonel A. B., first regiment of ——, President.

2. Colonel C. D.   3. Lieut.-Colonel E. F.

4. Lieut.-Colonel F. G.   5. Major W. T.

6. Major N. M.   7. Captain A. N.

8. Captain B. N.   9. Captain C. N.

10. Captain D. M.   11. Captain E. L.

12. Captain F. H.   13. Captain W. G.

⎱ Members.

Captain T. R., Judge-advocate.

The court then proceeded to the trial of Captain A.
B., of the —— regiment of ——, who, being called into
court, and having heard the general order read, was
asked if he had any objection to any of the members
named in the general order, to which he replied in the
negative.

The court was then duly sworn in his presence, and
Captain A. B. was arraigned on the following charge
and specifications, viz.:

(Here insert the charge and specifications.)

To which the prisoner pleaded as follows:

Not guilty to the first specification;

Not guilty to the second specification;

Not guilty to the charge.

All persons required to give evidence were directed
to withdraw, and remain in waiting until called
for.

Lieutenant A. B., of the second regiment of infantry, a witness for the prosecution, being duly
sworn, says: that on the —— day of ——, &c., —— &c.
——.

Question by the judge-advocate —— ?

Answer. ——.

Question by the prisoner. —— ?

Answer. ——.

Question by the court. —— ?

Answer. ——.

The prosecution was then closed, and the prisoner produced the following evidence:

Captain C. D., of the corps of ——, a witness for the defence, being duly sworn, says: that on the —— day of ——, &c., &c.

Question by the prisoner. —— ?

Answer. ——.

Question by the judge-advocate. —— ?

Answer. ——.

Question by the court. —— ?

Answer. ——.

The prisoner, having no further testimony to offer, requested to be indulged with —— days to prepare for his final defence. The court granted his request, and adjourned at —— o'clock, P. M., to meet again at —— o'clock, A. M., on ——, the —— day of ——.

SECOND DAY.

Wednesday, ——, 18 ——.

The court met pursuant to adjournment: present all the members.

The proceedings having been read over to the court by the judge-advocate, the prisoner, Captain A. B., made the following address in his defence: (here insert the defence, or if it be too long, it may be marked and annexed.)

The court then closed, and proceeded to deliberate

on the testimony adduced, and pronounced the following

Sentence.

The court, having maturely weighed and considered the evidence adduced, is of the opinion that, &c.
&c., ——, and does therefore, ——, &c., &c.

A. B., Colonel first regiment of ——,
President.

S. R., Captain —— regiment of ——,
   Judge-advocate.

FORM OF AN ORDER APPOINTING A GARRISON OR REGI-
MENTAL COURT-MARTIAL.

Orders, }   Head-quarters, Fort Columbus, N. Y., }
No. —. }   ——,18—. }

A garrison (or regimental) court-martial, to consist
of Captain C. D., ——, First-Lieutenant D. F., ——,
and Second-Lieutenant G. II., ——, will convene at
the president's quarters, to-morrow morning, at
eleven o'clock, for the trial of Sergeant D. E.,
of —— company, —— regiment of ——, and such
other prisoners as may be brought before it.

By order of
Colonel A. B., commanding.
J. A., adjutant.

FORM OF CHARGES AND SPECIFICATIONS AGAINST A
PRISONER.

Charges and specifications preferred against
Captain C. D., of the first regiment of infantry.

Charge 1st.—Disobedience of orders.

Specifications 1st.—In this, that he, the said
Captain C. D., of the first regiment of infantry, being
ordered, on the thirtieth of September, 18—, at the

recruiting depot, in the town of Newport, Kentucky, by Colonel A. B., of the first regiment of infantry, the commanding officer of said depot, to take command of, and march with a detachment of recruits to Jefferson Barracks, in the state of Missouri, did, at the town of Newport, at the time aforesaid, refuse to take command of, and march with said detachment of recruits, thereby disobeying the lawful commands and orders of his superior and commanding officer, the said Colonel A. B.

Specification 2d.—In this, that he, the said Captain C. D., &c., &c.

C. F.,
Major first reg't of infantry.

FORM OF A GENERAL ORDER APPROVING OR DISAPPROV-
ING THE PROCEEDINGS OF A GENERAL COURT-MAR-
TIAL.

General Orders,   Head-quarters of the Army,
No. —.   January —, 18—.

I.—At a general court-martial, which convened at ——, on the —— day of ——, 18—, pursuant to general orders, No. —, of January, 18—, and of which brevet Brigadier-General —— is president, was tried Captain ——, of the —— regiment of ——, on the following charges and specifications, preferred by Major ——, of the —— regiment of ——, to wit:

Charge.

(Here insert charges and specifications—see a previous form.)

To which charges and specifications the prisoner pleaded as follows:

To the first specification, first charge. (plea.)

To the second specification, first charge. (plea.)
To the first charge. (plea.)

Findings and Sentence.

The court, after mature deliberation on the testimony adduced, find the prisoner, Captain——, of the —— regiment of ——, as follows:

Of the first specification, first charge. (finding.)

Of the second specification, first charge. (finding.)

And guilty (or not guilty) of the charge.

And the court do therefore sentence him, Captain ——, of —— regiment of artillery, to (insert sentence.)

II.—The proceedings, findings, and sentence in the case of —— are approved (or disapproved), &c., (here the authority which constituted the court will add such remarks as he may think proper.)

III.—The general court-martial, of which Brevet Brigadier-General —— is president, is hereby dissolved.

By command of
Major-General ——,
——, Adj't Gen'l.

In appointing a general court-martial, as many members will be detailed, from five to thirteen inclusively, as can be assembled without manifest injury to the service. The decision of the officer appointing the court, as to the number that can be assembled without manifest injury to the service, is conclusive.

A president of the court will not be appointed. The officer highest in rank present will be president.

The members will take place in the court in the order of their rank. A decision of the proper authority in regard to the rank of the members cannot be reversed by the court. The place of holding a court is appointed by the authority convening it.

Application for postponement or delay of trial must, when practicable, be made to the authority convening the court. When made to the court, it must be before plea, and will then, if in the opinion of the court well founded, be referred to the authority convening the court, to decide whether the court should be adjourned or dissolved, and the charged reserved for another court.

Upon application by the accused for postponement on the ground of absence of a witness, it ought distinctly to appear on his oath, 1st, that the witness is material, and how; 2d, that the accused has used due diligence to procure his attendance; 3d, that he has reasonable ground to believe, and does believe, that he will be able to procure such attendance, within a reasonable time stated.

The president of a court-martial, besides his duties and privileges as member, is the organ of the court, to keep order and conduct its business. He speaks and acts for the court in each case where the rule has been prescribed by law, regulation, or its own resolution. In all their deliberations the law secures the equality of the members.

The seventy-sixth article of war does not confer on a court-martial the power to punish its own members. For disorderly conduct, a member is liable as in other offences against military discipline; improper words are to be taken down, and any disorderly conduct of a member reported to the authority convening the court.

The judge-advocate shall summon the necessary witnesses for the trial; but he shall not summon any witness at the expense of the United States, nor any officer of the army, without the order of the court, unless he is satisfied that his testimony is material and necessary to the ends of justice.

Every court-martial shall keep a complete and accurate record of its proceedings, to be authenticated by the signatures of the President and judge-advocate; who shall also certify, in like manner, the sentence pronounced by the court in each case. The record must show that the court was organized as the law requires; that the court and judge-advocate were duly sworn in the presence of the prisoner; that he was previously asked whether he had any objection to any member, and his answer thereto. A copy of the order appointing the court will be entered on the record of each case.

Wherever the same court-martial tries more prisoners than one, and they are arraigned on separate and distinct charges, the court is to be sworn at the commencement of each trial, and the proceedings in each case will be made up separately.

The record will be clearly and legibly written; as far as practicable, without erasures or interlineations. The pages to be numbered, with a margin of one inch on the left side of each page, and at the top of the odd and bottom of the even pages; through this last margin the sheets to be stitched together; the documents accompanying the proceedings to be marked and noted in such manner as to afford an easy reference.

No recommendation will be embraced in the body

of the sentence. Those members only who concur in the recommendation will sign it.

The legal punishments for soldiers by sentence of a court-martial, according to the offence and the jurisdiction of the court, are death, confinement, confinement on bread-and-water diet, solitary confinement, hard labor, ball and chain, forfeiture of pay and allowances, discharge from service, reprimands. Solitary confinement, or confinement on bread and water, shall not exceed fourteen days at a time, with intervals between the periods of such confinement not less than such periods, and not exceeding eighty-four days in any one year.

The judge-advocate shall transmit the proceedings without delay to the officer having authority to confirm the sentence, who shall state, at the end of the proceedings in each case, his decision and orders thereon. The original proceedings of all general courts-martial, after the decision on them of the reviewing authority, and all proceedings that require the decision of the President, under the sixty-fifth and eighty-ninth articles of war, and copies of all orders confirming or disapproving, or remitting the sentences of courts-martial, and all official communications for the judge-advocate of the army, will be addressed to the "Adjutant-General of the Army, War Department," marked on the cover—"Judge-Advocate." The proceedings of garrison and regimental courts-martial will be transmitted without delay by the garrison or regimental commander to the department head-quarters for the supervision of the department commander. The power to pardon or mitigate the punishment ordered by a court-martial is vested in the authority confirming the proceedings, and in the President of the United States. A superior military commander to the officer confirming the proceedings may suspend the execution of the sentence, when in his judgment it is void upon the face of the proceedings, or when he sees a fit case for executive clemency. When a court-martial or court of inquiry adjourns without day, the members will return to their respective posts and duties unless otherwise ordered. When a court adjourns for three days, the judge-advocate shall report the facts to the commander of the port or troops, and the members belonging to the command will be liable to duty during the time.

COURTS OF INQUIRY.

In cases where the general or commanding officer may order a court of inquiry to examine into the nature of any transaction, accusation, or imputation against any officer or soldier, the said court shall consist of one or more officers, not exceeding three, and a judge-advocate, or other suitable person as a recorder, to reduce the proceedings and evidence to writing, all of whom shall be sworn to the faithful performance of duty. This court shall have the same power to summon witnesses as a court-martial, and to examine them on oath. But they shall not give their opinion on the merits of the case, excepting they shall be thereto specially required. The parties accused shall also be permitted to cross-examine and interrogate the witnesses, so as to investigate fully the circumstances in the question. (Art. 91.)

The proceedings of a court of inquiry must be authenticated by the signatures of the recorder and the president, and delivered to the commanding officer, and the said proceedings may be admitted as evidence by a court-martial, in cases not capital, or extending to the dismissal of an officer, provided that the circumstances are such that oral testimony cannot be obtained. But courts of inquiry are prohibited unless directed by the President of the United States or demanded by the accused. (Art. 92.)

The court may be ordered to report the *facts* of the case, with or without an opinion thereon. Such an order will not be complied with by merely reporting the evidence or testimony: facts being the result or conclusion established by weighing all the testimony, oral and documentary, before the court.

When a court of inquiry is directed to be assembled, the order should state whether the court is to report the facts or not, and also whether or not it is to give an opinion on the merits. The court should also be instructed whether its attention is to be extended to a general investigation, or to be confined to the examination of particular points only, as the case may seem to require, in the judgment of the officer under whose authority it is assembled. When the subject is multifarious, the court shall be directed to state its opinion on each point separately, that the proper authority may be able to form his judgment.

The court may sit with open or closed doors according to the nature of the transaction to be investigated. The court generally sits with open doors; but there may be delicate matters to be examined into that might render it proper to sit with doors closed.

The form of proceedings in courts of inquiry is nearly the same as in courts-martial; the members being assembled, and the parties interested called into court, the judge-advocate or recorder, by direction of the president, reads the order by which the court is constituted, and then administers to the members the following oath: "You shall well and truly examine and inquire, according to your evidence, into the matter now before you, without partiality, favor, affection, prejudice, or hope of reward, so help you God." (Art. 93.)

The accusation is then read, and the witnesses are examined by the court, and the parties accused are also permitted to cross-examine and interrogate the witnesses, so as to investigate fully the circumstances in question. (Art. 91.)

The examination of witnesses being finished, the parties before the court may address the court, should they see fit to do so, after which the president orders the court to be cleared. The recorder then reads over the whole of the proceedings, as well for the purpose of correcting the record, as for aiding the memory of the members of the court. After mature deliberation on the evidence adduced, they proceed to find a state of facts, if so directed by the order assembling the court, and to declare whether or not the grounds of accusation are sufficient to bring the matter before a general court-martial, and also to give their opinion of the merits of the case, if so required. The court shall be careful to examine the order by which it is constituted, and be particular in conforming to the directions contained therein, either by giving a general opinion on the whole matter, a statement of facts only, or an opinion on such facts. The proceedings of courts of inquiry have been returned to be reconsidered, when the court has been unmindful of these points.

It has been settled that a member of a court of inquiry may be objected to for cause.

Transactions may become the subject of investigation by courts of inquiry after the lapse of any number of years, on the application of the party accused, or by order of the President of the United States: the limitation mentioned in the eighty-eighth article of war being applicable only to general courts-martial.

It is not necessary to publish the proceedings or opinion of the court, although it is usually done in general orders.

The court is dissolved by the authority that ordered it to convene.

ART. 107.—Retirement of Officers from Active Duty.

The law of August 3, 1861, provides that if any commissioned officer of the army, or of the marine corps, shall have become, or shall hereafter become, incapable of performing the duties of his office, he shall be placed upon the retired list, and withdrawn from active service and command, and from the line of promotion, with the following pay and emoluments, namely: the pay proper of the highest rank held by him at the time of his retirement, whether by staff or regimental commission, and four rations per day, and without any other pay, emoluments or allowances; and the next officer in rank shall be promoted to the place of the retired officer, according to the established rules of the service. And the same rule of promotion shall be applied successively to the vacancies consequent upon the retirement of an officer; provided that should the brevet lieutenant-general be retired under this act, it shall be without deduction in his current pay, subsistence or allowances; and provided further, that there shall not be on the retired list, at any one time, more than seven per centum of the whole number of officers of the army, as fixed by law.

To carry out the law, the secretary of war, under the direction and approval of the President of the United States, shall, from time to time, as occasion may require, assemble a board of not more than nine, nor less than five commissioned officers, two-fifths of whom shall be of the medical staff; the board, except those taken from the medical staff, to be composed, as far as may be, of his seniors in rank, to determine the facts as to the nature and occasion of the disability of any officer appearing disabled to perform such military service, such board being invested with the powers of a court of inquiry and court-martial, and their decision shall be subject to like revision as that of such courts, by the President of the United States.

The board, whenever it finds an officer incapacitated for active service, will report whether, in its judgment, the said incapacity result from long and faithful service, from wounds or injury received in the line of duty, from exposure or sickness therein, or from any other incident of service. If so, and the President approve such judgment, the disabled officer shall thereupon be placed upon the list of retired officers, according to the provisions of this act. If otherwise, and the President concur in opinion with the board, the officer shall be retired as above, either with his pay proper alone, or with his service rations, at the discretion of the President, or he shall be wholly retired from the service with one year's pay and allowances; and in this last case his name shall be thenceforward omitted from the army register; provided that in every case the members of the board shall be sworn to an honest and impartial discharge of their duties, and that no officer of the army shall be retired either partially or wholly from the service, without having had a fair and full hearing before the board, if upon due summons, he shall demand it.

The officers partially retired are entitled to wear the uniform of their respective grades, shall continue to be borne upon the register of the army, and shall be subject to the rules and articles of war, and to trial by general court-martial, for any breach of the said articles.

Any commissioned officer of the army, who shall have served for forty consecutive years, may, upon his own application to the President of the United States, be placed upon the list of retired officers, with the pay and emoluments allowed by this act.

Retired officers of the army may be assigned to such duties as the President may deem them capable of performing, and such as the exigencies of the public service may require.

ART. 108.—Prisoners of War. Captured Property.

A return of prisoners, and a report of the number and description of the killed and wounded of the enemy, should be forwarded to the adjutant-general's office, in Washington.

A return of all property captured should be made by the commanding officer of the troops by whom such capture is made, to the adjutant-general at Washington, in order that it may be disposed of according to the orders of the war department.

Prisoners of war should be disarmed and sent to the rear, and reported as soon as practicable to the head-quarters. The return of prisoners from the head-quarters of the army to the war department will specify the number, rank, and corps, and as far as possible, names of individuals.

The private property of prisoners should be respected, and each should be treated with the respect due to his rank. They are to obey the necessary orders given them. They receive for subsistence one ration each, without regard to rank; and the wounded are to be treated with the same care as the wounded of the army. Other allowances to them will depend upon conventions with the enemy. Prisoner's horses will be taken for the army.

Exchanges of prisoners and release of officers on parole depend on the orders of the general commanding in chief, under the instructions of the government.

After an action or affair, a return of the killed, wounded, and missing will be made, in which the name, rank, and regiment of each officer and soldier will be specified, with such remarks and explanations as may be requisite for the records of the department of war, or be necessary to establish the just claims of any individual who may have been wounded, or

of the heirs and representatives of any killed in
action (taking care to specify the nature of the
wound, the time and place of its occurrence, the
company, regiment or corps, and the name of the
captain, colonel, or other commanding officer).

ART. 109.—Travelling Expenses of Officers.

An officer who travels not less than ten miles without troops, escort, or military stores, and under special orders, in the case, from a superior, or a summons to attend a military court, shall receive ten
cents mileage, or, if he prefer it, the actual cost of his
transportation and of the transportation of his
allowance of baggage for the whole journey, provided he has travelled in the customary reasonable manner. Mileage will not be allowed where the travel is
by government conveyances, which will be furnished
in case of necessity.

If the journey be to cash treasury drafts, the necessary and actual cost of transportation only will be
allowed; and the account must describe the draft
and state its amount, and set out the items of
expense, and be supported by a certificate that the
journey was necessary to procure specie for the draft
at par.

If an officer travels on urgent public duty without
orders, he shall report the case to his superior who
had authority to order the journey; and his approval,
if then given, shall allow the actual cost of transportation. Mileage is computed by the shortest mail
route, and the distance by the general post-office
book. When the distance cannot be so ascertained,

it shall be reckoned subject to the decision of the quartermaster-general.

Orders to an officer, on leave of absence, to rejoin the station or troops he left, will not carry transportation.

In changes of station, an officer entitled to mileage or actual cost of transportation, shall be entitled to actual cost of transportation of his authorized servants; and in other cases than change of station, an officer entitled to transportation, who, from wounds or disability, requires and takes one servant, shall be entitled to the actual cost of his transportation.

Citizens receiving military appointments join their stations without expense to the public; but assistant-surgeons approved by an examining board and commissioned, receive transportation in the execution of their first order to duty, and graduates of the military academy receive transportation from the academy to their stations.

When officers are permitted to exchange stations, the public will not be put to expense of transportation, which would have been saved if such transportation had not taken place.

ART. 110.—Honors to be Paid by the Troops.

The President or Vice-President is to be saluted with the highest honors—all standards and colors dropping, officers and troops saluting, drums beating, and trumpets sounding.

A general commanding in chief is to be received by cavalry with sabres presented, trumpets sounding the march, and all the officers saluting, standards dropping; by infantry, with drums beating the march, colors dropping, officers saluting, and arms presented. A major-general is to be received, by cavalry with sabres presented, trumpets sounding twice the trumpet flourish, and officers saluting; by infantry, with three ruffles, colors dropping, officers saluting, and arms presented.

A brigadier-general is to be received by cavalry with sabres presented, trumpets sounding once the trumpet flourish, and officers saluting; by infantry, with two ruffles, colors dropping, officers saluting, arms presented. An adjutant-general or inspector-general, if under the rank of a general officer, is to be received, at a review or inspection of the troops under arms, by cavalry, with sabres presented, officers saluting; by infantry, officers saluting, and arms presented. The same honors to be paid to any field officer authorized to review and inspect the troops. When the inspecting officer is junior to the officer commanding the parade, no compliments will be paid; he will be received only with swords drawn and arms shouldered.

All guards are to turn out and present arms to general officers as often as they pass them, except the personal guards of general officers, which only turn out to the generals whose guards they are, and to officers of superior rank.

To commanders of regiments, garrison or camp, their own guard turn out and present arms once a day; after which, they turn out with shouldered arms.

To the members of the cabinet, to the chief-justice, the president of the Senate, and speaker of the House of Representatives of the United States, and to governors within their respective states and territories, the same honors will be paid as to a general commanding in chief.

Officers of a foreign service may be complimented with the honors due to their rank. American and foreign envoys and ministers will be received with the compliments due to a major-general.

The colors of a regiment passing a guard are to be saluted, the trumpets sounding, and the drums beating a march.

When general officers or persons entitled to salute, pass in the rear of a guard, the officer is only to make his men stand shouldered, and not to face his guard about, or beat his drum.

When general officers or persons entitled to a salute, pass guards while in the act of relieving, both guards are to salute, receiving the word of command from the senior officer of the whole.

All guards are to be under arms when armed parties approach their posts; and to parties commanded by commissioned officers they are to present arms, drums beating a march, and officers saluting.

No compliments by guards or sentinels will be paid between retreat and reveille, except as prescribed for grand rounds.

All guards and sentinels are to pay the same compliments to the officers of the navy, marines, and militia in the service of the United States, as are directed to be paid to the officers of the army, according to their relative ranks.

It is equally the duty of non-commissioned officers and soldiers, at all times, and in all situations, to pay the proper compliments to officers of the navy and marines, and to officers of other regiments, when in uniform, as to offices of their own particular regiments and corps.

Courtesy among military men is indispensable to discipline. Respect to superiors should not be confined to obedience on duty, but should be extended to all occasions. It is always the duty of the inferior to accost, or to offer first the customary salutation, and of the superior to return such complimentary notice.

Sergeants, with swords drawn, will salute by bringing them to a present; with muskets, by bringing the left hand cross the body, so as to strike the musket near the right shoulder. Corporals out of the ranks, and privates not sentries, will carry their muskets at a shoulder as sergeants, and salute in like manner.

When a soldier without arms, or with side-arms only, meets an officer, he is to raise his hand to the right side of the visor of his cap, palm to the front, elbow raised as high as the shoulder, looking at the same time in a respectful and soldier-like manner at the officer, who will return the compliment thus offered.

A non-commissioned officer or soldier being seated, and without particular occupation will rise on the approach of an officer, and make the customary salutation. If standing, he will turn toward the officer form the same purpose. If the parties remain in the same place, or on the same ground, such compliments need not be repeated.

SALUTES.

The national salute is determined by the number of states composing the Union, at the rate of one gun for each state.

The President of the United States alone is to receive a salute of twenty-one guns. The Vice-President is to receive a salute of seventeen guns.

The heads of the great executive department of the national government; the general commanding the army; the governors of states and territories, within their respective jurisdictions, fifteen guns. A major-general, thirteen guns. A brigadier-general, eleven guns. Foreign ships of war will be saluted in return for a similar compliment, gun for gun, on notice being officially received of such intention. If there be several posts in sight of, or within six miles of each other, the principal only shall reciprocate compliments with ships passing.

Officers of the navy will be saluted according to relative rank. Foreign officers, invited to visit a fort or post, may be saluted according to their relative rank.

Envoys and ministers of the United States and foreign powers, are to be saluted with thirteen guns.

A general officer will be saluted but once in a year at each post, and only when notice of his intention to visit the post has been given.

Salutes to individuals must be fired on their arrival only.

A national salute will be fired at meridian on the anniversary of the Independence of the United States, at each military post and camp provided with artillery and ammunition.

ESCORTS OF HONOR.

Escorts of honor may be composed of cavalry or infantry, or both, according to circumstances. They are guards of honor for the purpose of receiving and escorting personages of high rank, civil or military. The troops for this purpose will be selected for their soldierly appearance and superior discipline.

The escort will be drawn up in line, the center opposite to the place where the personage presents himself, with an interval between the wings, to receive him and his retinue. On his appearance, he will be received with the honors due to his rank. When he has taken his place in the line, the whole will be wheeled into platoons or companies, as the case may be, and take up the march. The same ceremony will be observed and the same honors paid on his leaving the escort.

When the position of the escort is at a considerable distance from the point where he is expected to be received, as for instance, where a court-yard or wharf intervenes, a double line of sentinels will be posted from that point to the escort, facing inward, and the sentinels will successively salute as he passes.

An officer will be appointed to attend him, to bear such communications as he may have to make to the commander of the escorts.

FUNERAL HONORS.

On the receipt of official intelligence of the death of the President of the United States, at any post or camp, the commanding officer shall, on the following day, cause a gun to be fired at sunrise, and at every succeeding half-hour until sunset. When posts are contiguous, the firing will take place only at the post commanded by the superior officer.

On the day of the interment of a general commanding in chief, a gun will be fired at every half-hour, until the procession moves, beginning at sunrise.

The funeral escort of a general commanding in chief, consists of a regiment of infantry, a squadron of cavalry, and six pieces of artillery.

Of a major-general, a regiment of infantry, a squadron of cavalry, and four pieces of artillery.

Of a brigadier-general, a regiment of infantry, one company of cavalry, and two pieces of artillery.

Of a colonel, a regiment: of a lieutenant-colonel, six companies; of a major, four companies; of a captain, one company; of a subaltern, half a company.

The funeral escort should be commanded by an officer of the same rank with the deceased; or, if none such be present, by one of next inferior grade.

The funeral escort of a non-commissioned staff officer should consist of sixteen rank and file, commanded by a sergeant.

Of a sergeant, of fourteen rank and file, commanded by a sergeant. Of a corporal, of twelve rank and file, commanded by a corporal; of a private, of eight rank and file, commanded by a corporal.

The escort will be formed in two ranks, opposite to the quarters or tent of the deceased, with shouldered arms and bayonets unfixed; the artillery and cavalry on the right of the infantry.

The pall-bearers, six in number, will be selected from the grade of the deceased.

ART. 111.—Inspection Reports.

These should show the discipline of the troops; their instruction in all military exercises and duties; the state of their arms, clothing, equipments, and accoutrements of all kinds; of their kitchens and messes; of the barracks and quarters of the post; of the guard-house, prisons, hospital, bake-house, magazines, store-houses, and stores of every description: of the stables and horses; the condition of the post school; the management and application of the post and company funds; the state of the post, and regimental, and company books, papers, and files; the zeal and ability of the officers in command of the troops; the capacity of the officers conducting the administrative and staff services, the fidelity and economy of their disbursements; the condition of all public property, and the amount of money in the hands of each disbursing officer; the regularity of issues and payments; the mode of enforcing discipline by courts-martial, and by the authority of the officer; the propriety and legality of all punishments inflicted; and any information whatsoever, concerning the service in any matter or particular that may merit notice, or aid to correct defects or introduce improvements.

Inspectors are required particularly to report if any officer is of intemperate habits, or unfit for active service by infirmity or any other cause.

The periodical inspections are the following:

1st. The commanders of the regiments and posts make an inspection of their commands on the last day of every month.

2d. Captains will inspect their companies every

Sunday morning. No soldier should be excused from Sunday inspection except the guard, the sick, and the necessary attendants in the hospital.

3d. Medical officers having charge of hospitals, will also make a thorough inspection of them every Sunday morning.

4th. Inspections when troops are mustered for payment.

ART. 112.—List of Books every Officer will find of Great Use in the Field.

Army Regulations. Mahan's Works on Field Fortifications and Outpost Service. Scott's Military Dictionary. Marcy's Prairie Traveller. The engineers should carry in addition Laisné's Aide-memoire du genie; The Ordnance and Artillery. The Ordnance Manual and Gibbon's Artillerist's Manual. Every office should carry the Tactics of the arm to which he belongs. At every head-quarters should be a copy or two of Callan's Military Laws and De Hart's Courts-Martial.

ART. 113.—General Principles.

Fathom your heart and endeavor to know yourself. See what you can do, that you undertake nothing but what you can accomplish. Do not entertain too high an opinion of your abilities, and do not distrust those of others.

If you are free, never accept a command or a mission above your skill, your courage or power. If you are not free, and if a responsibility is imposed upon you, endeavor to be convinced that you are worthy of the trust, and act up to the best of your ability.

Ascertain if your mind received inspiration in difficult circumstances, and if your courage rises at the moment of danger; if such is the case, venture boldly among the chances of war.

A strong will and the sense of duty often lead to greater results than enthusiasm; do not therefore despair, if necessity more than inclination detains you in the army.

A recruit, who deserts during his first engagement, may afterward become a hero. Persevering toil, practice and reflection, can in time make a good general of an indifferent officer.

Have in every thing and at all times an aim, either remote or near, either material or abstract. When we know well where to go, it seldom happens we fail to reach our destination.

As long as your mind is in suspense, and you do not see plainly what is to be done, do not engage in a course the end of which is not clearly defined; it is far better to remain still than to go no one knows whither. There is, however, danger in considering too much; the mind wanders whilst weighing the pros and cons, and generally quick decisions are the best. Minutes are often precious; you must not then waver, and a firm and vigorous execution will frequently atone for the deficiencies of your plan.

Your resolution once fixed, never lose sight of it until it is carried out. Overthrow or turn aside all obstacles, but reach your aim sooner or later without deviating or flinching. Dogged perseverance has often compensated for the lack of genius.

There are successful men favored by fortune, whose undertakings prosper to their utmost desire. Do not fancy yourself to be one of them; lay hold of every chance to insure success. Neglect no means, not even the slightest. A great final result is more frequently brought about by several ordinary combinations, either united or successive, than by a single and powerful effort.

Calculate every thing, foresee every thing, organize every thing, and ascertain exactly the means at your disposal, in order to rely upon them alone.

Responsibility is the only true inspirer, but it must be individual and entire; therefore let us have no combined operations between two men, independent of one another, for the same clear and defined purpose.

If you are commander-in-chief, never call a council of war, for in so doing you place your capacity in doubt, and destroy the reliance the army may have in you; whilst in return you only receive advice too various to be followed, and besides mostly dictated by evil feelings, jealousy, fear, &c., and every officer would be offended at your not having adopted his views.

If you are in need of the advice of your inferiors, ask for it skillfully and in an indirect manner, and reflect twice before adopting it, even if it seem judicious at first sight.

If you seriously believe yourself unfit for your position, do not have any false pride; resign the command or the direction to the most worthy, openly if you can, secretly if rank or any other cause prevents you from so doing.

No man is perfect. Confine yourself as much as possible to the specialty for which you have most aptitude, and as a rule intrust every one of your subordinates with the employment he can best fulfil. Endeavor, therefore, to know well all those about you.

Be active and vigilant in the execution of your duties; considerate, and above all, just toward your inferiors.

Are you subordinate, never criticise the orders of your superiors. Respect a position full of difficulties. If you cannot alter a plan which appears to you defective, remember that it may still succeed through your bravery and your good will. Do not discourage your comrades, who may be less quick-sighted than yourself; you would damp their ardor, which might have been sufficient to make up for the most absurd conceptions.

Be patient, brave, devoted to your duties, to your chief, to your comrades.

INDEX.